ELAINE (ROENNFELDT) ALLEN'S

watercolours of Kalamunda and surrounds

National Library of Australia Cataloguing-in-Publication entry

Creator: Allen, Elaine 1936, artist
Title: Elaine (Roennfeldt) Allen's watercolours of Kalamunda and surrounds
Elaine (Roennfeldt) Allen, the artist
Sandler, David Solly, the compiler

ISBN: 9780994619228 (paperback)

Subjects: Allen, Elaine born 1936 -
Watercolour painting--Western Australia--Kalamunda.
Landscapes in art.
Landscapes--Western Australia--Kalamunda.
Landscapes--Western Australia--Perth.

Other Creators/Contributors:
Sandler, David Solly, compiler

Dewey Number: 751.422099411

This edition first published August 2016

E-mail: <sedsand@iinet.net.au>
ISBN 978-0-9946192-2-8

Views of Perth

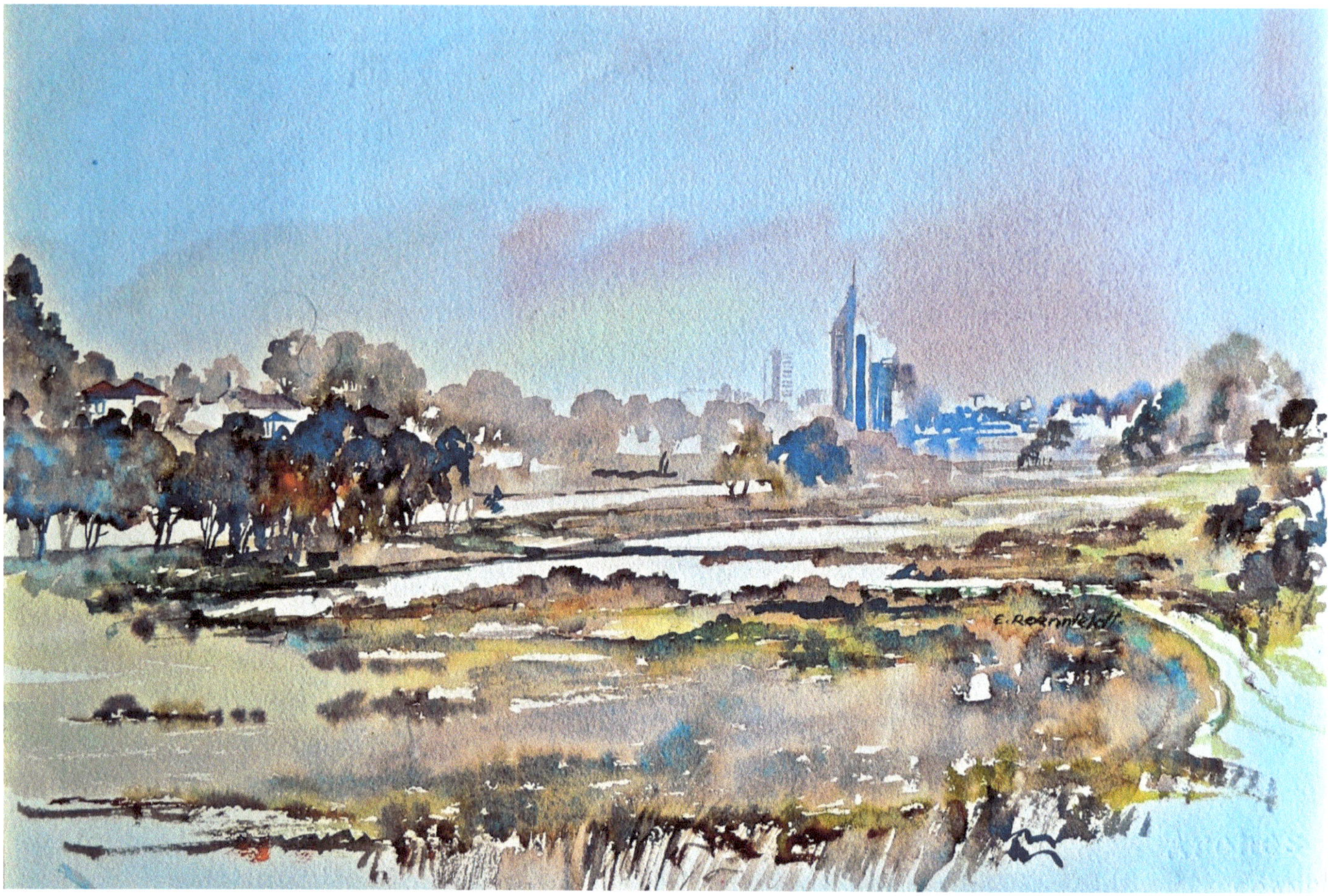

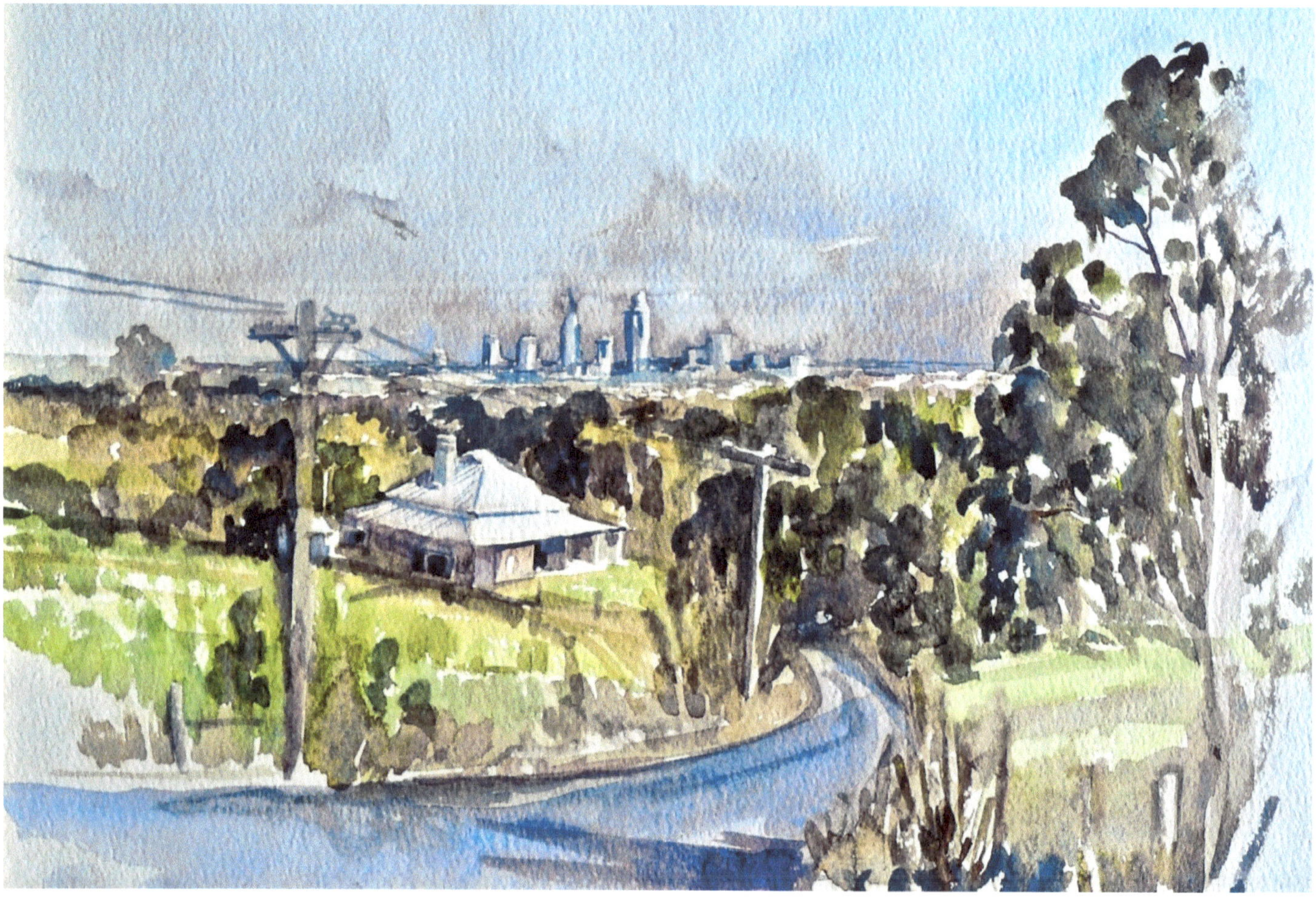

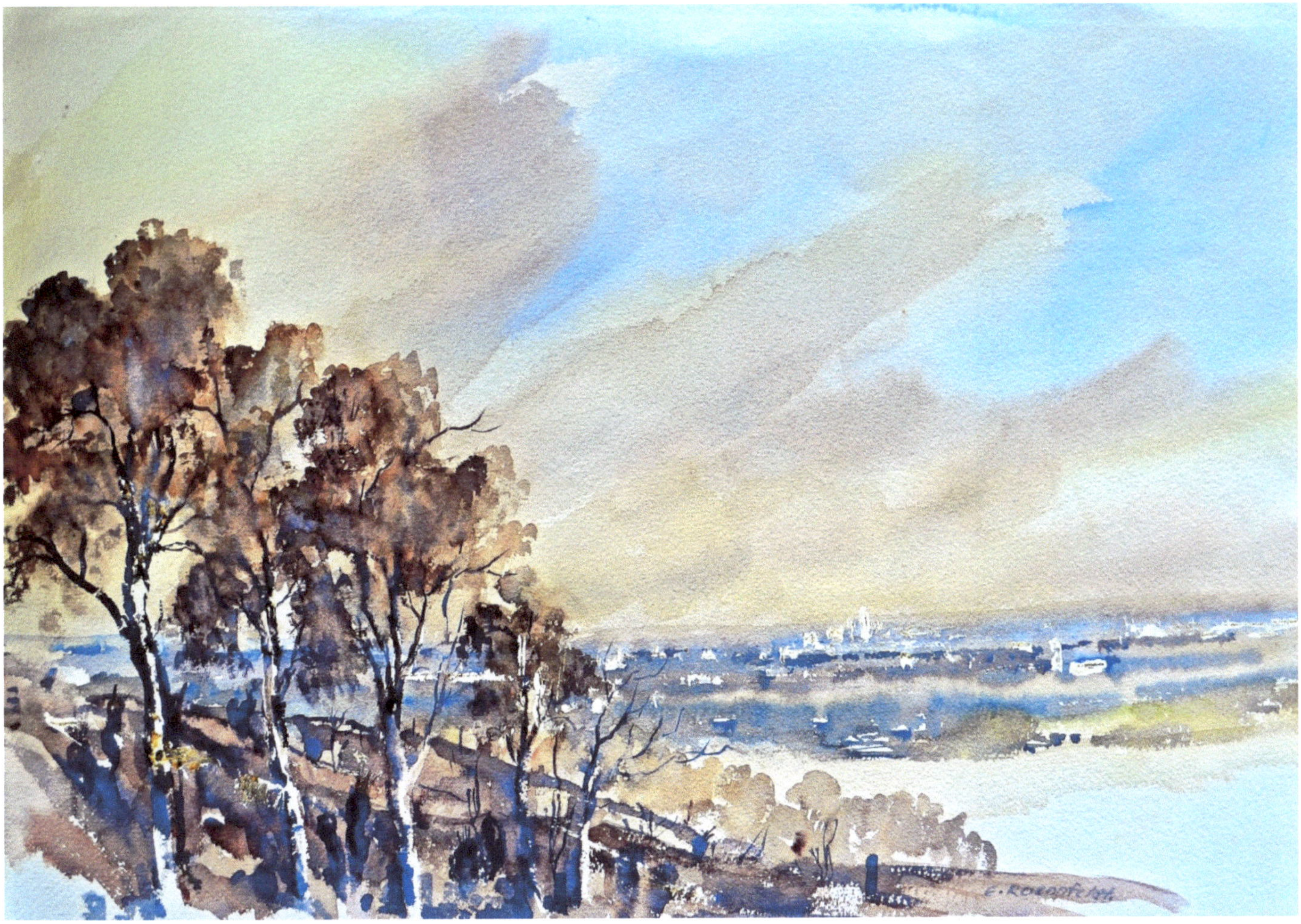

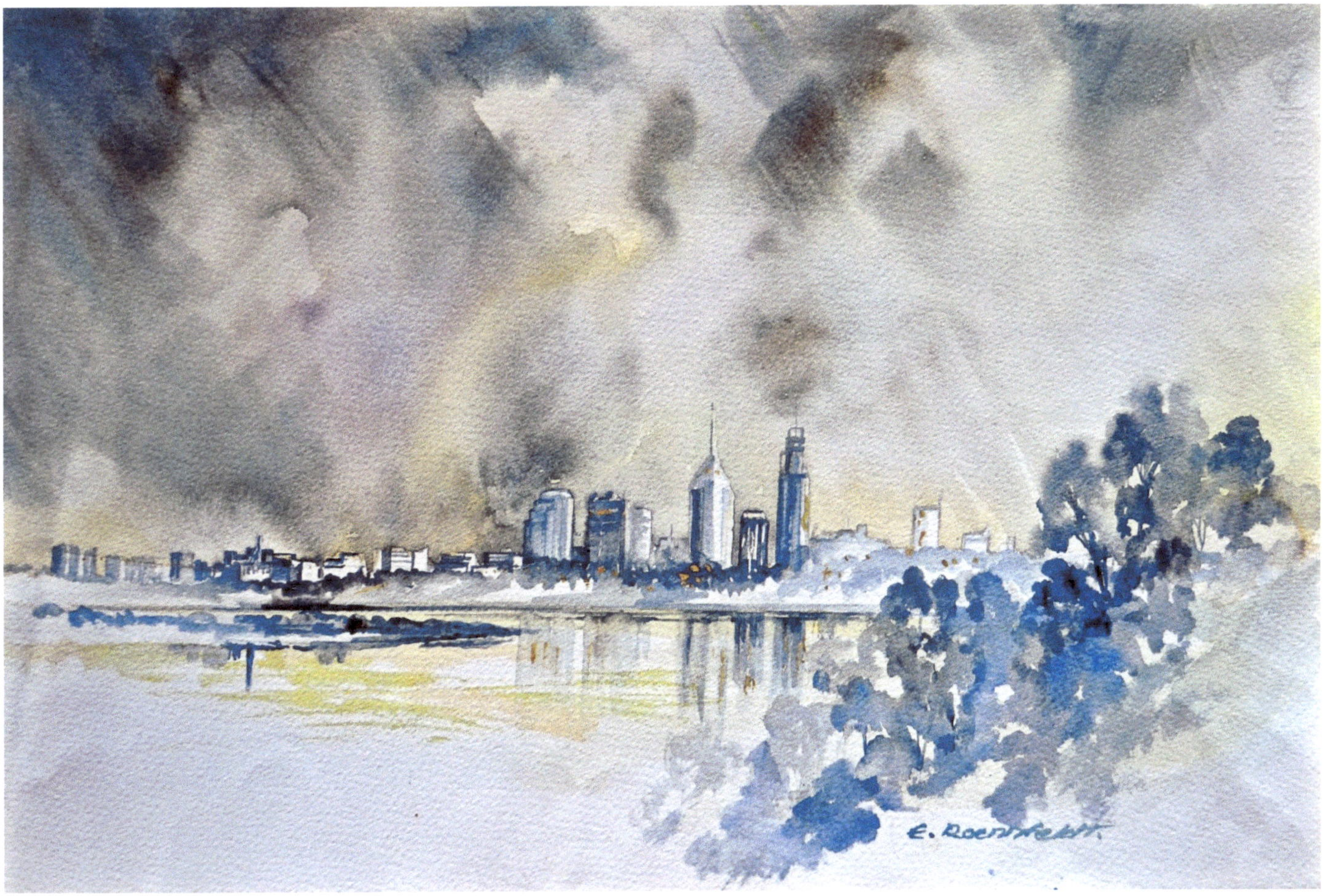

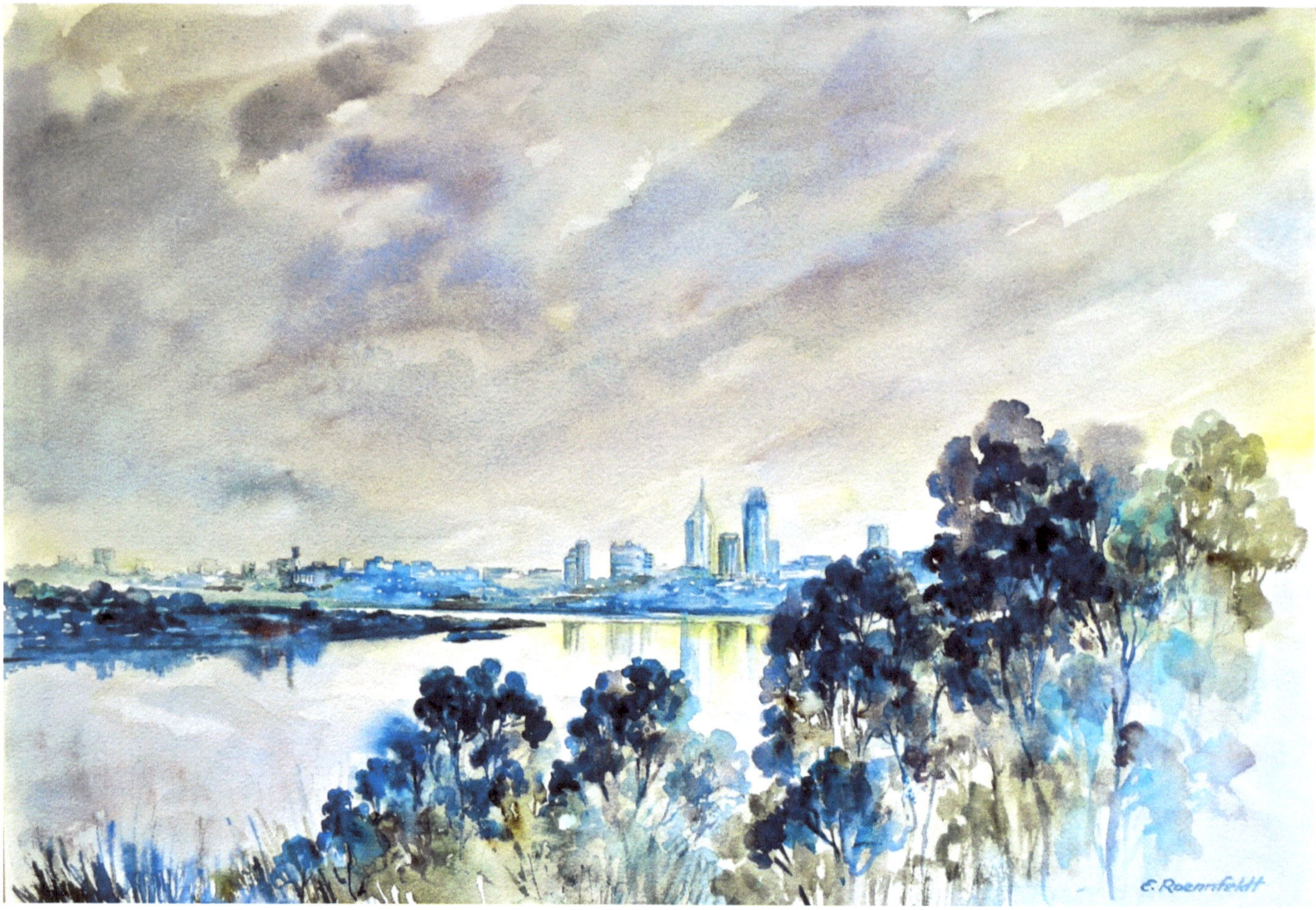

E. Roennfeldt

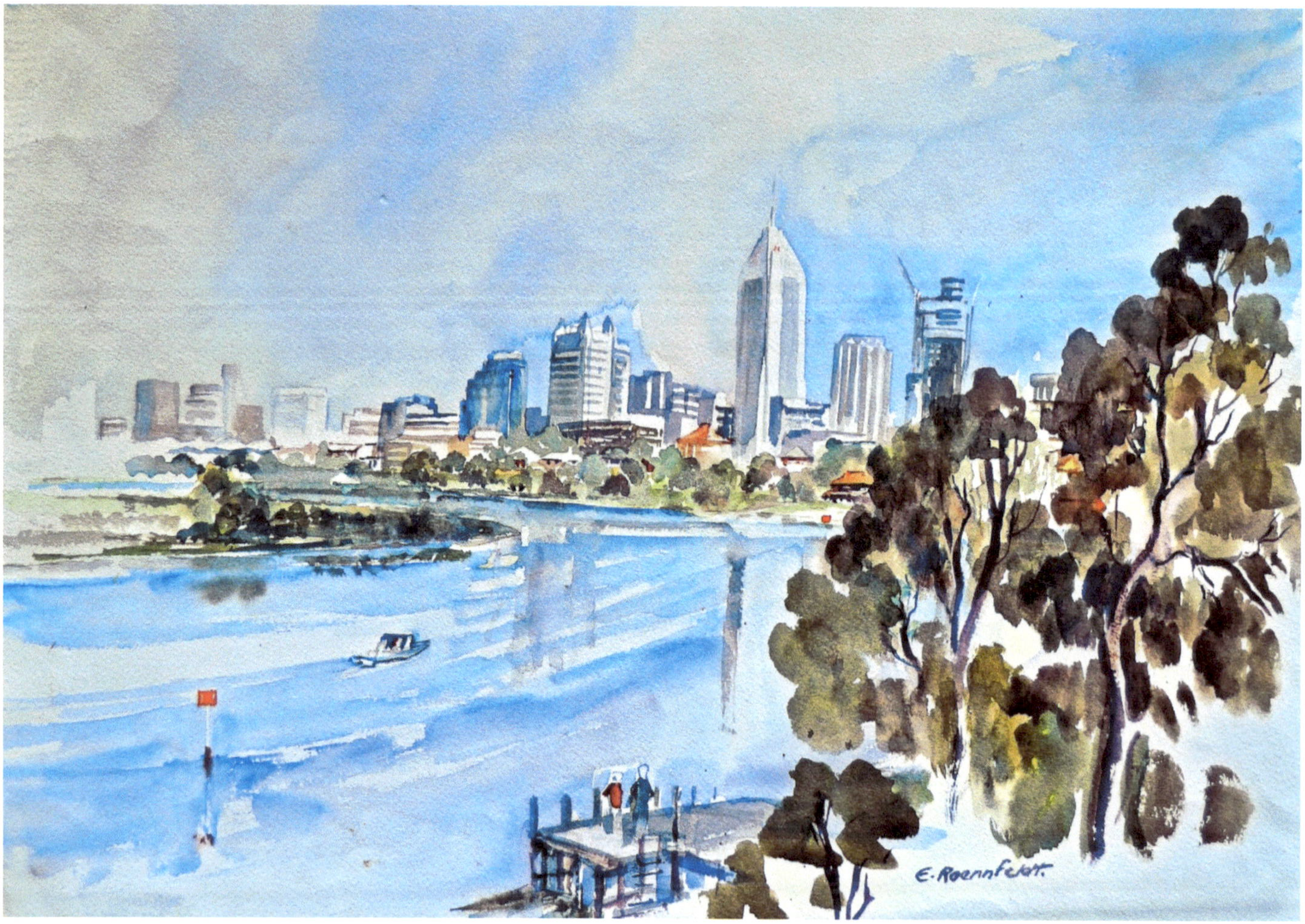

E. Roennfeldt

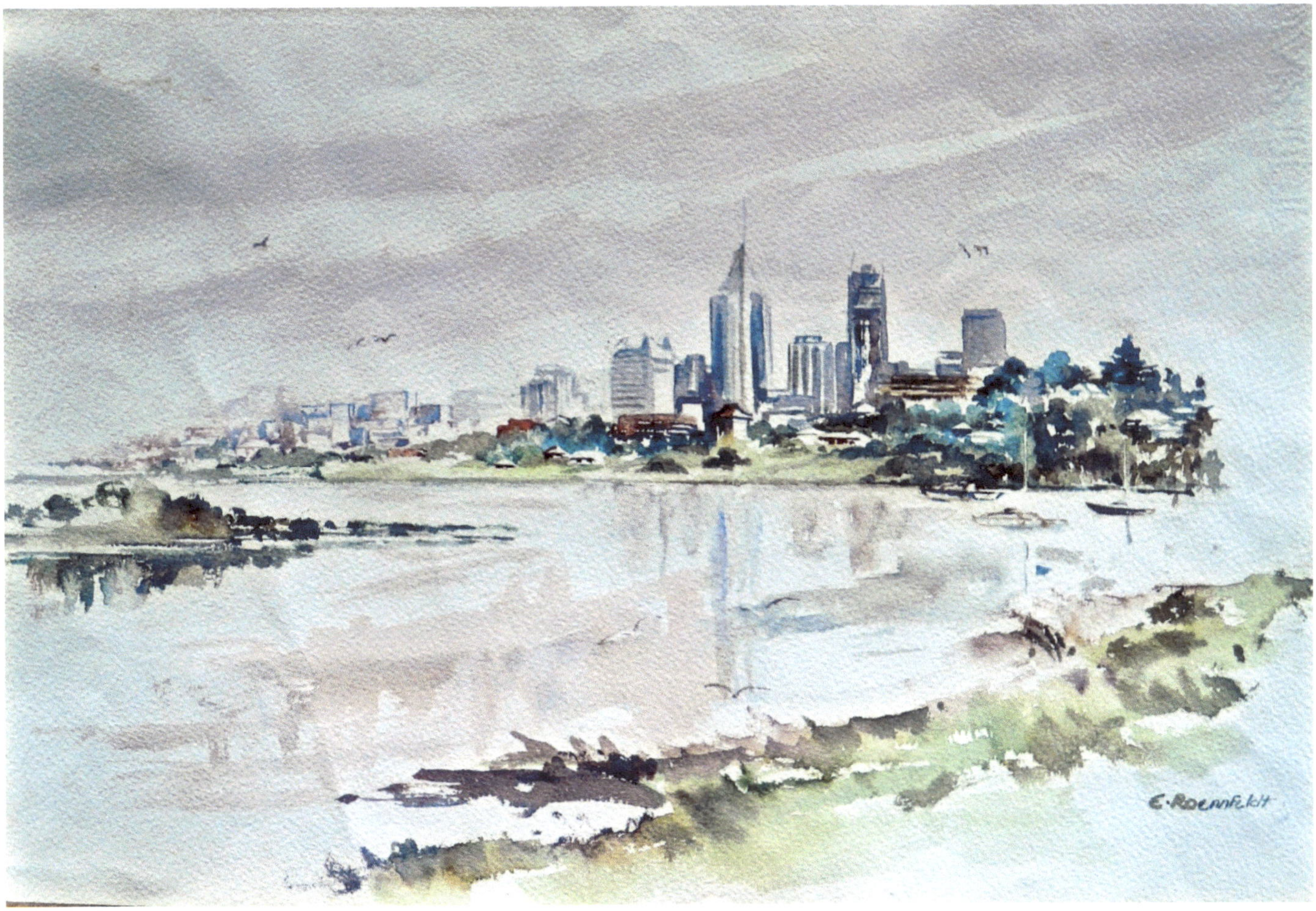

E. Roennfeldt

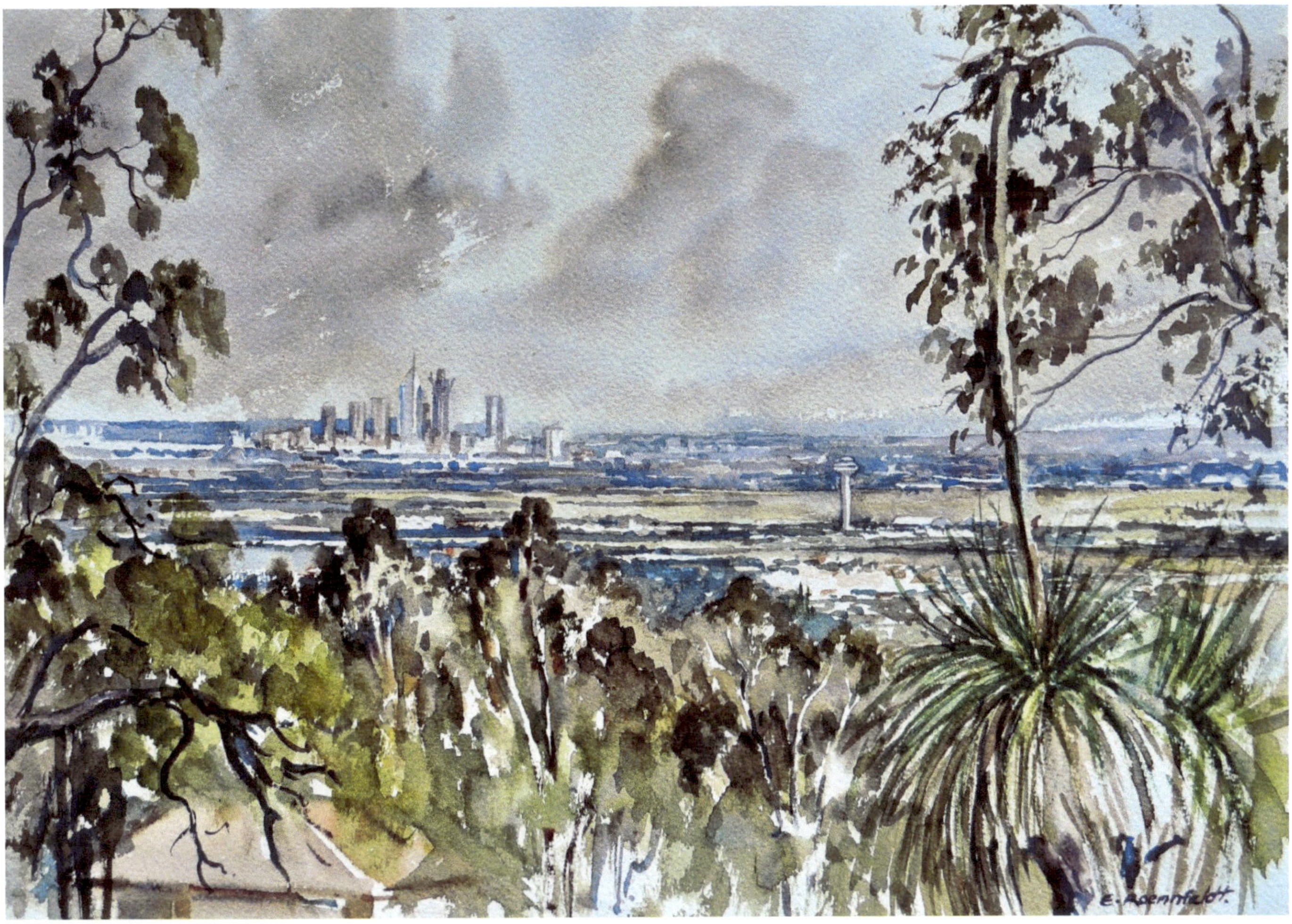

E. Roennfeldt.

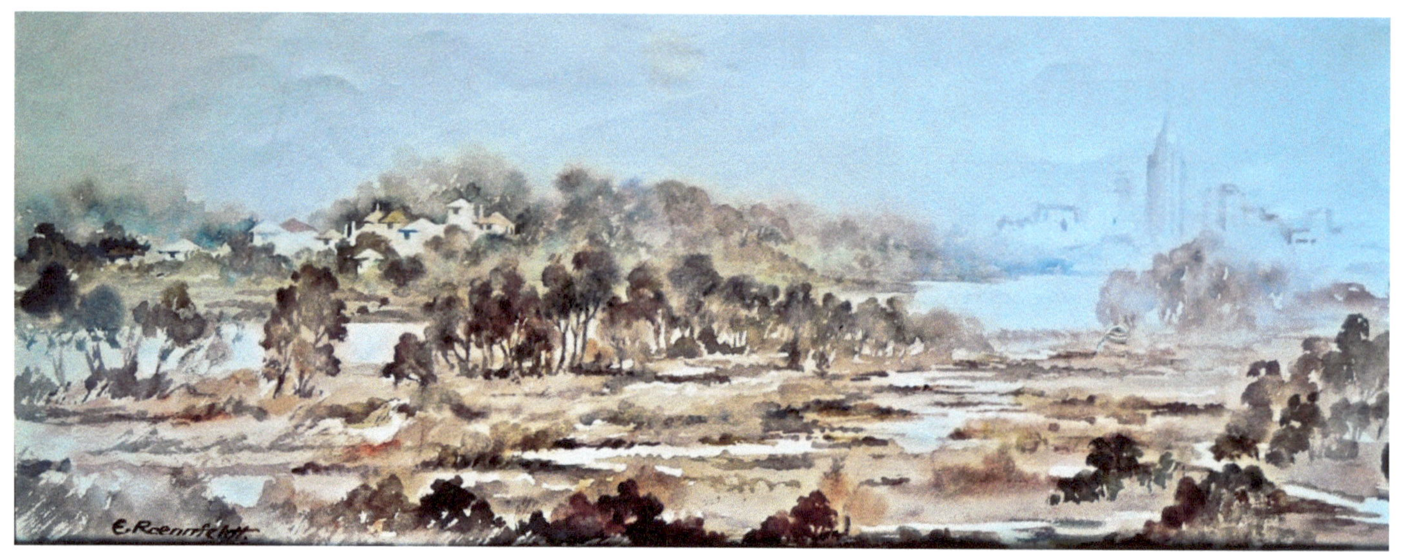
E.Roennfeldt

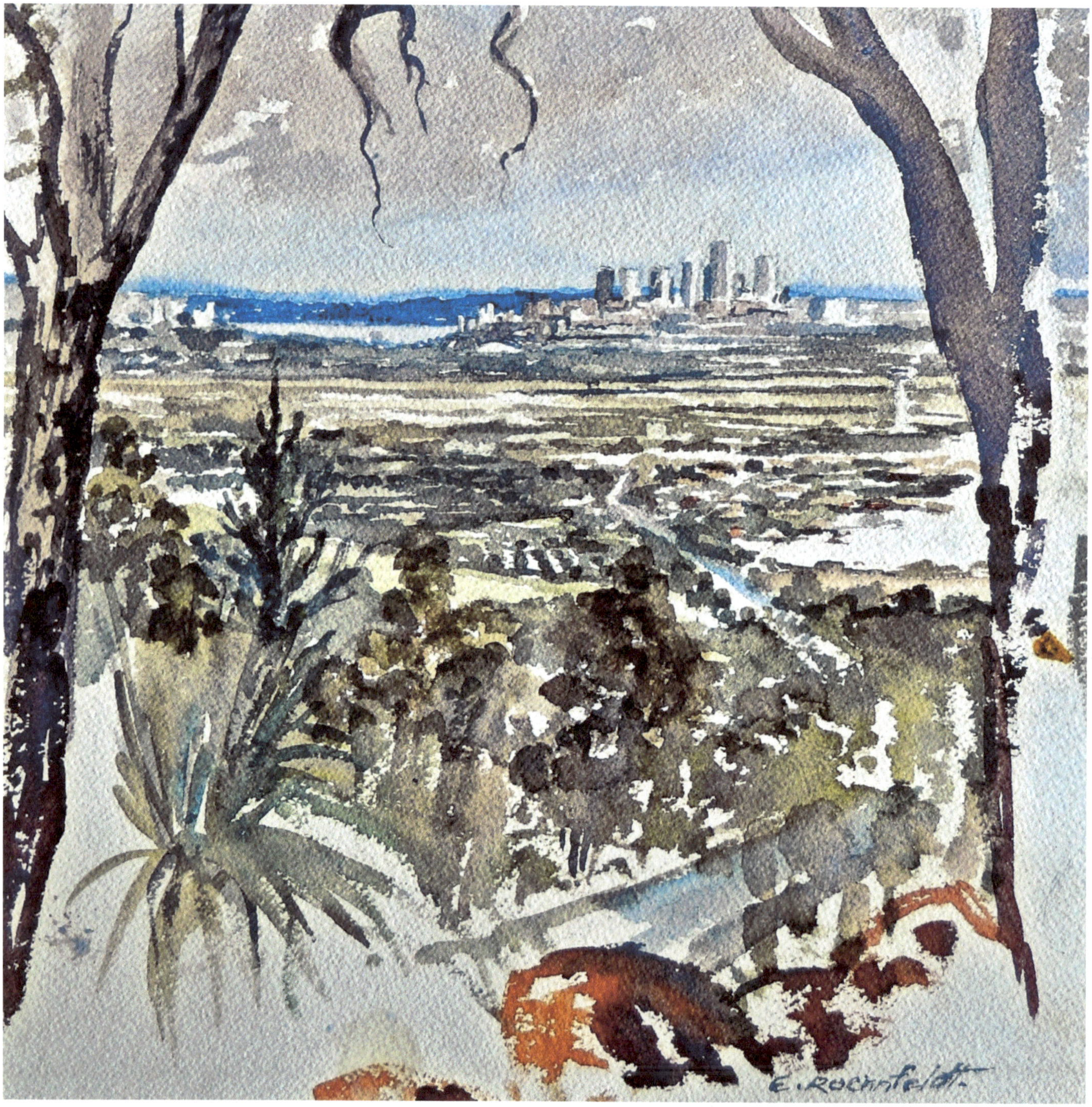

Landscapes of Kalamunda and surrounds

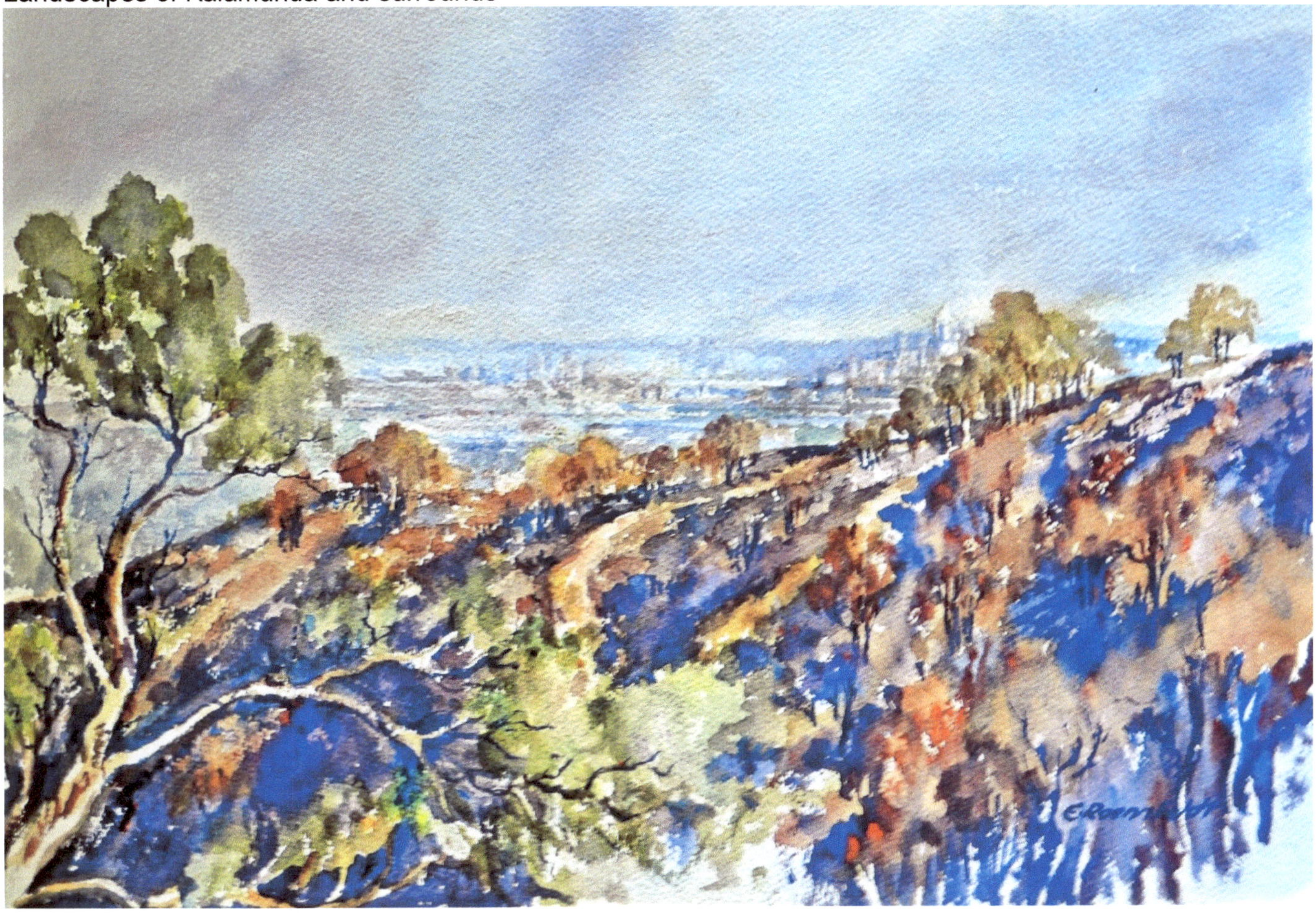

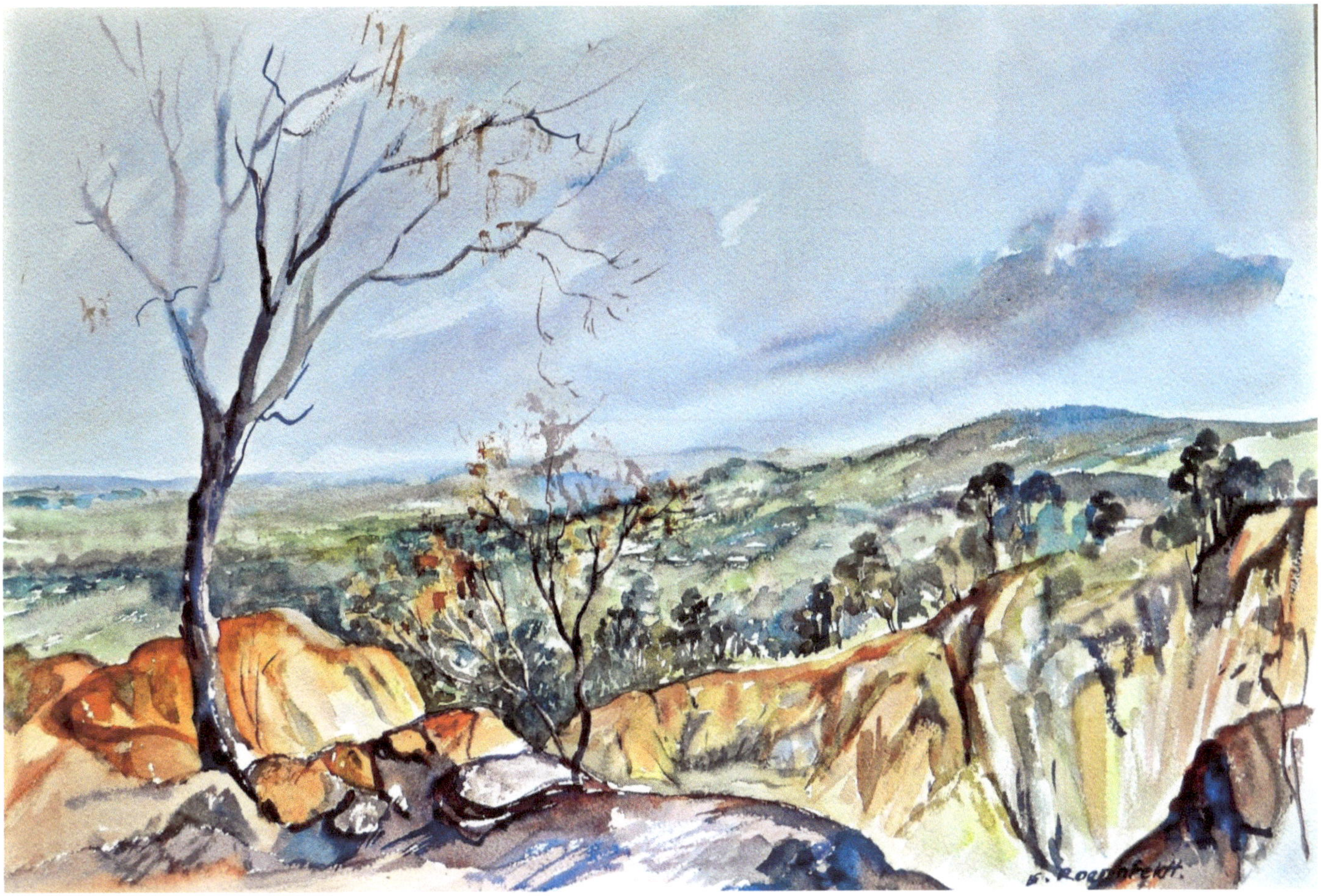

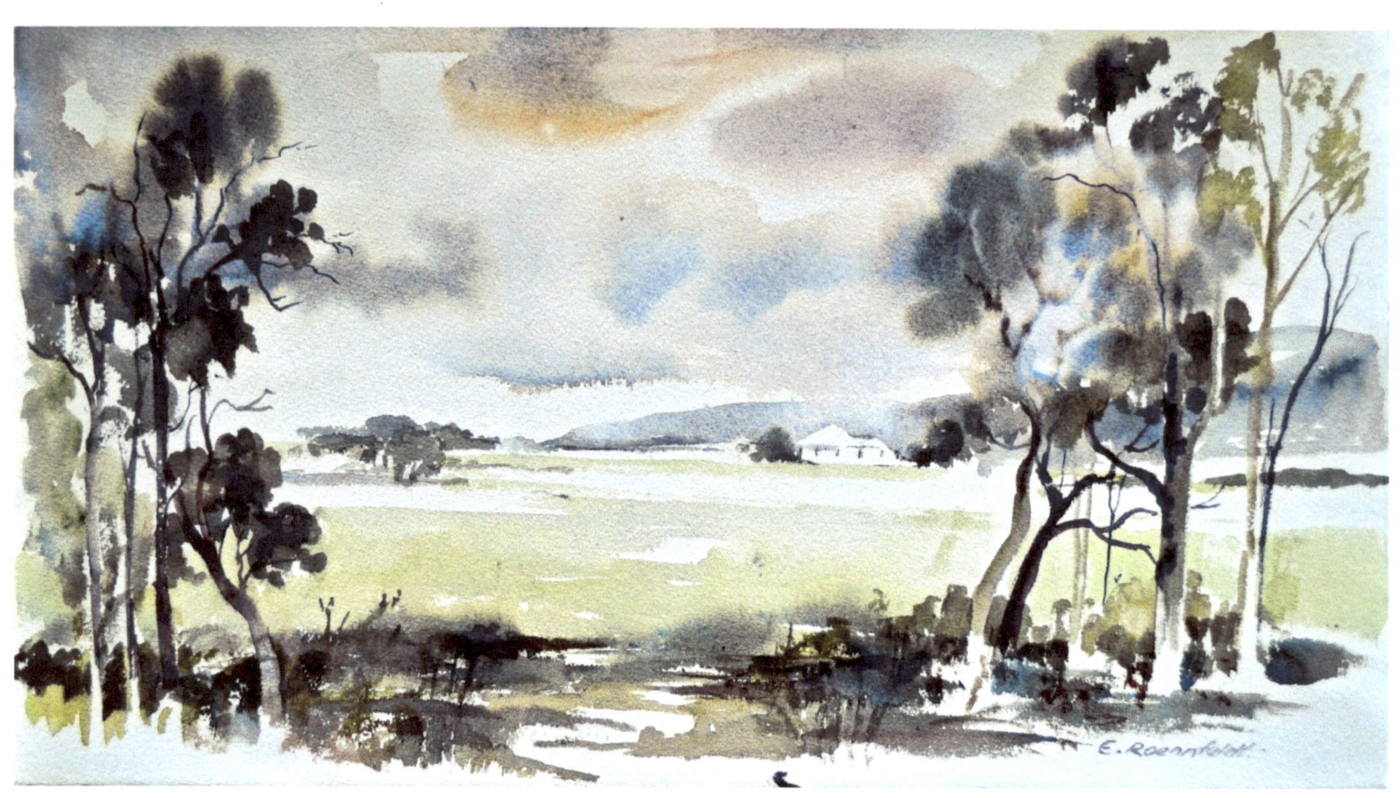

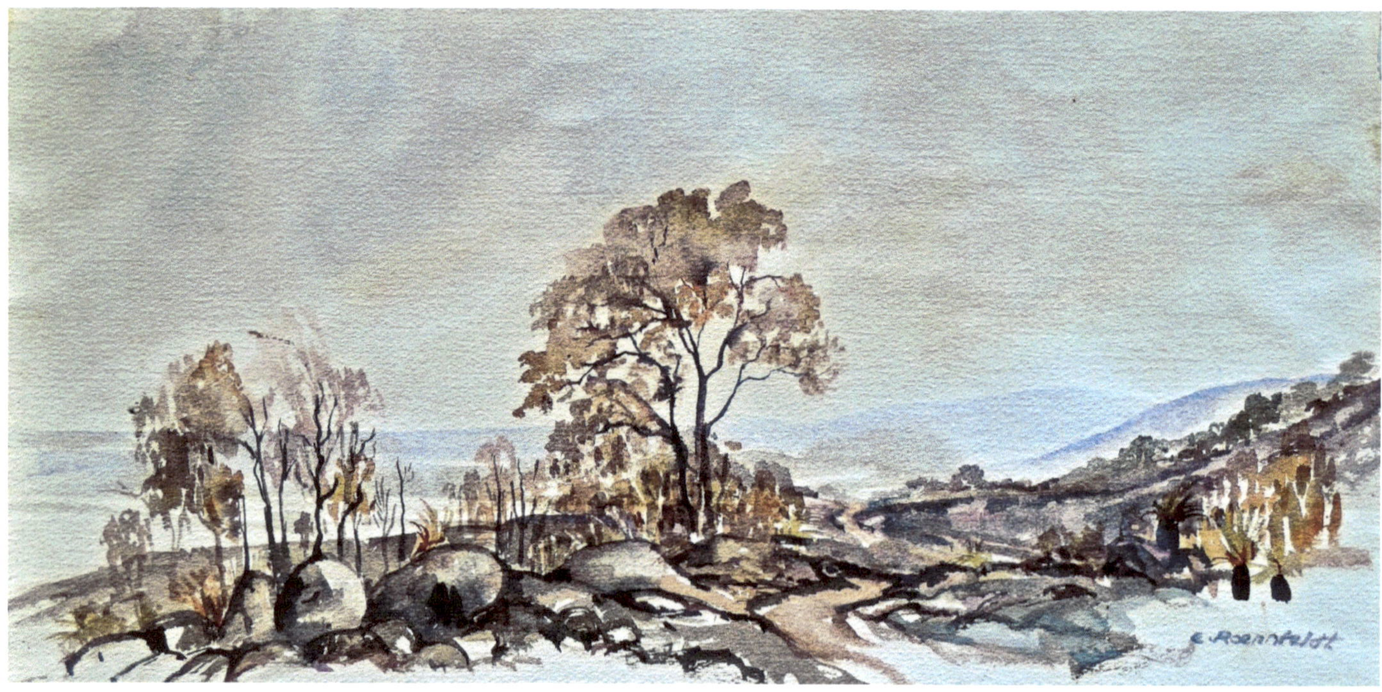

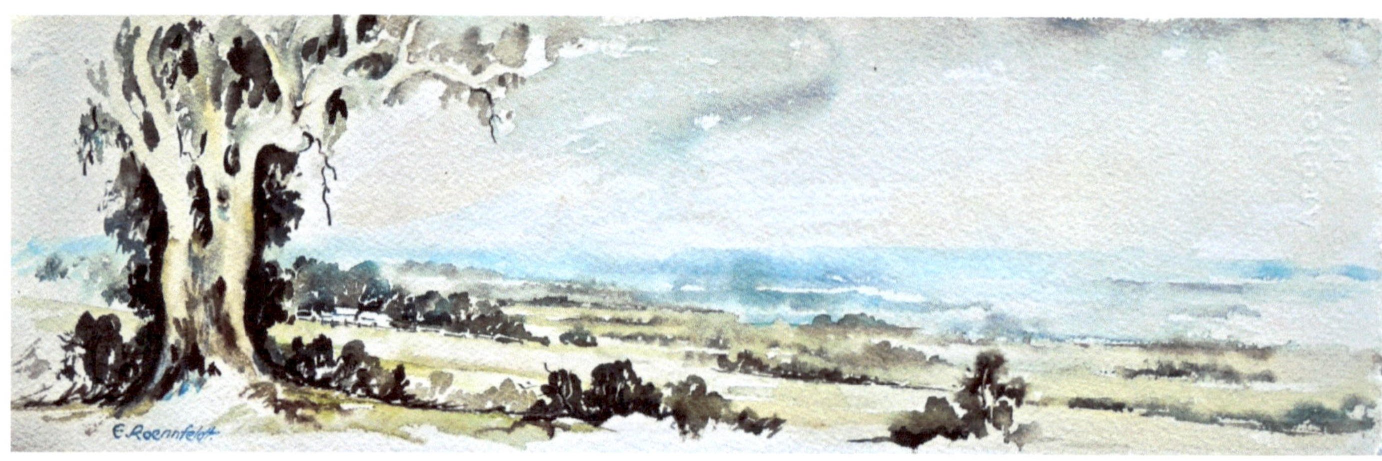

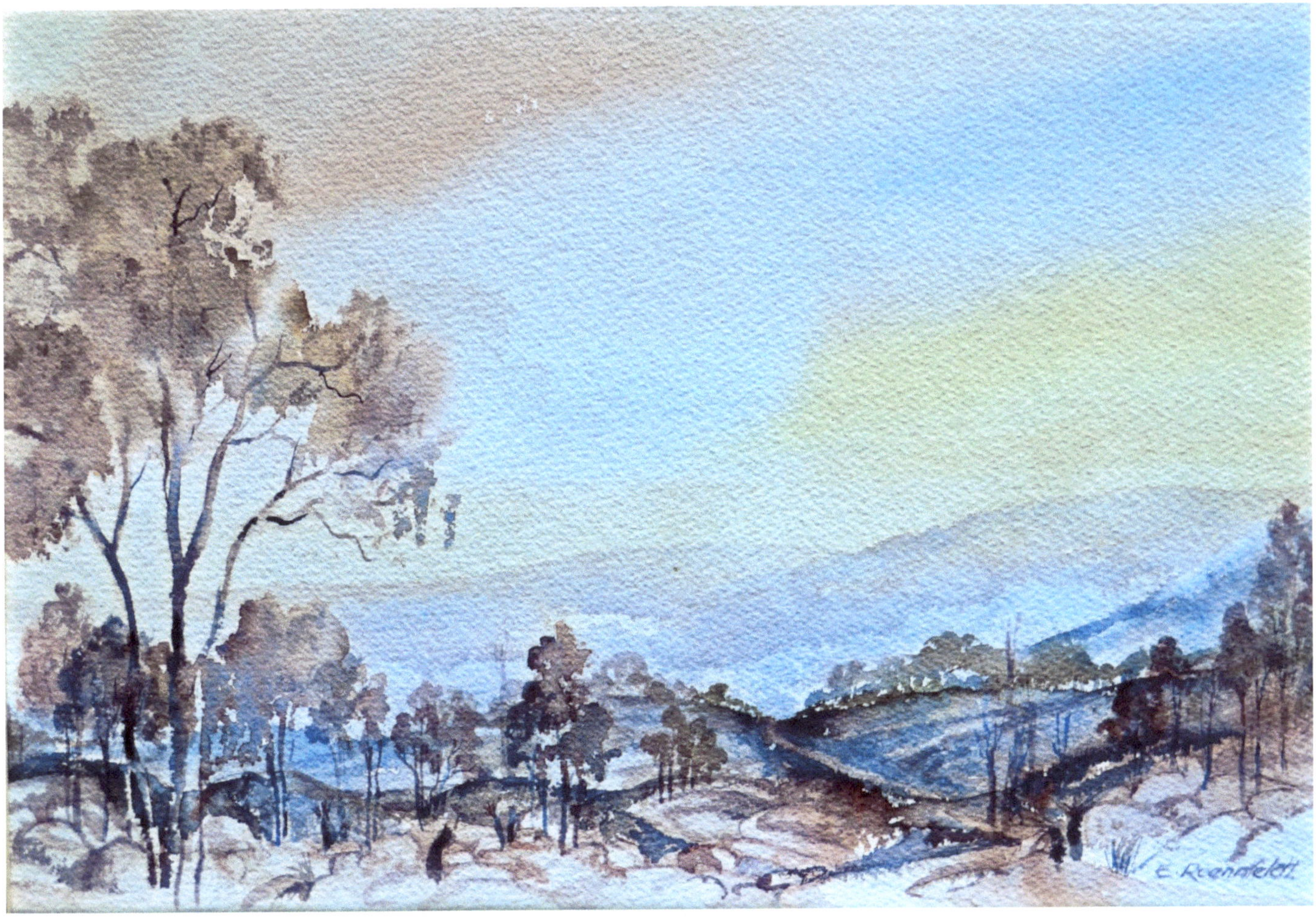

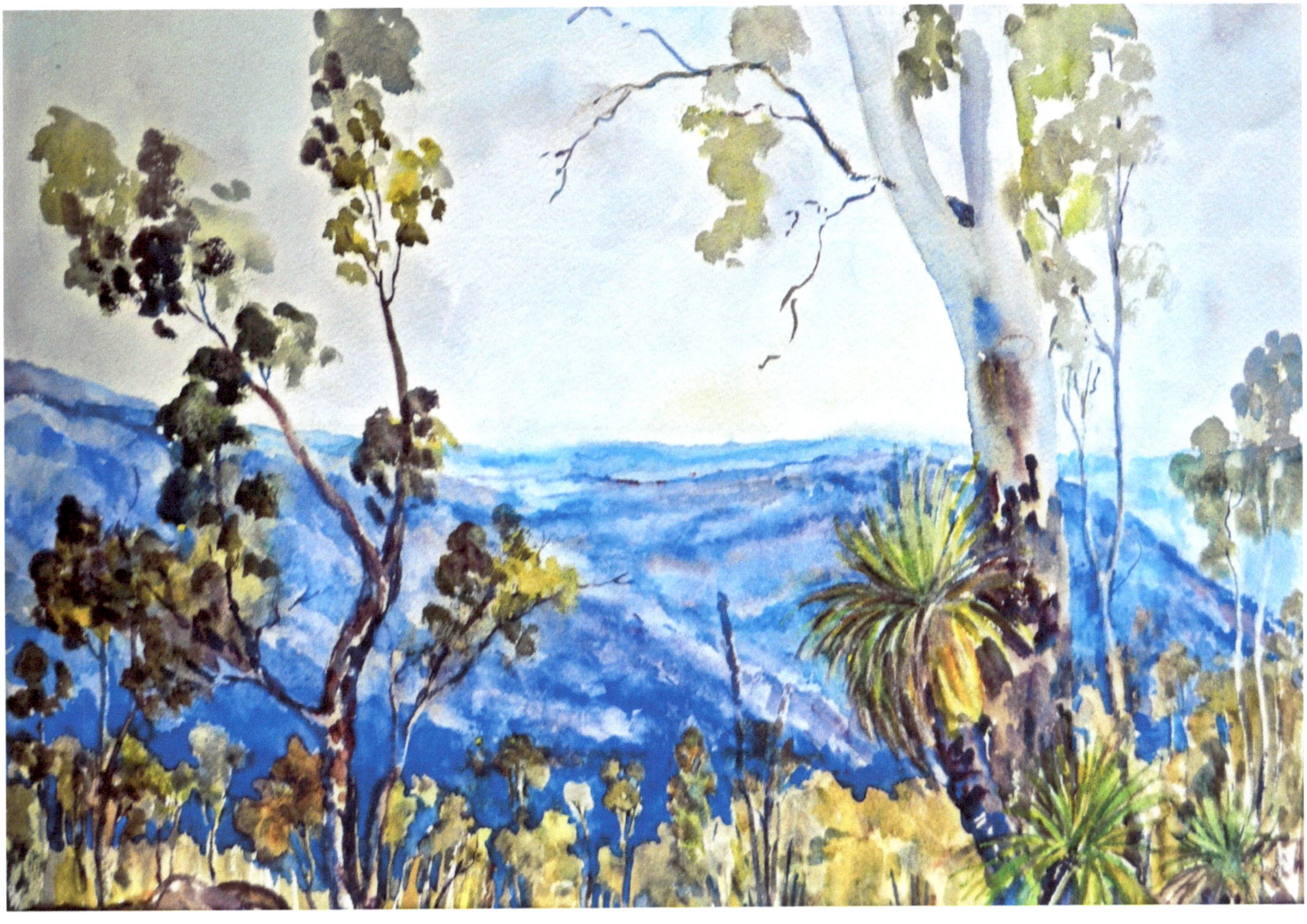

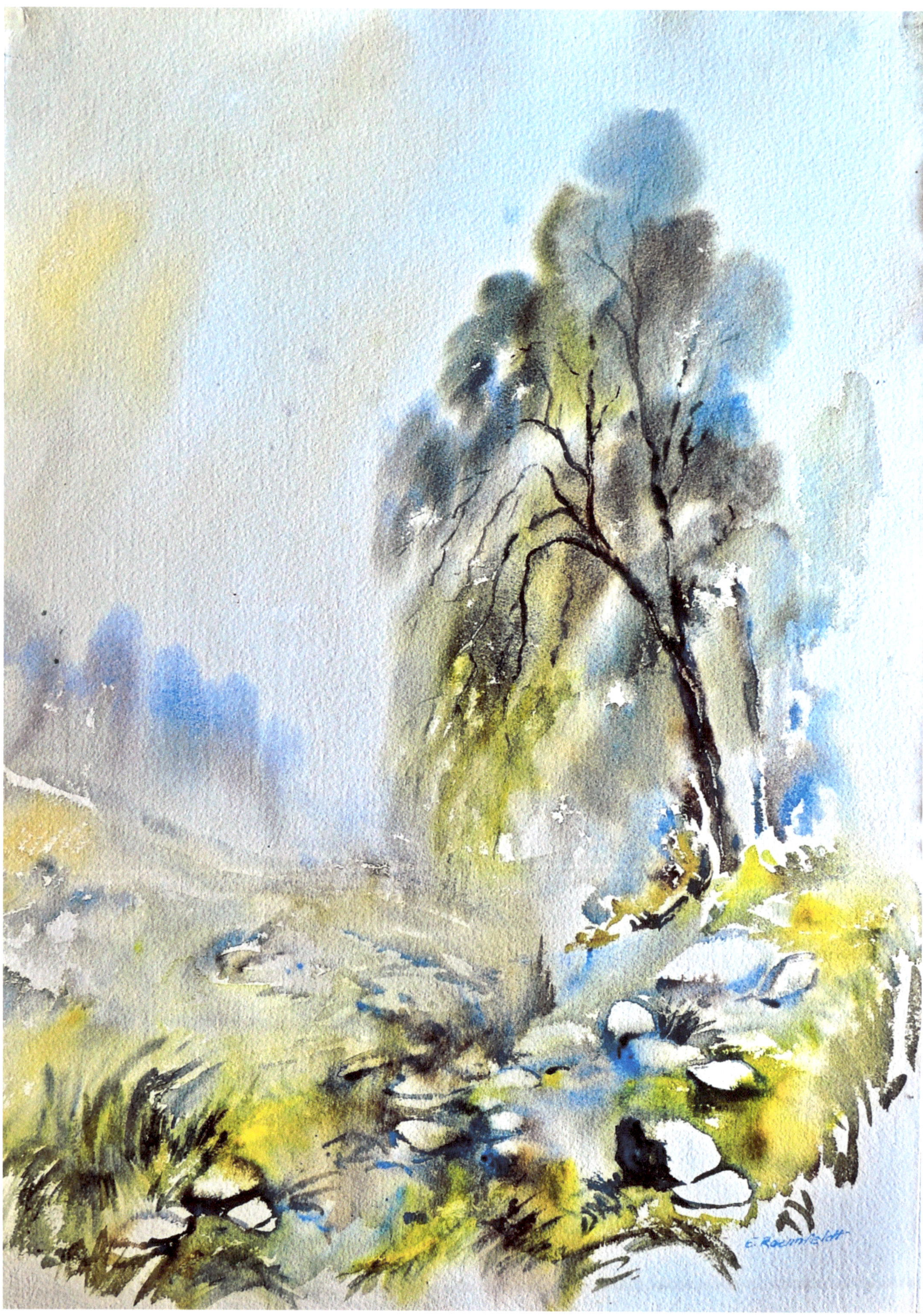

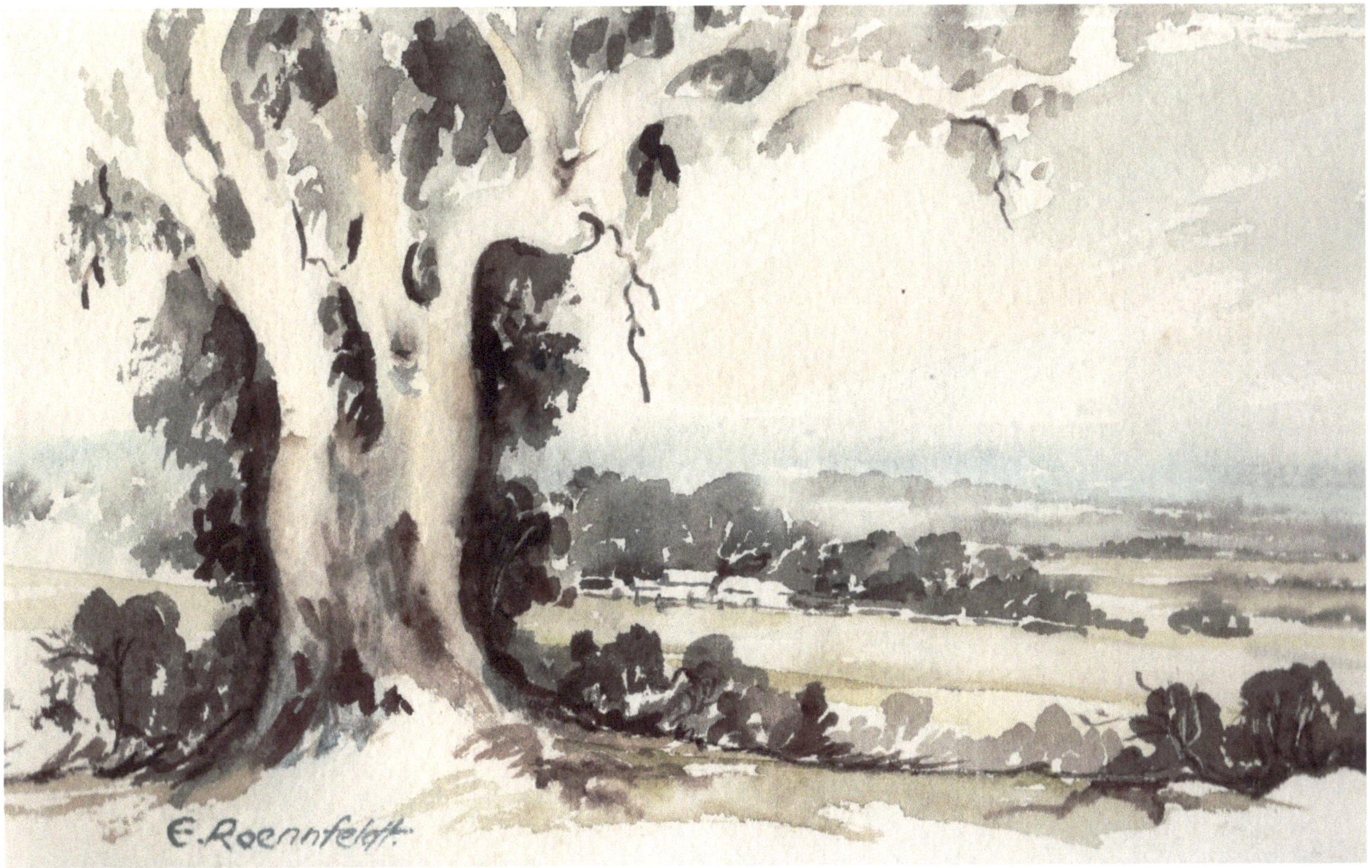

E. Roennfeldt

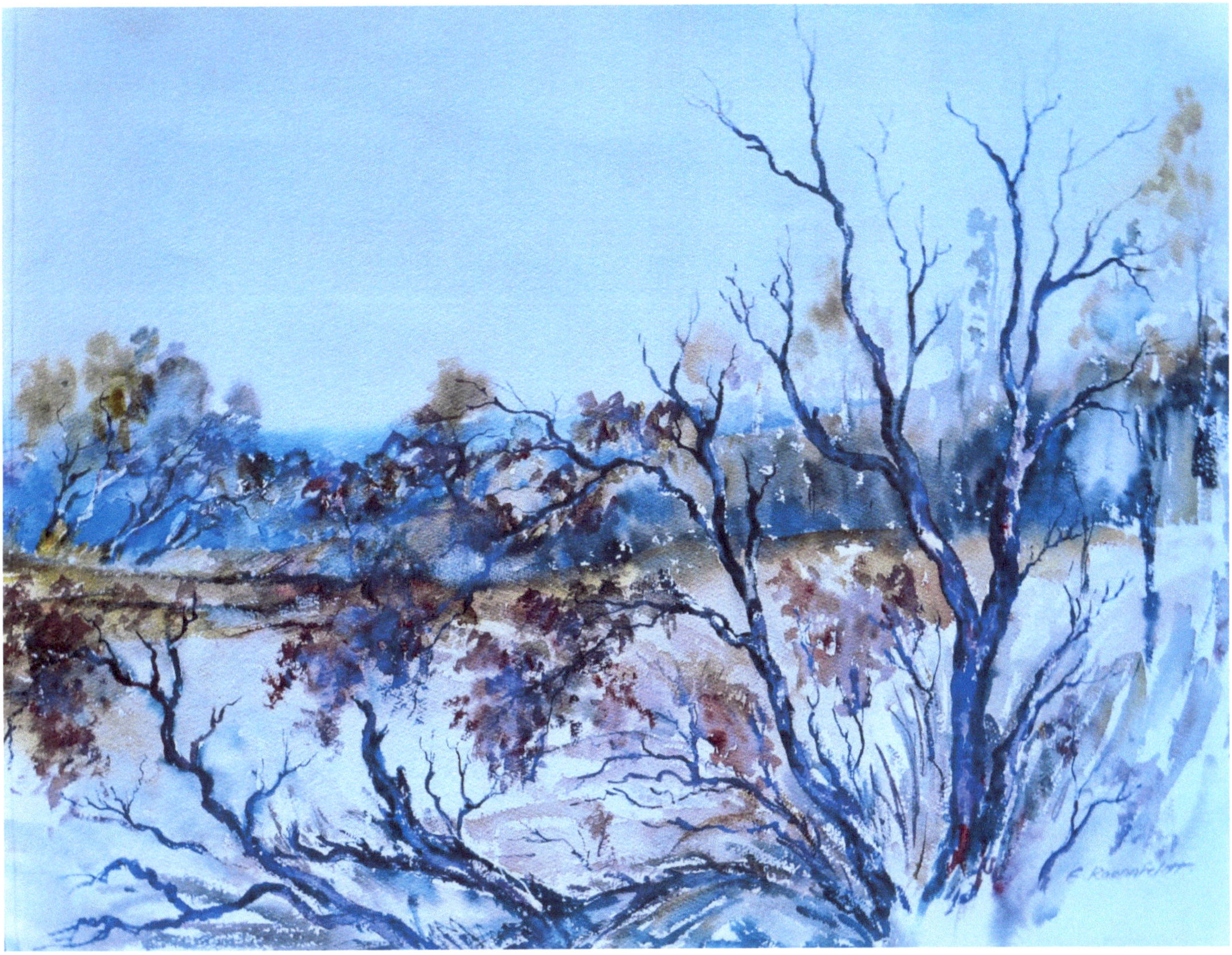

E. Roennfeldt

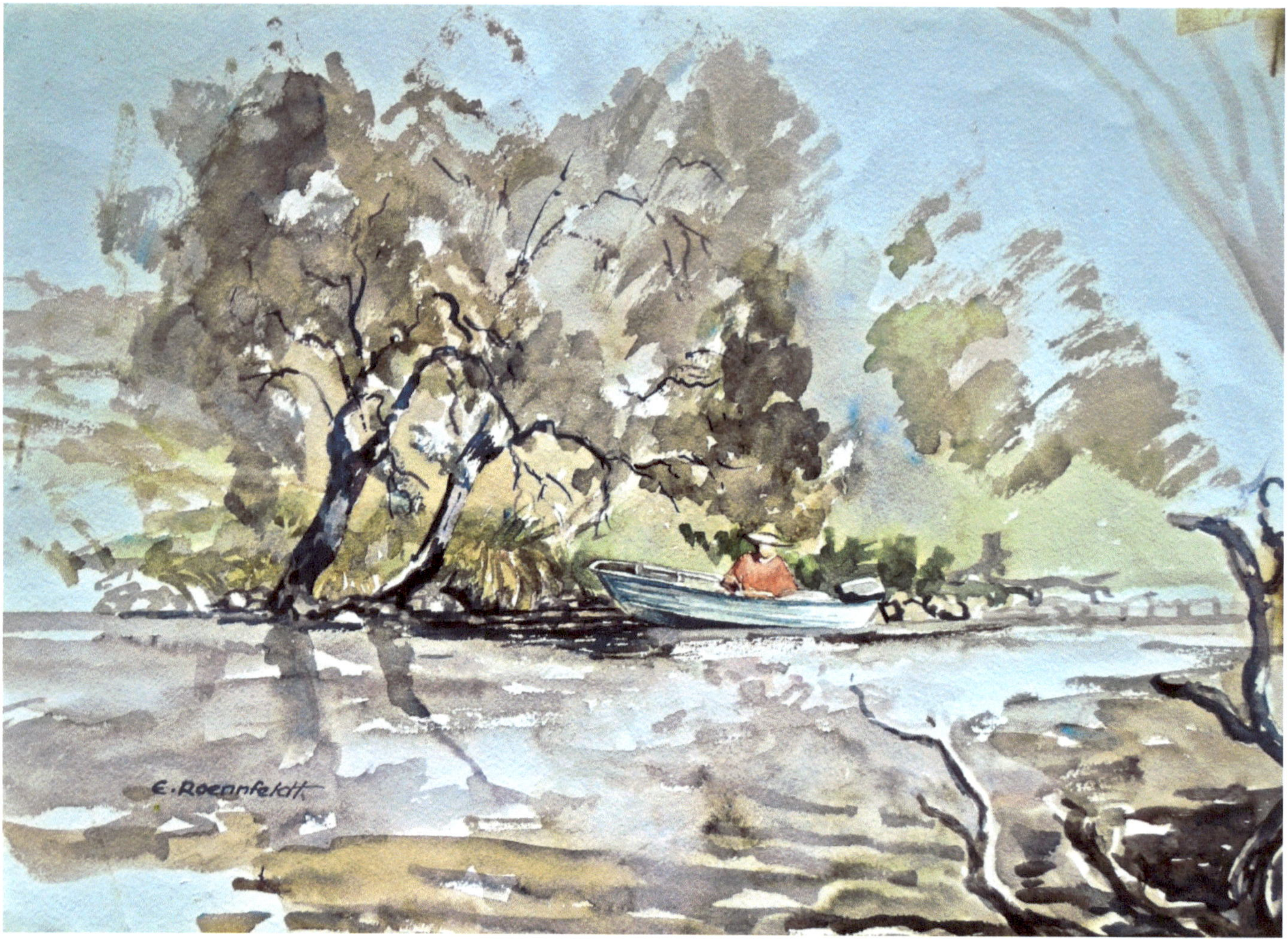

E. Roennfeldt

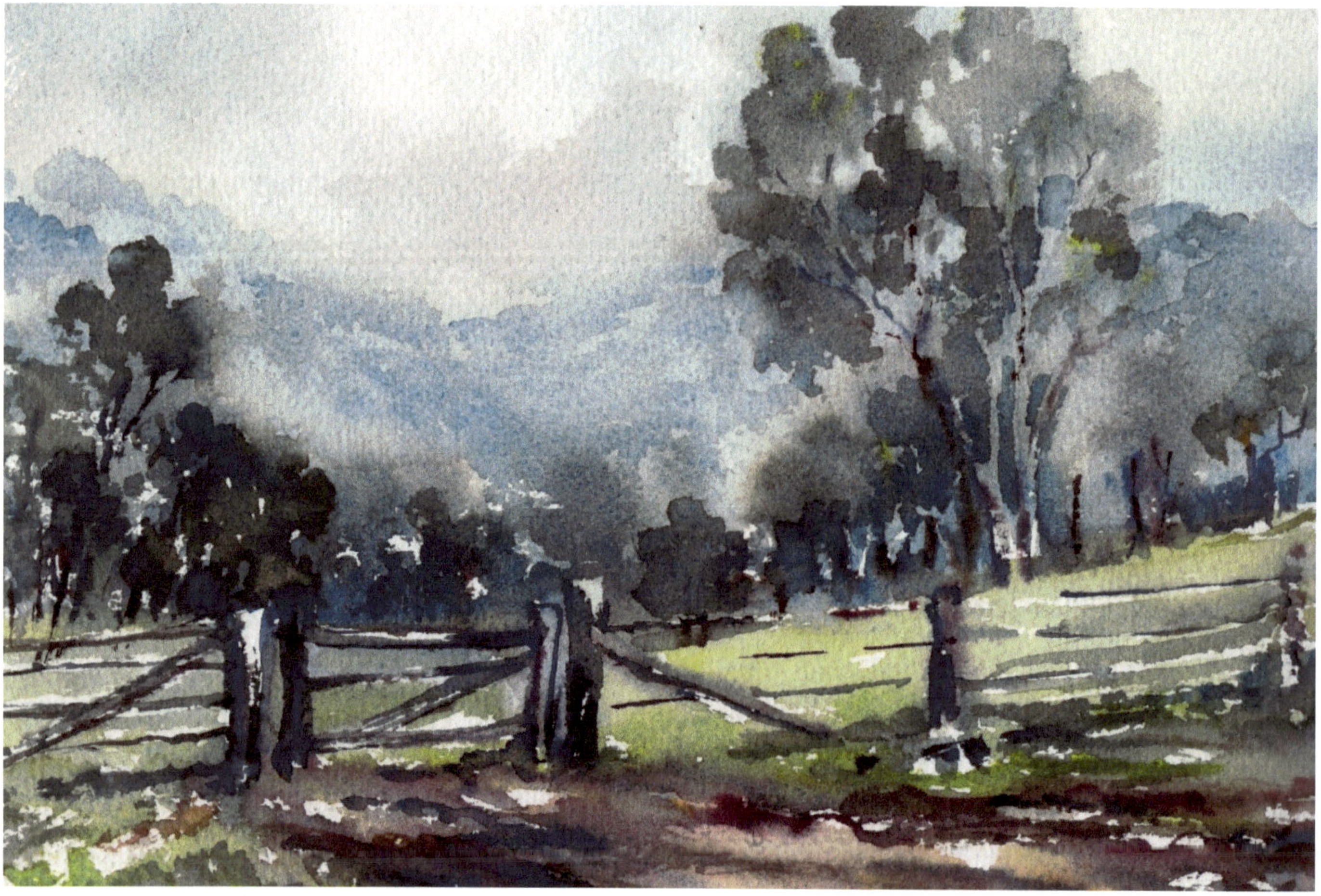

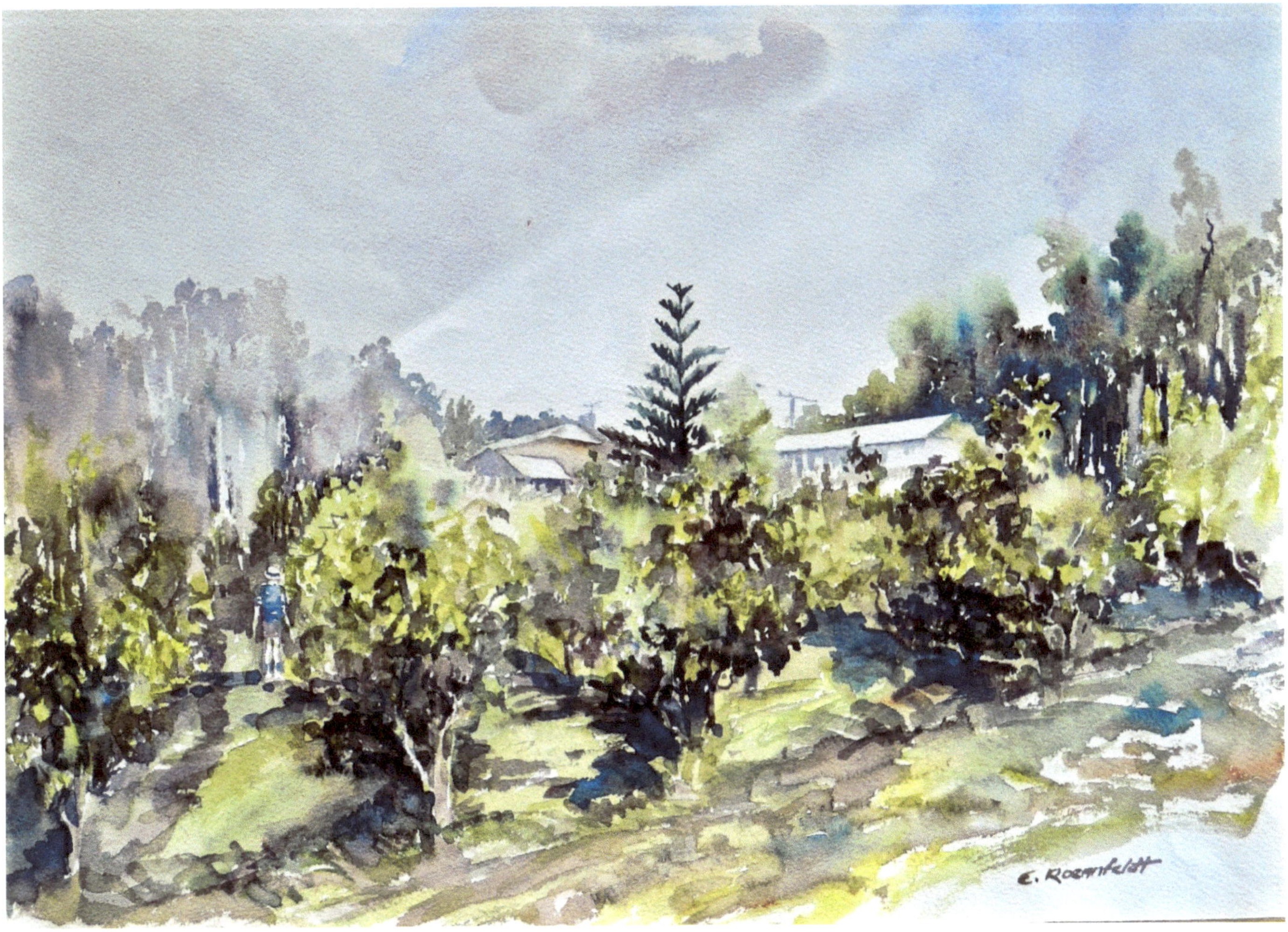

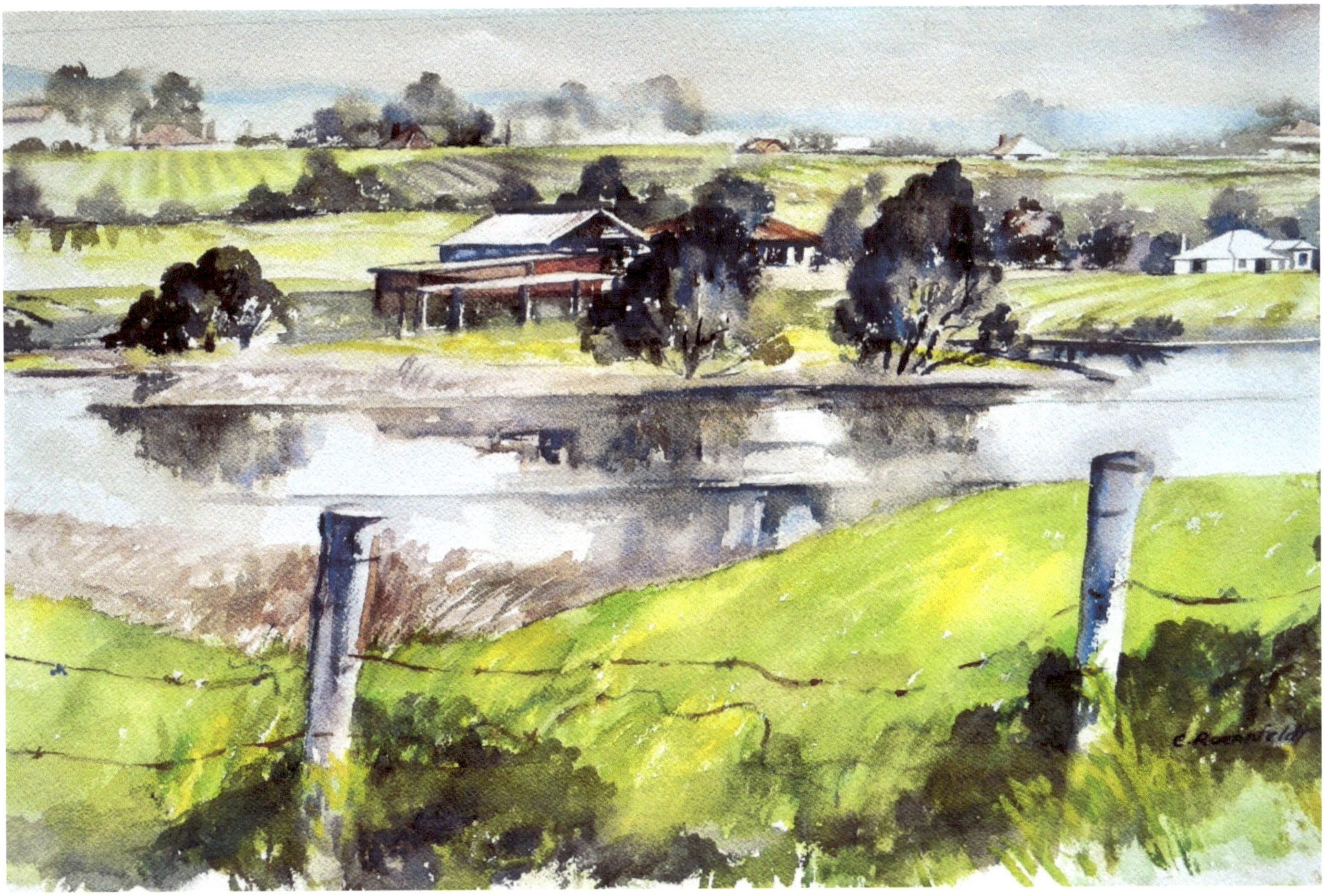

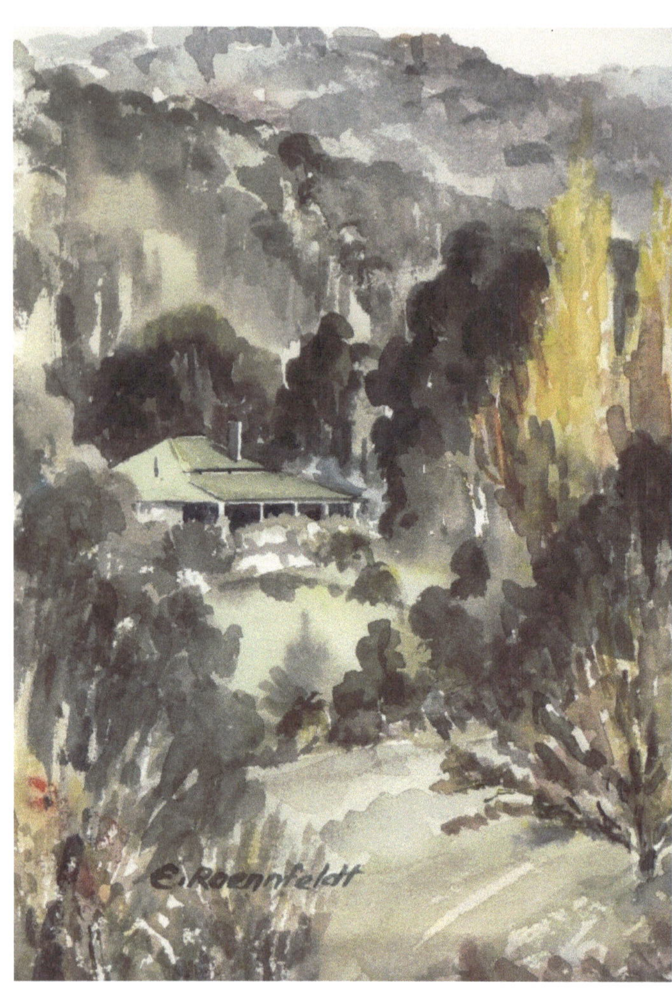
E.Roennfeldt

E.Roennfeldt

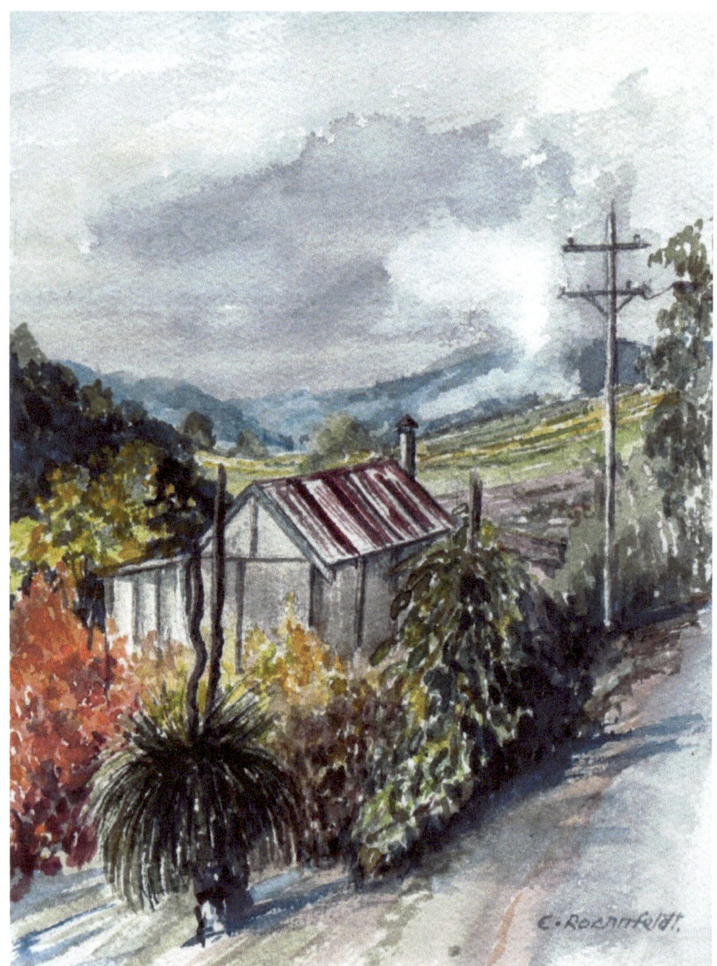
E.Roennfeldt.

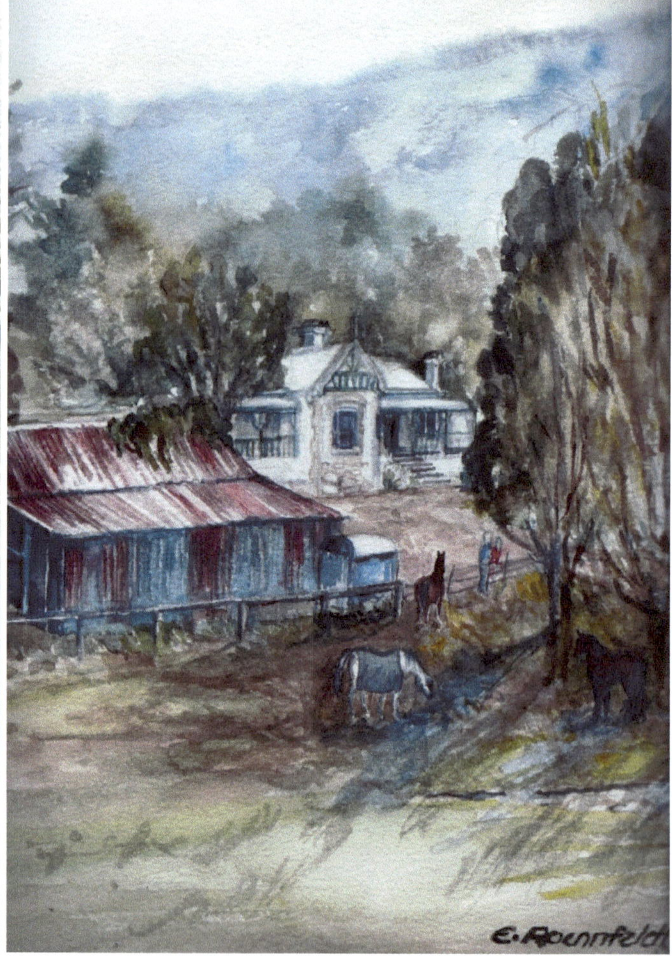
E.Roennfeldt

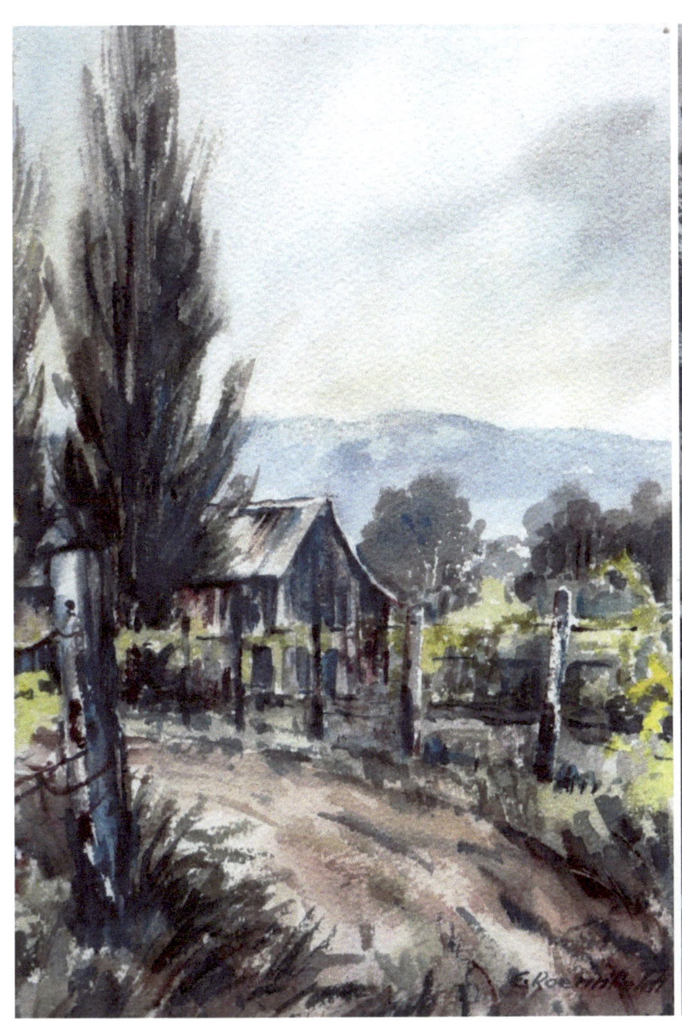

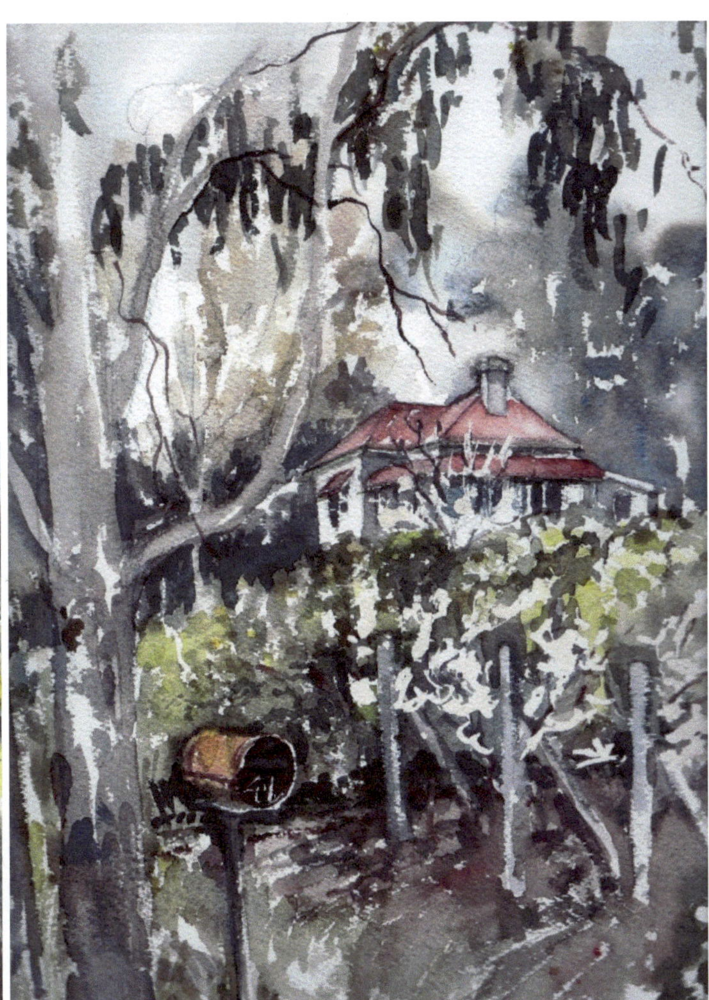

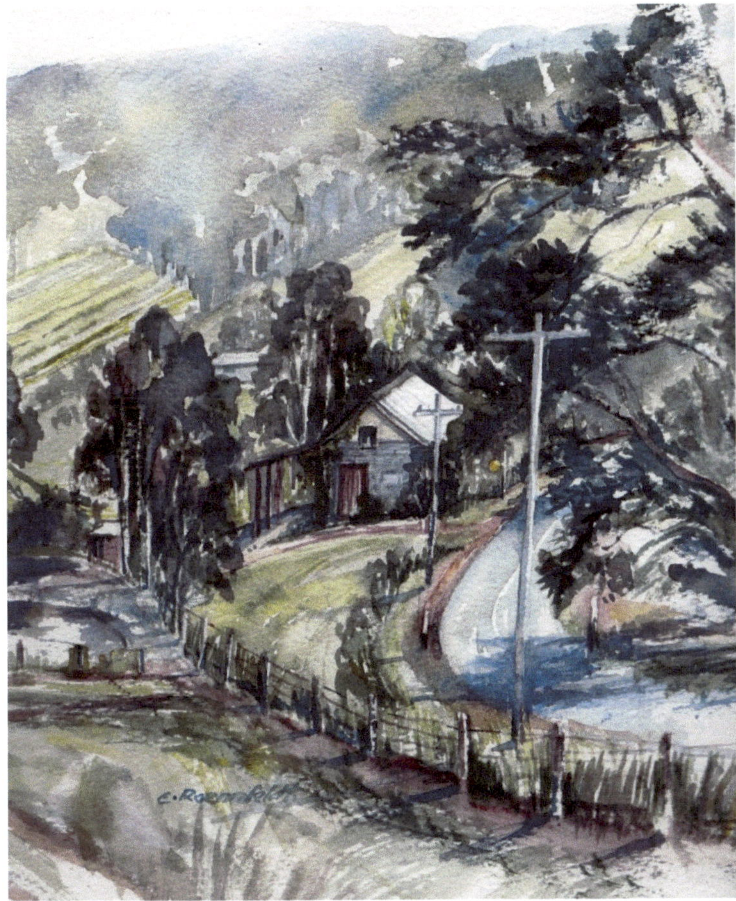

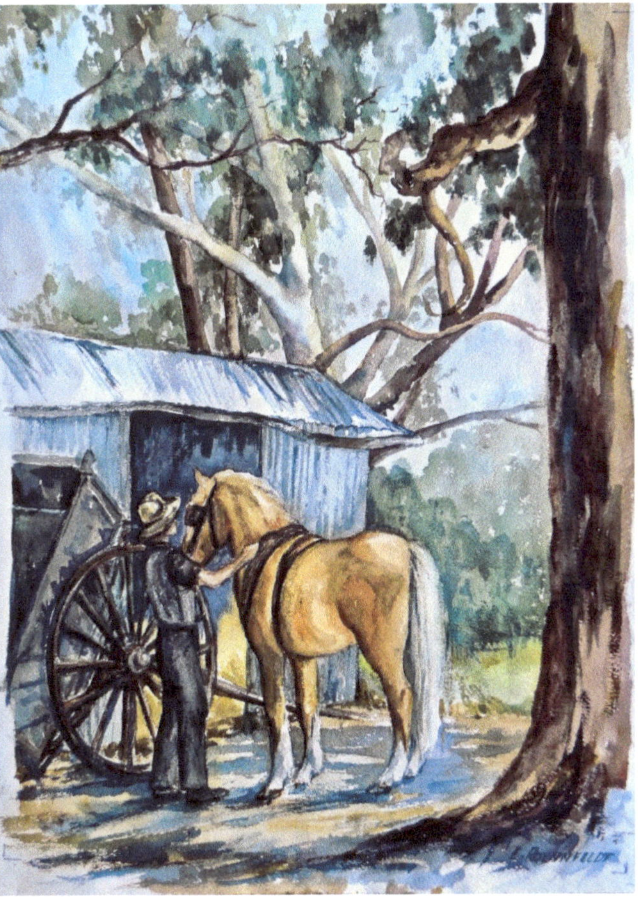

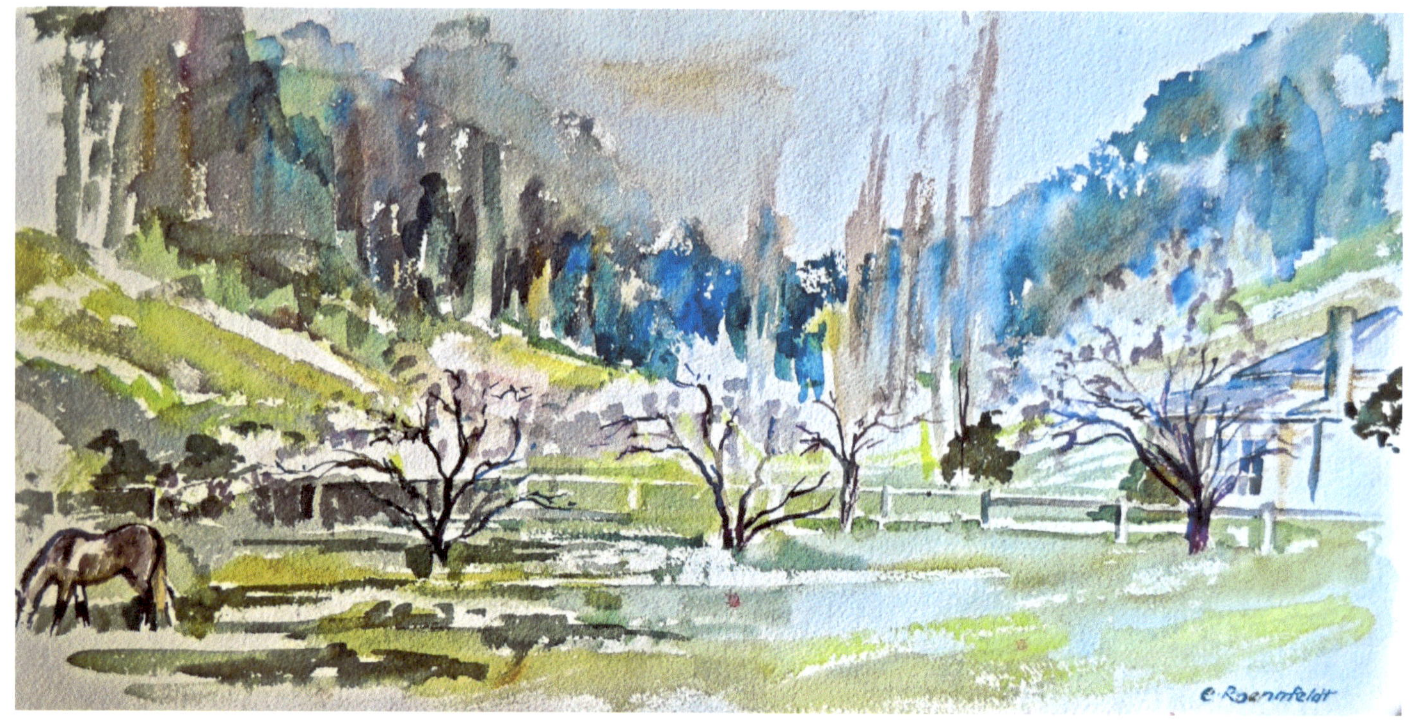
E Roennfeldt

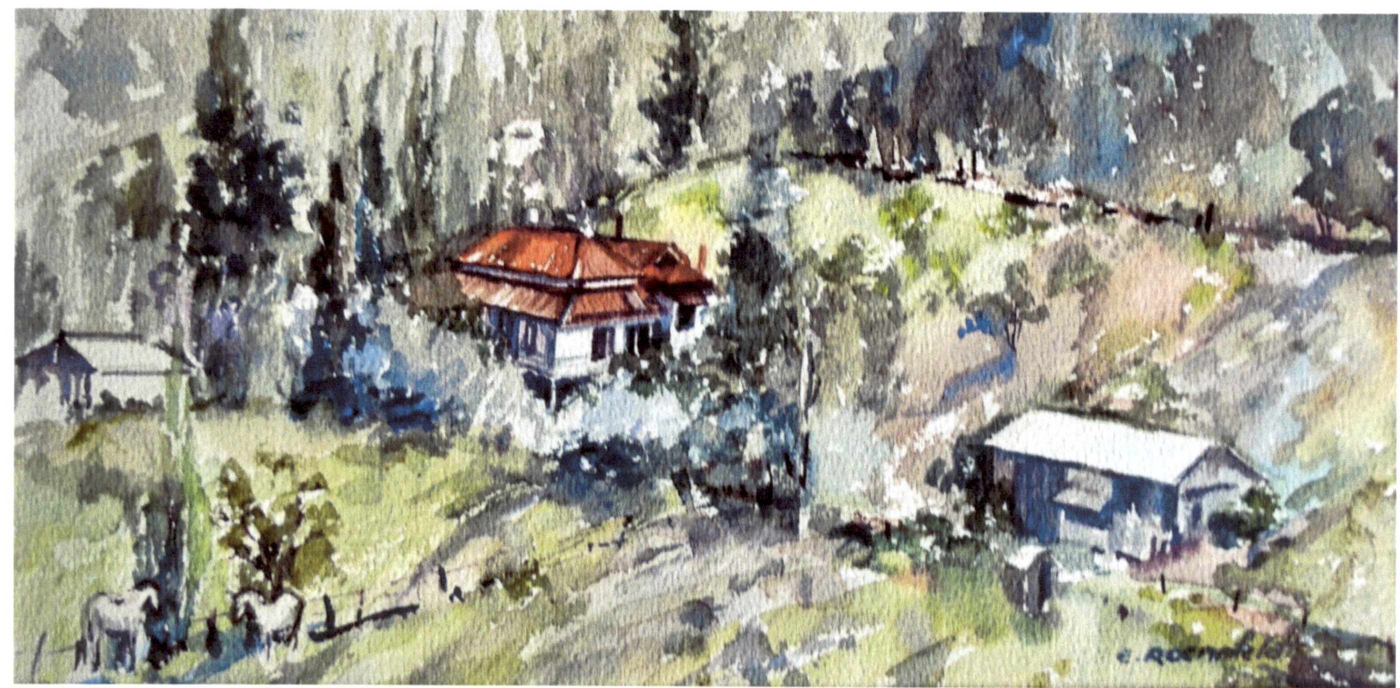

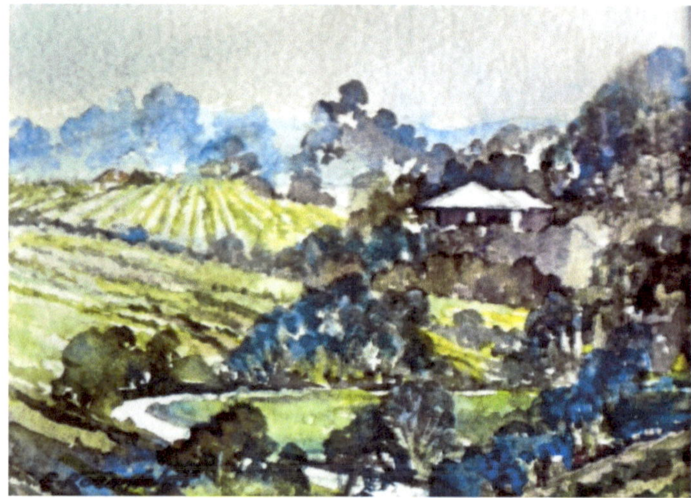

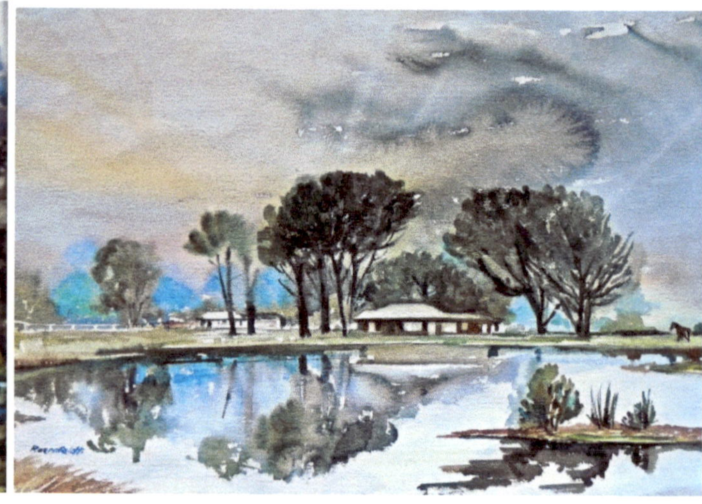

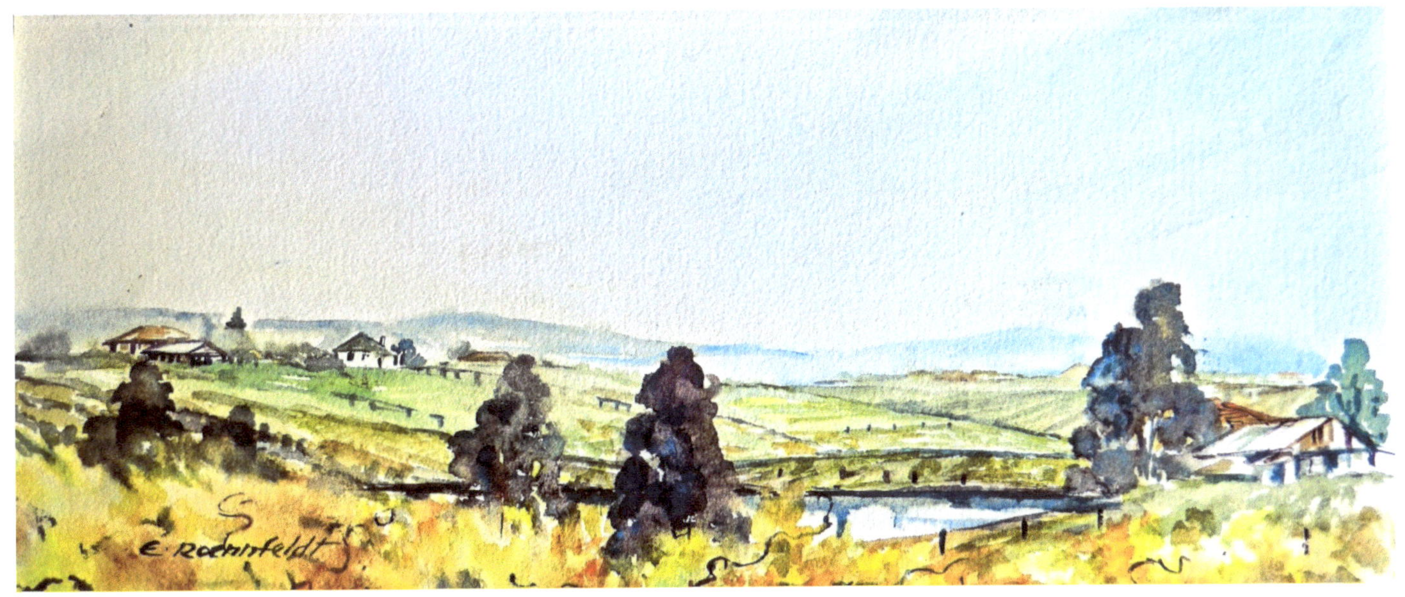
E.Roennfeldt

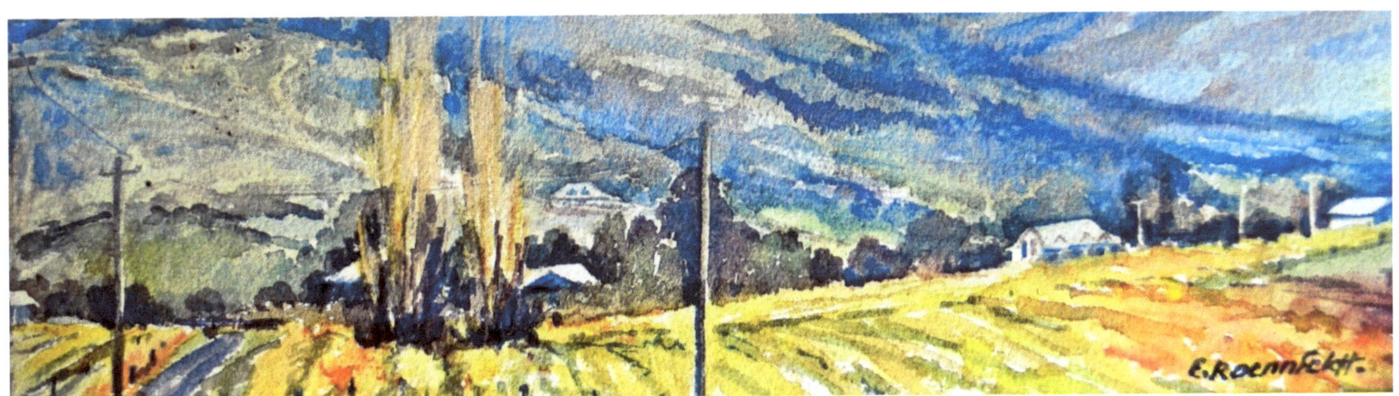
E.Roennfeldt.

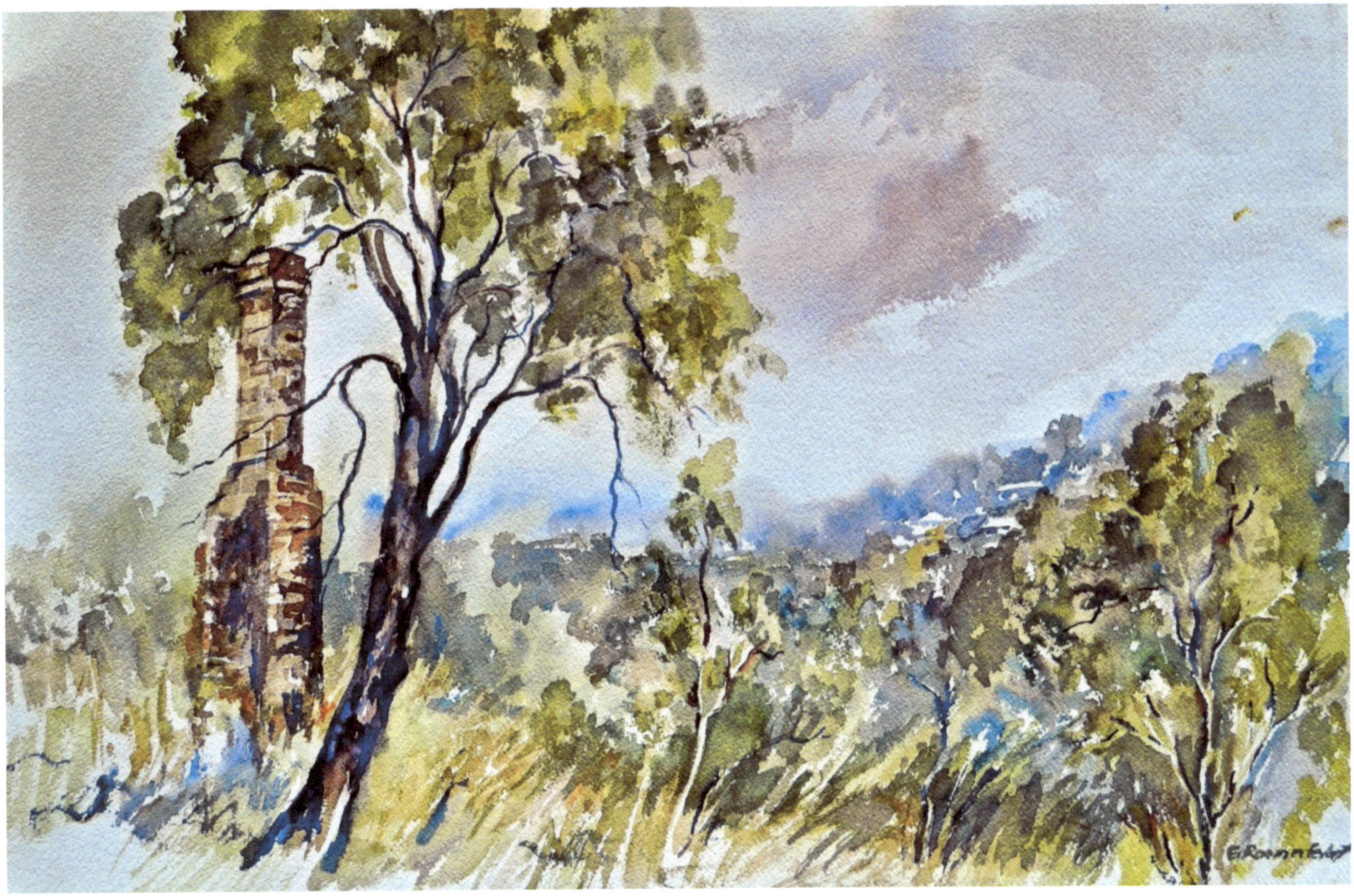

Old houses

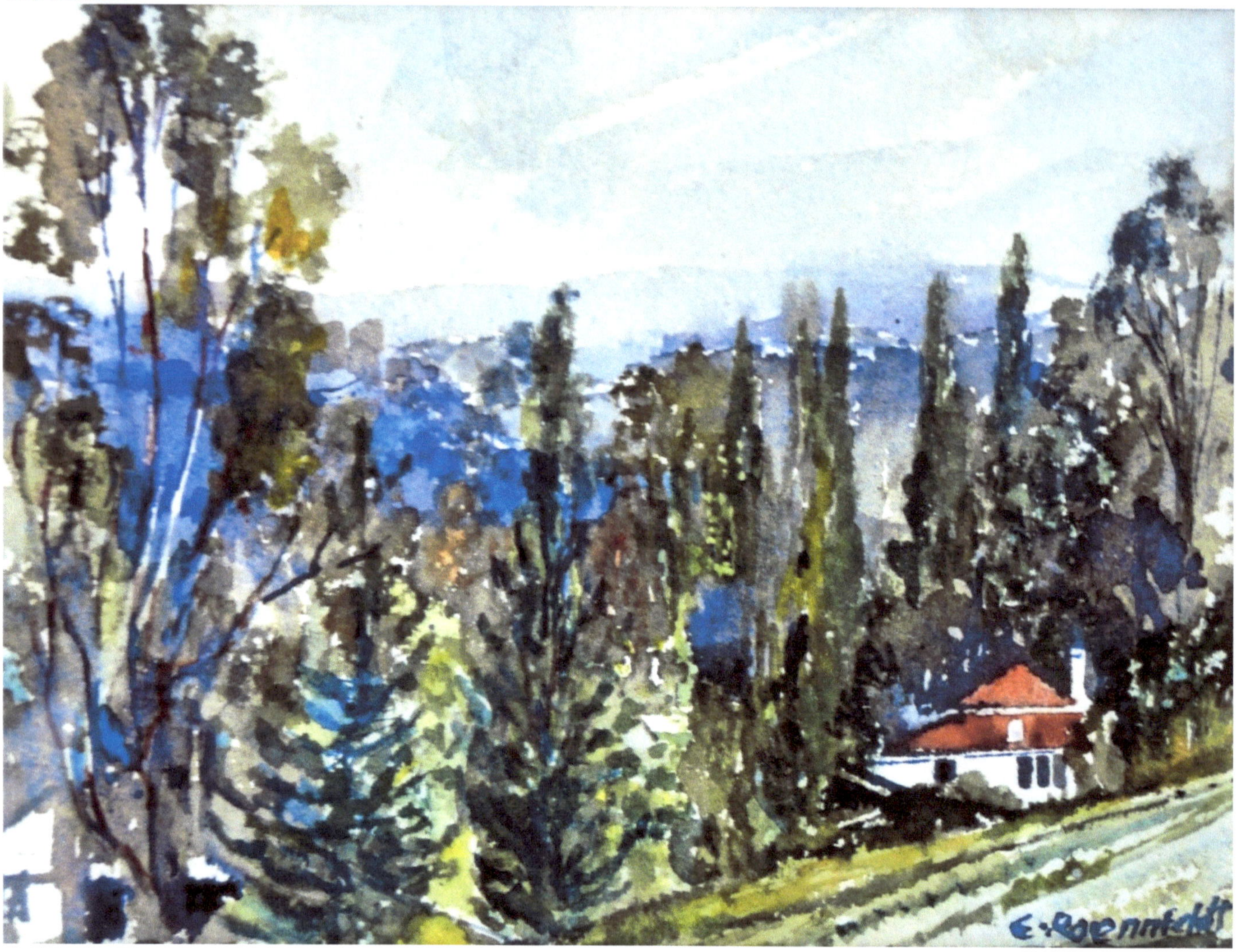

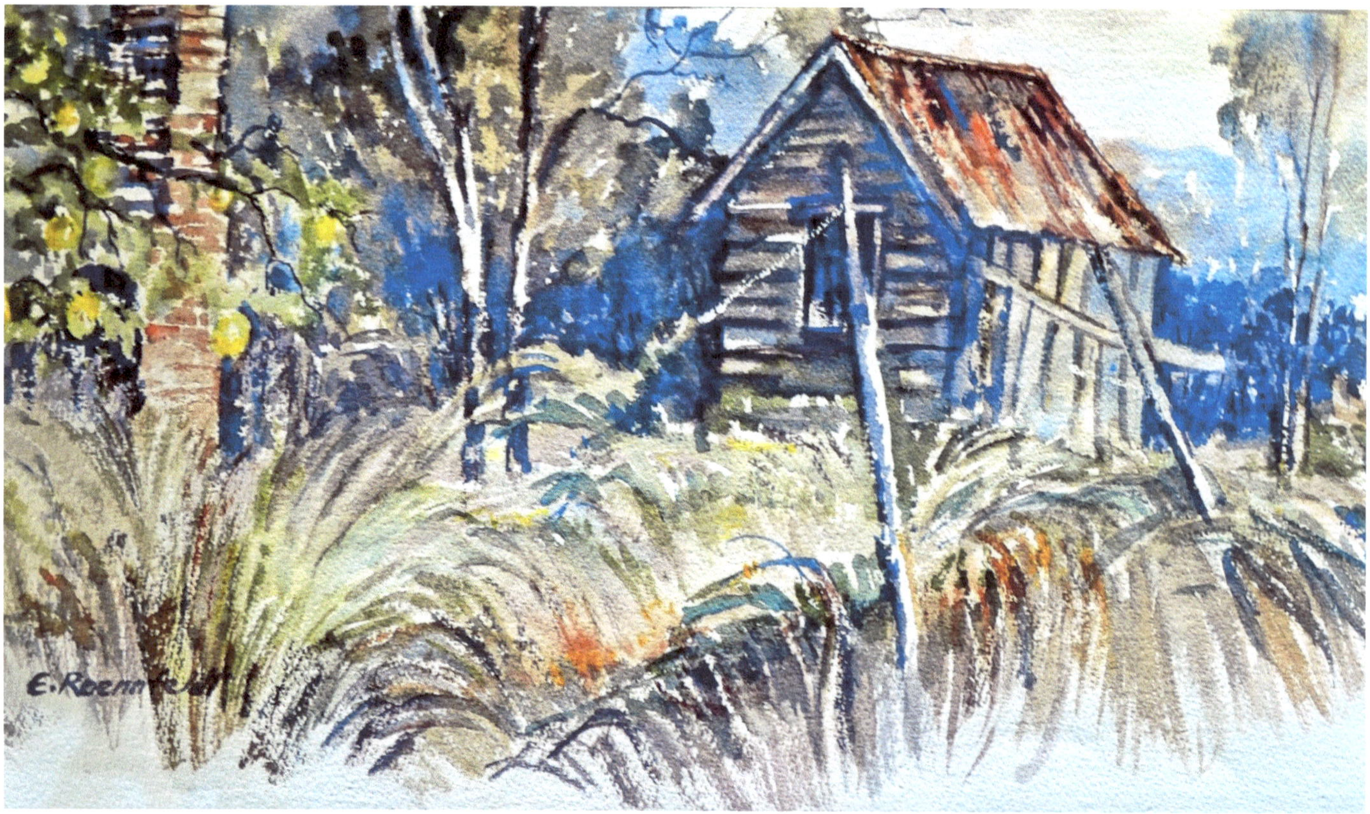

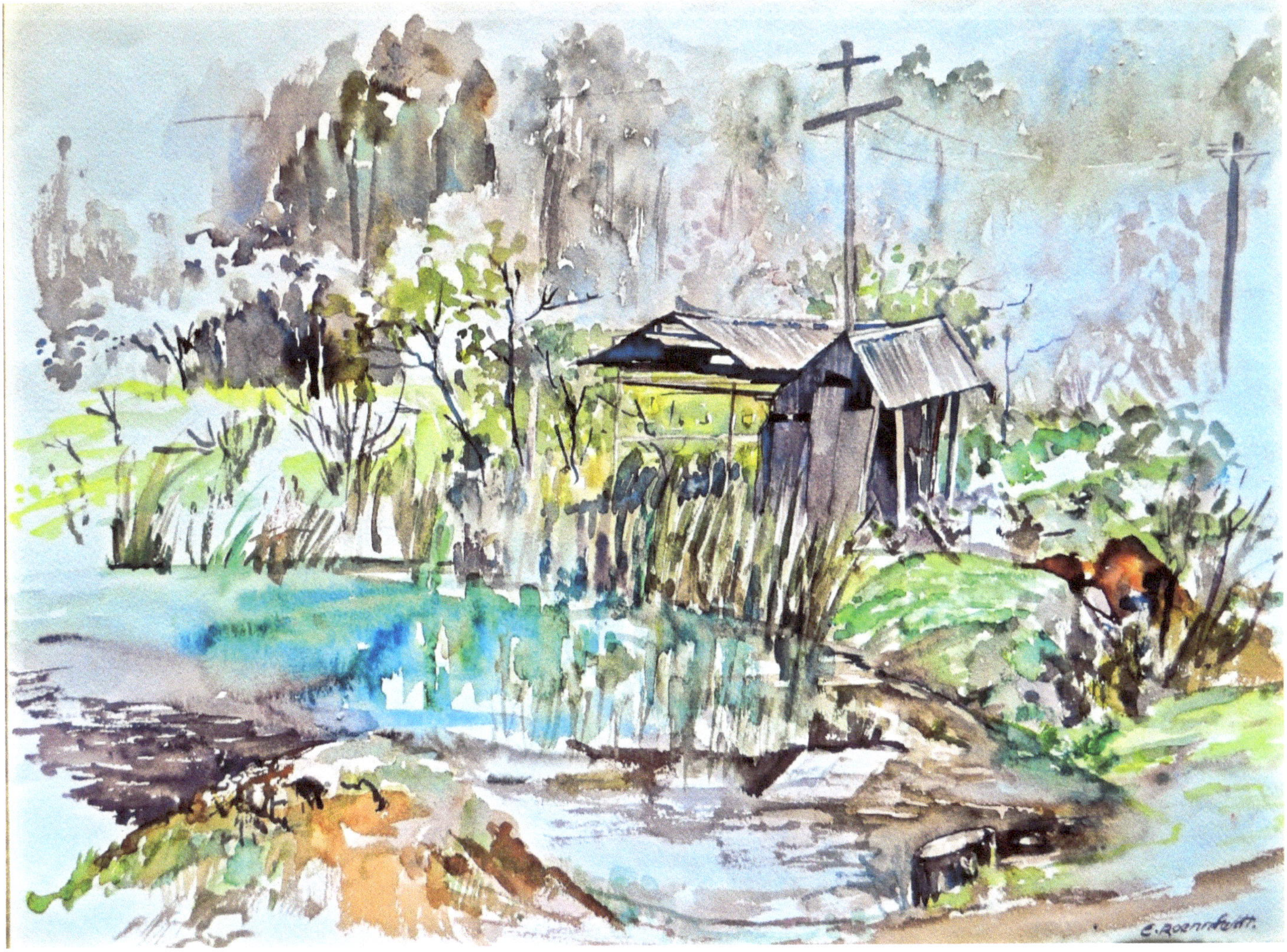

E. Roennfeldt.

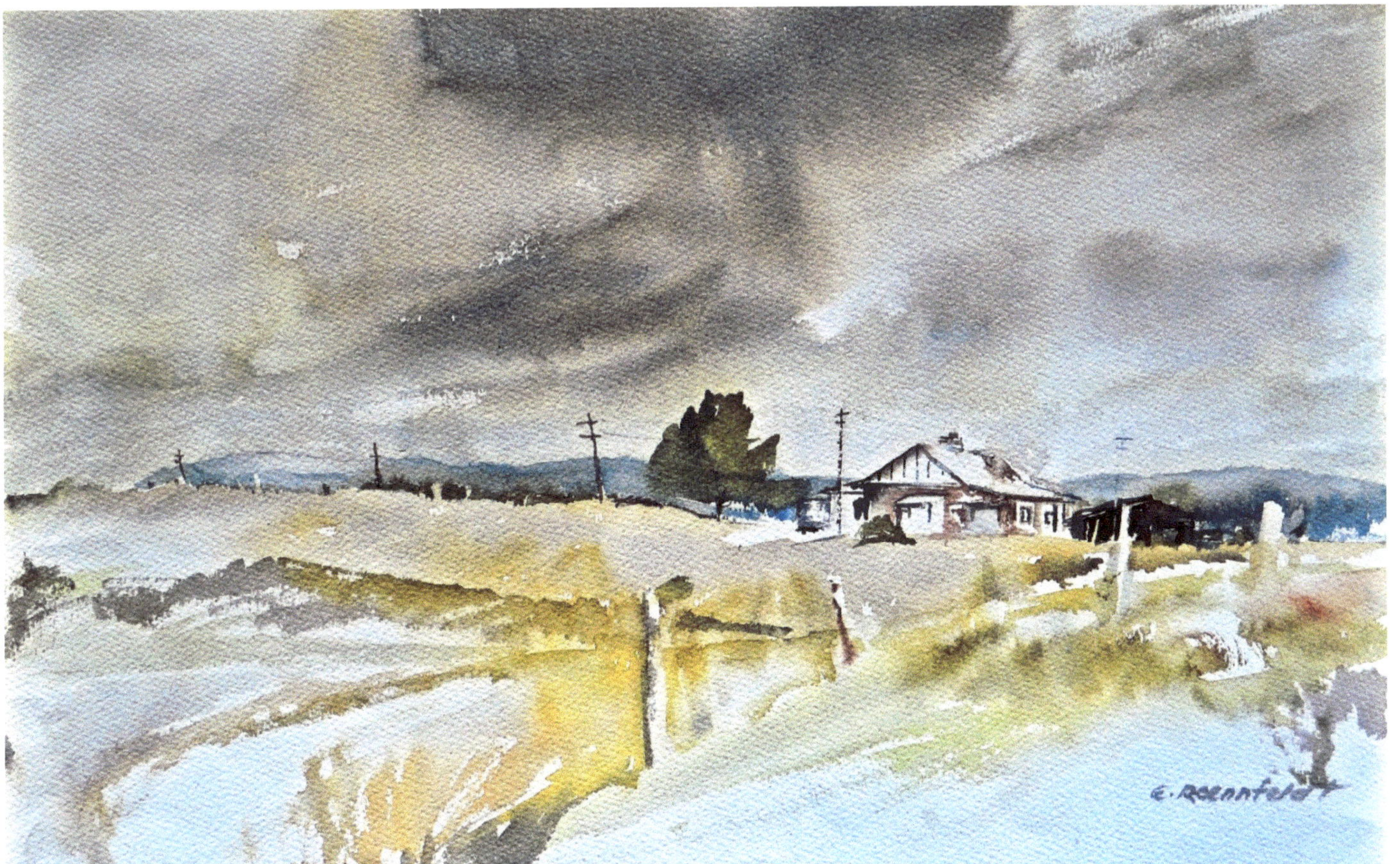

E. Roennfeldt

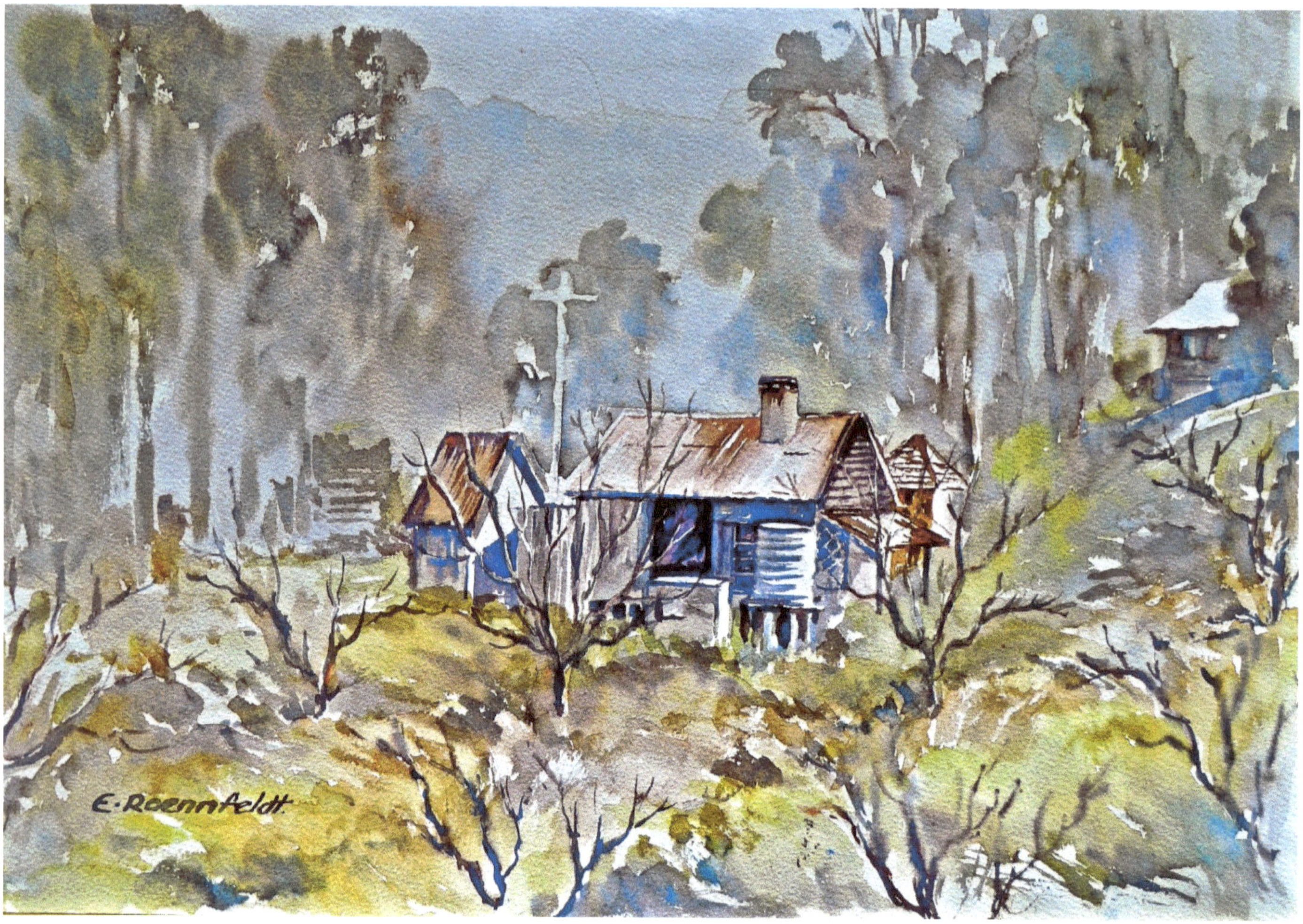

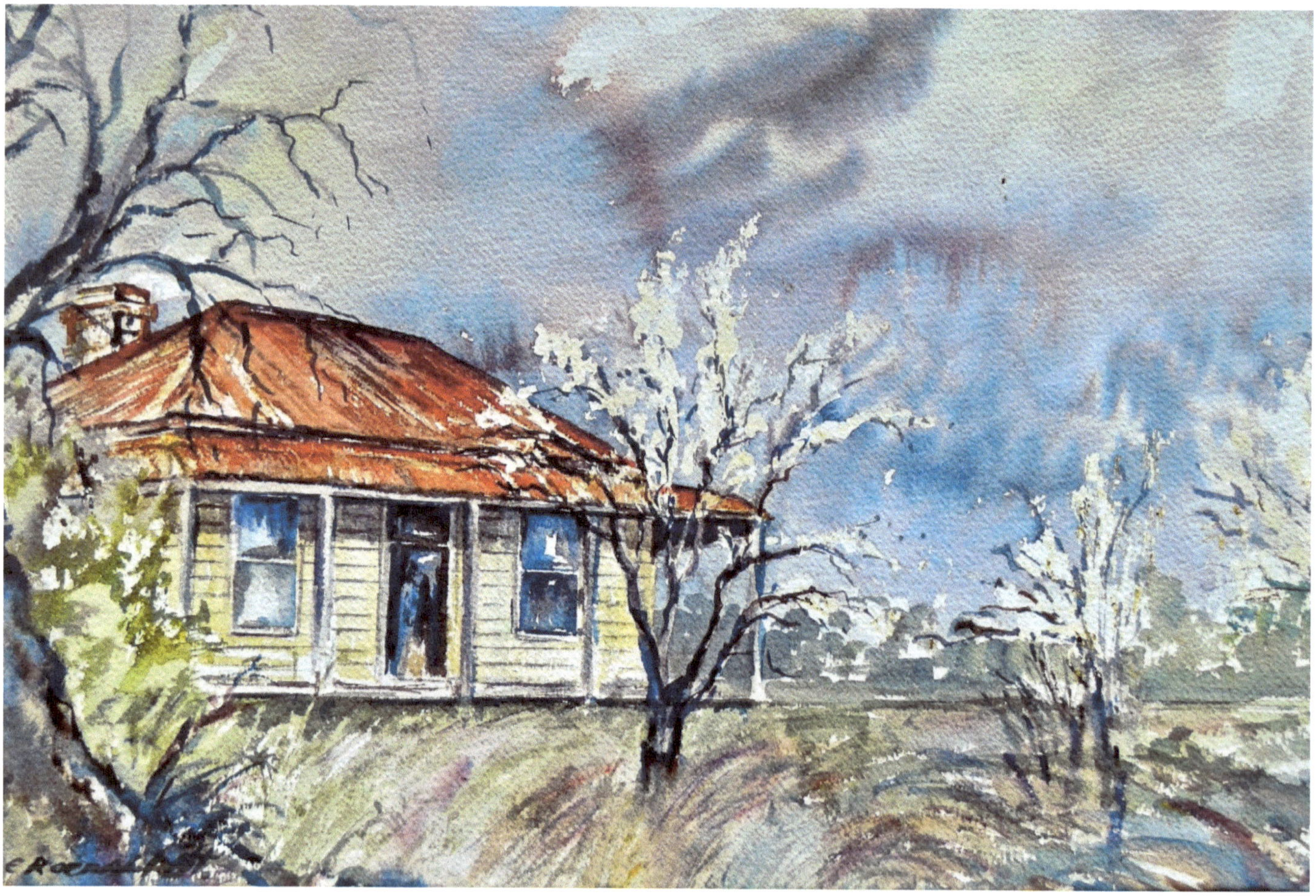

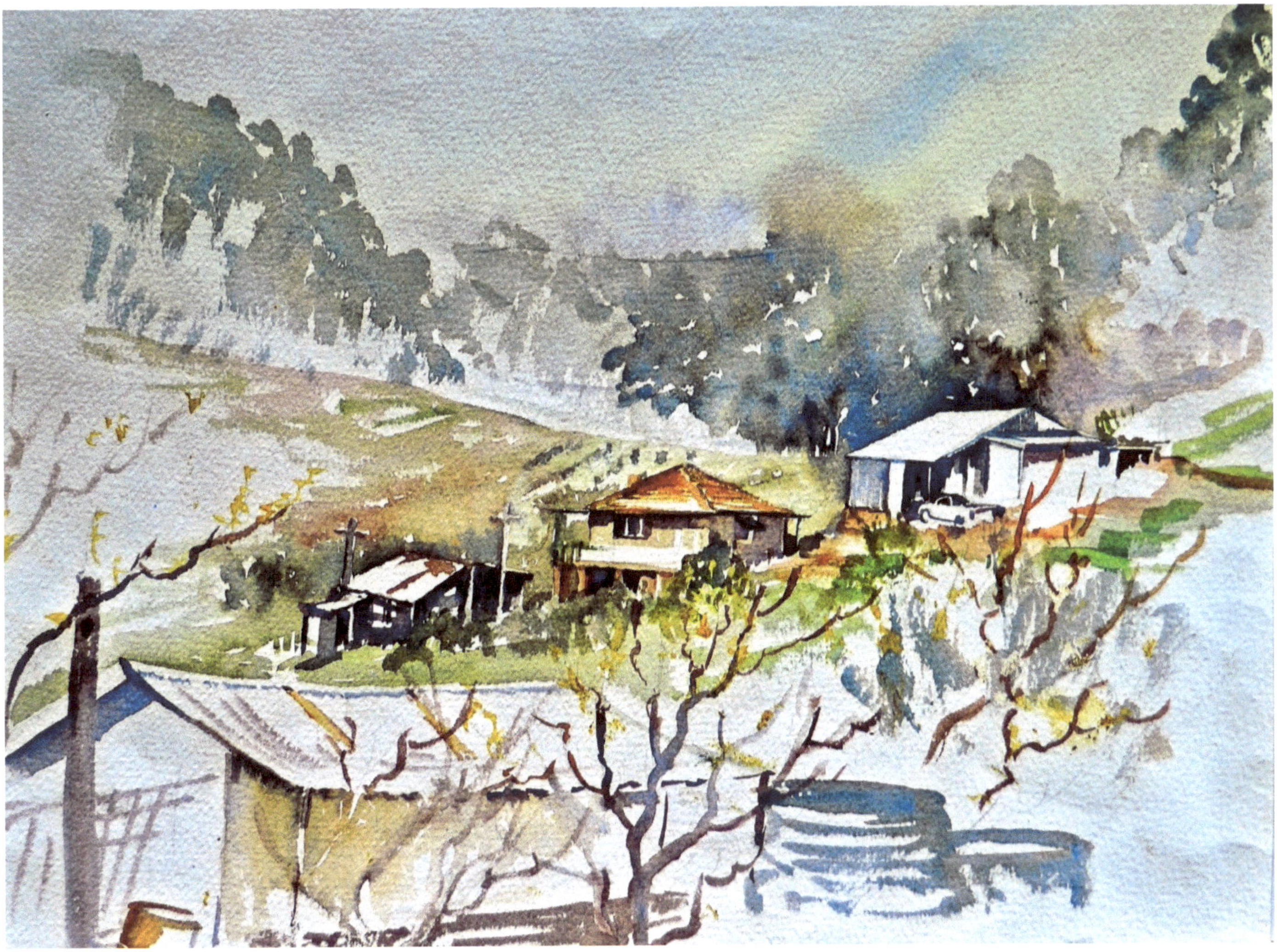

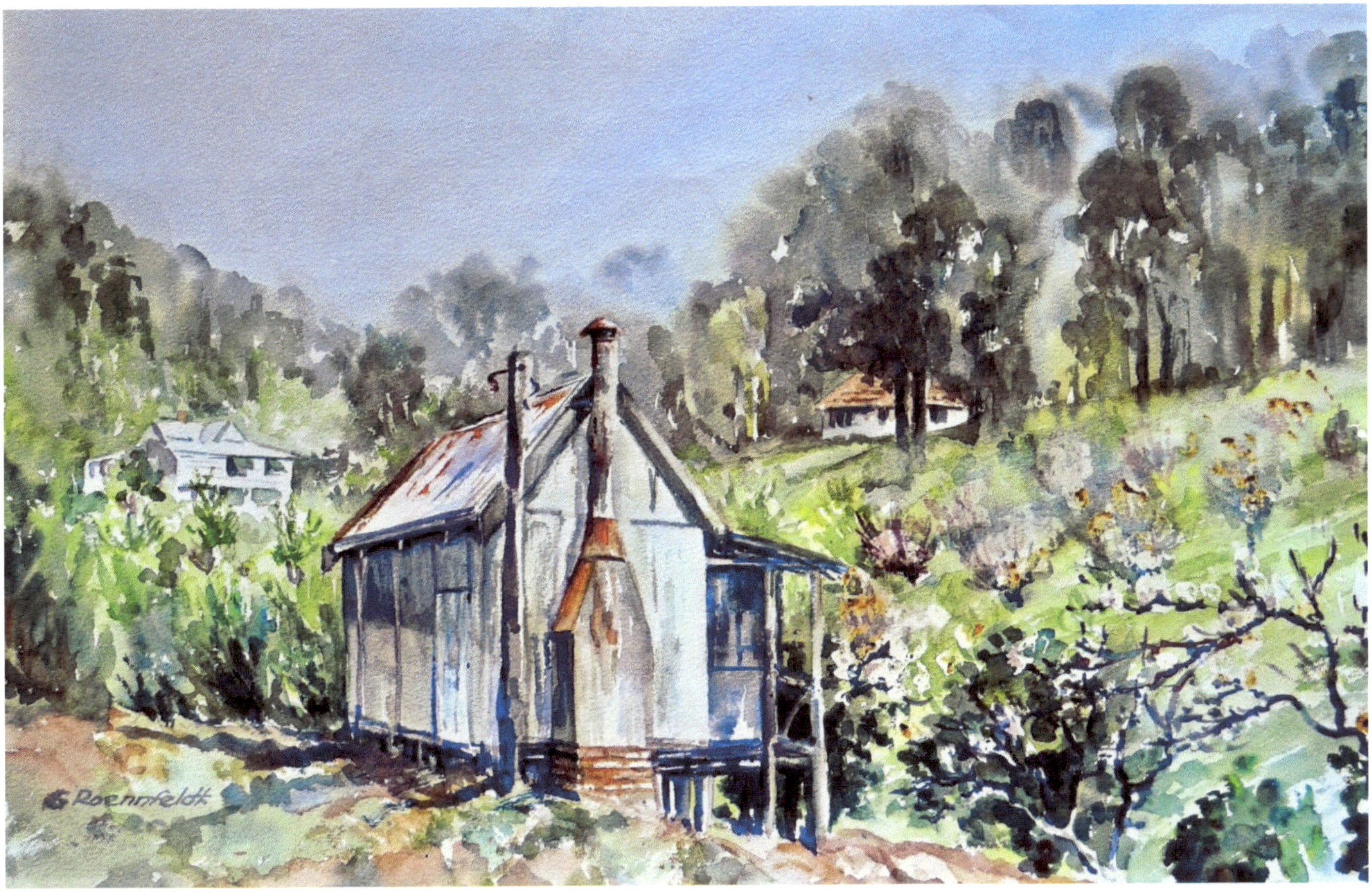

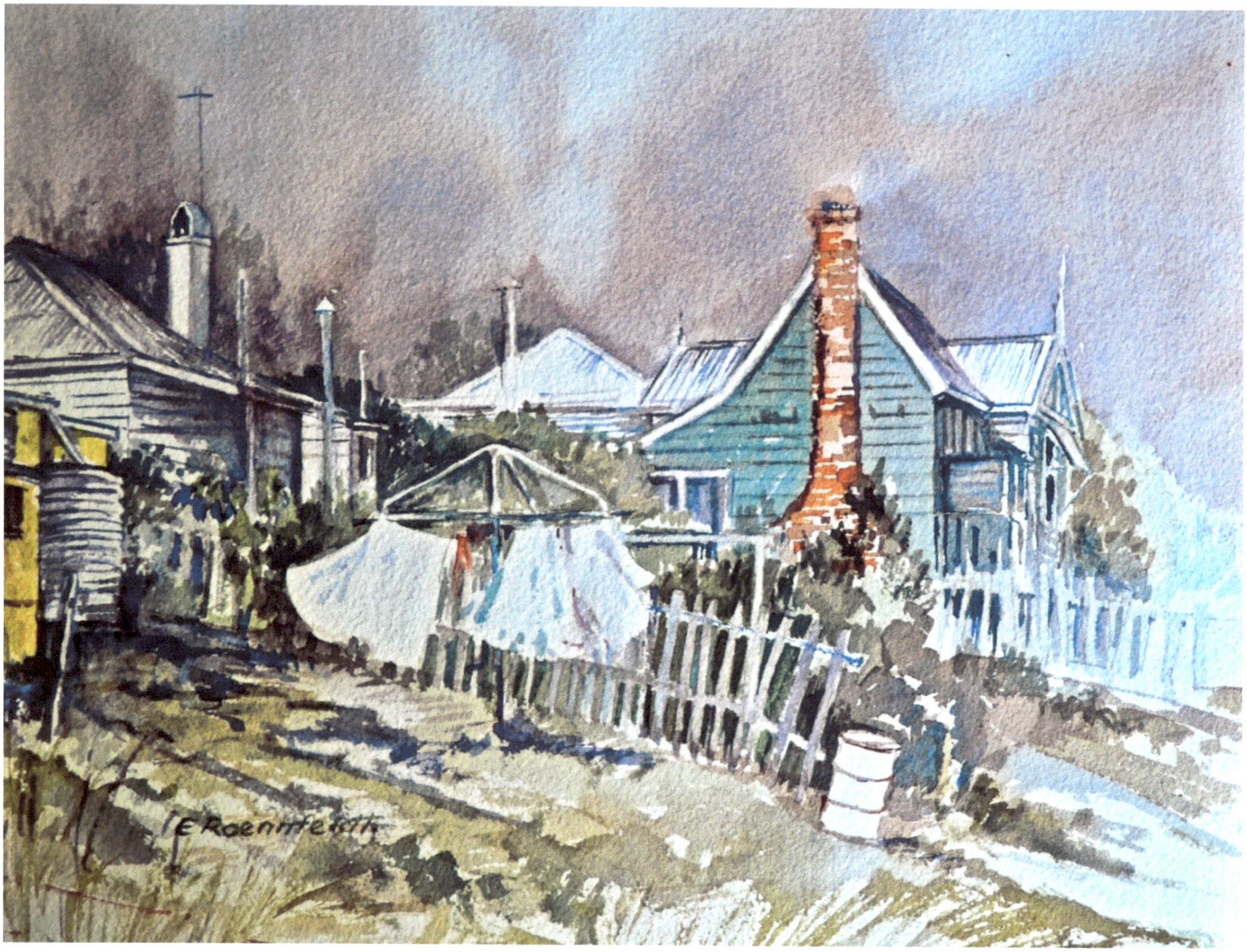

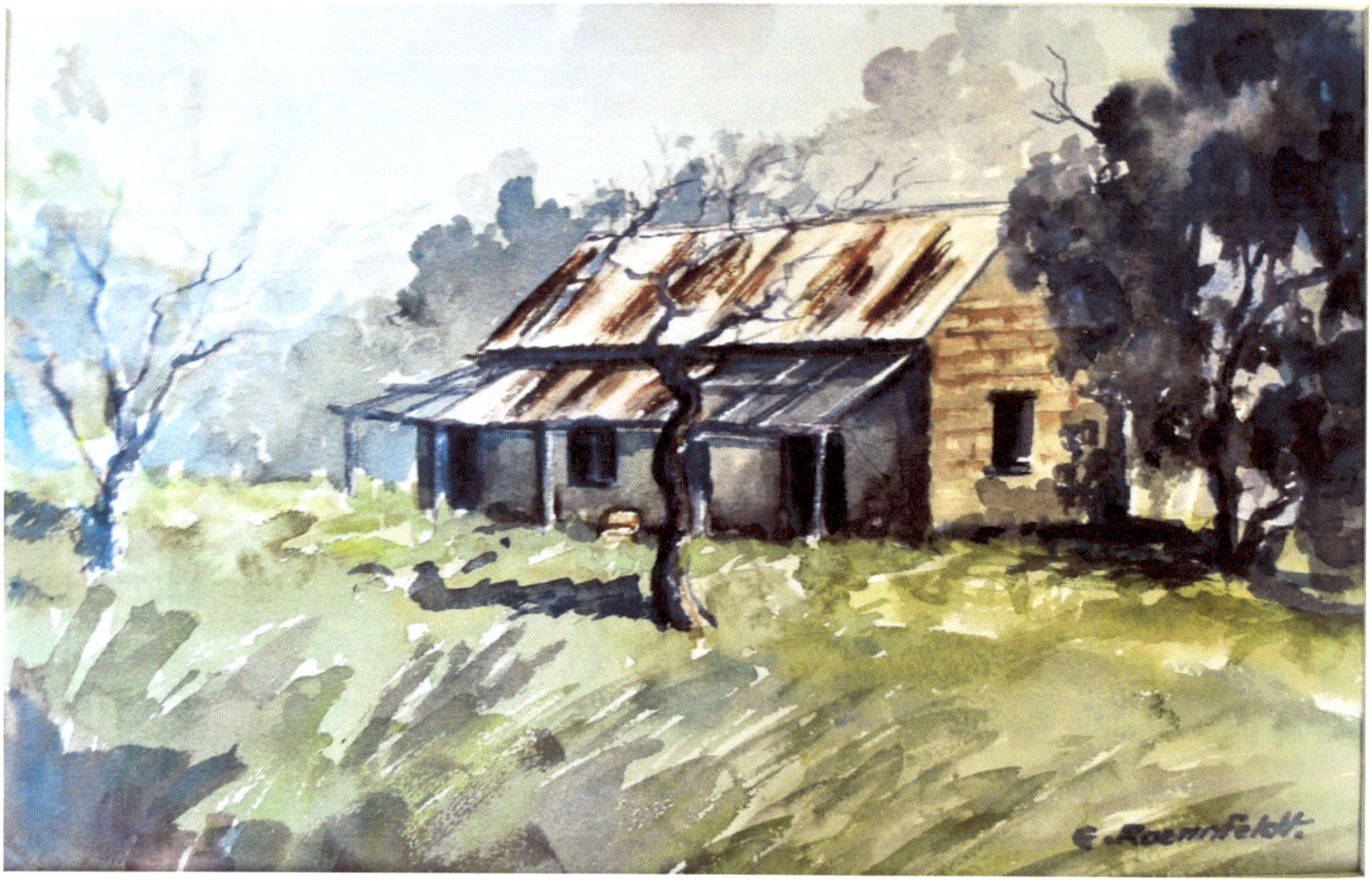

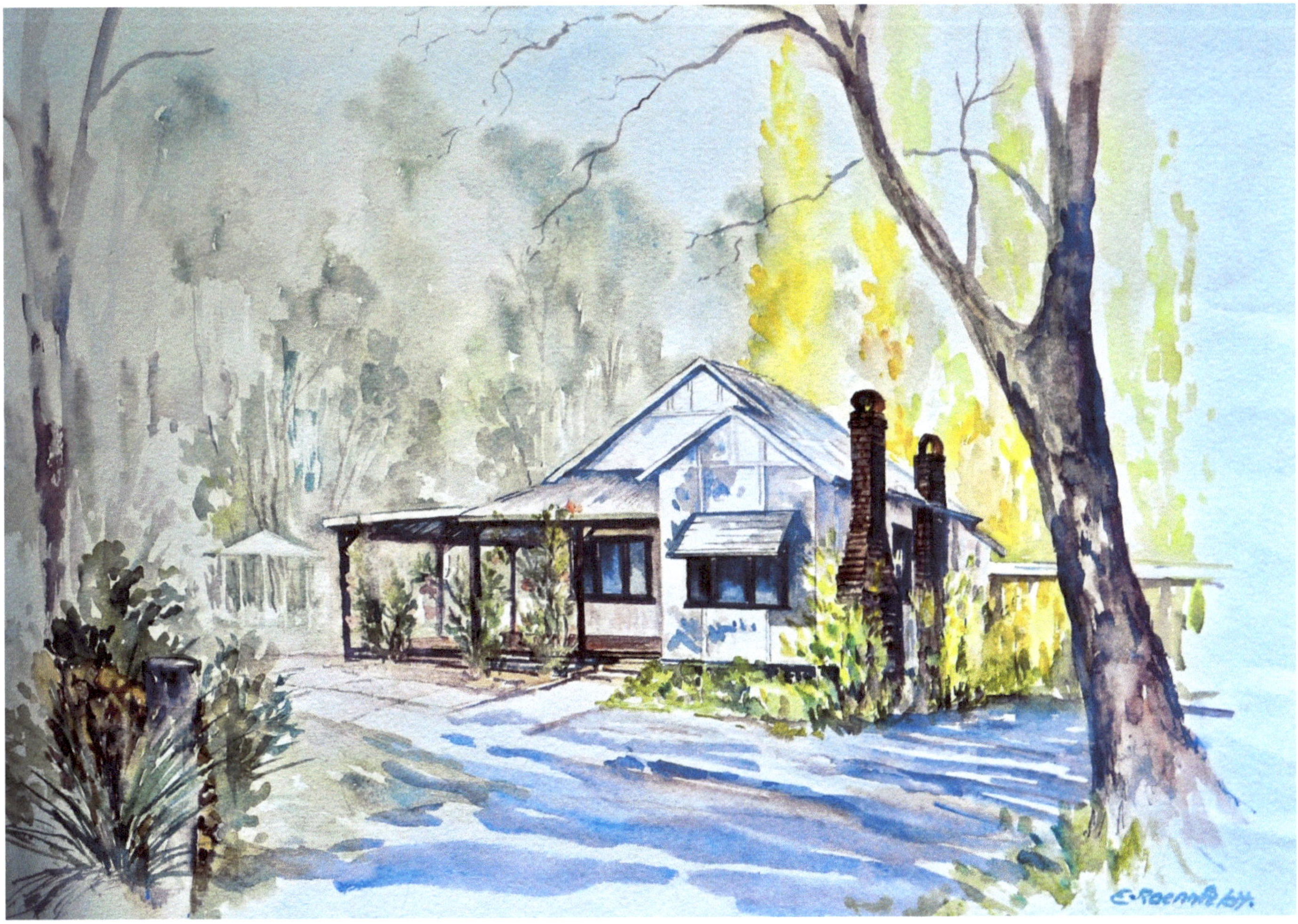

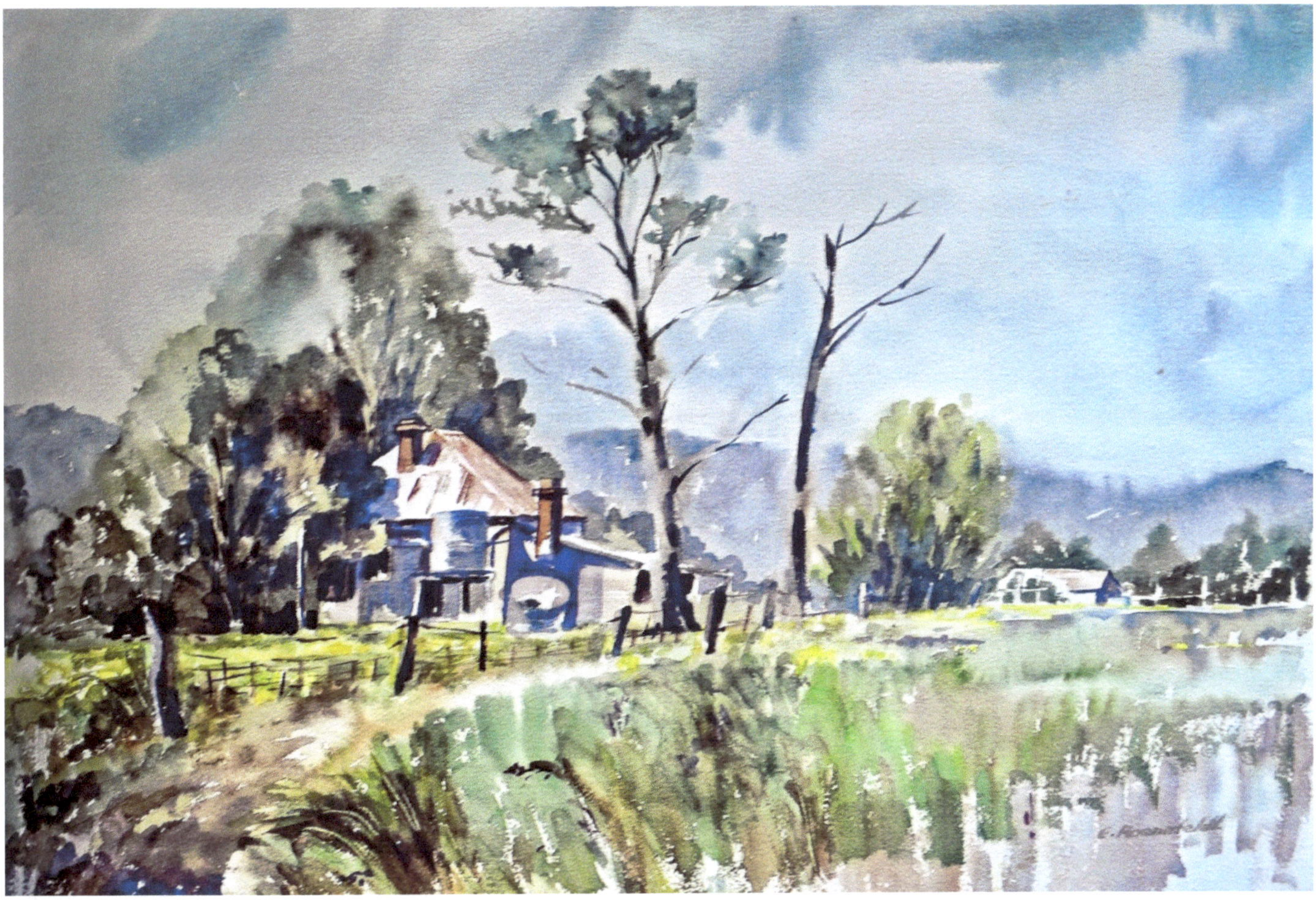

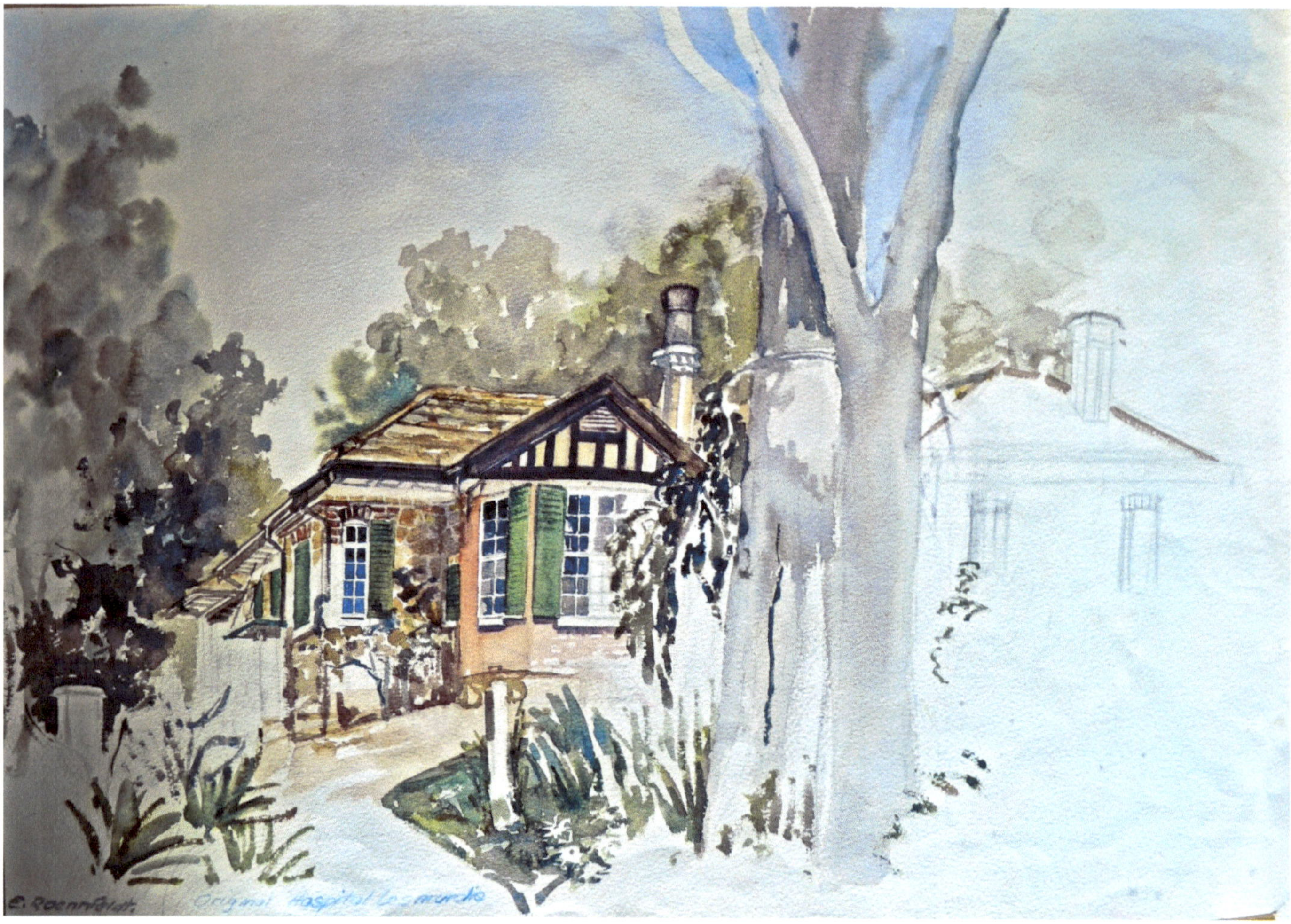

E. Roennfeldt. Original Hospital Lesmurdie

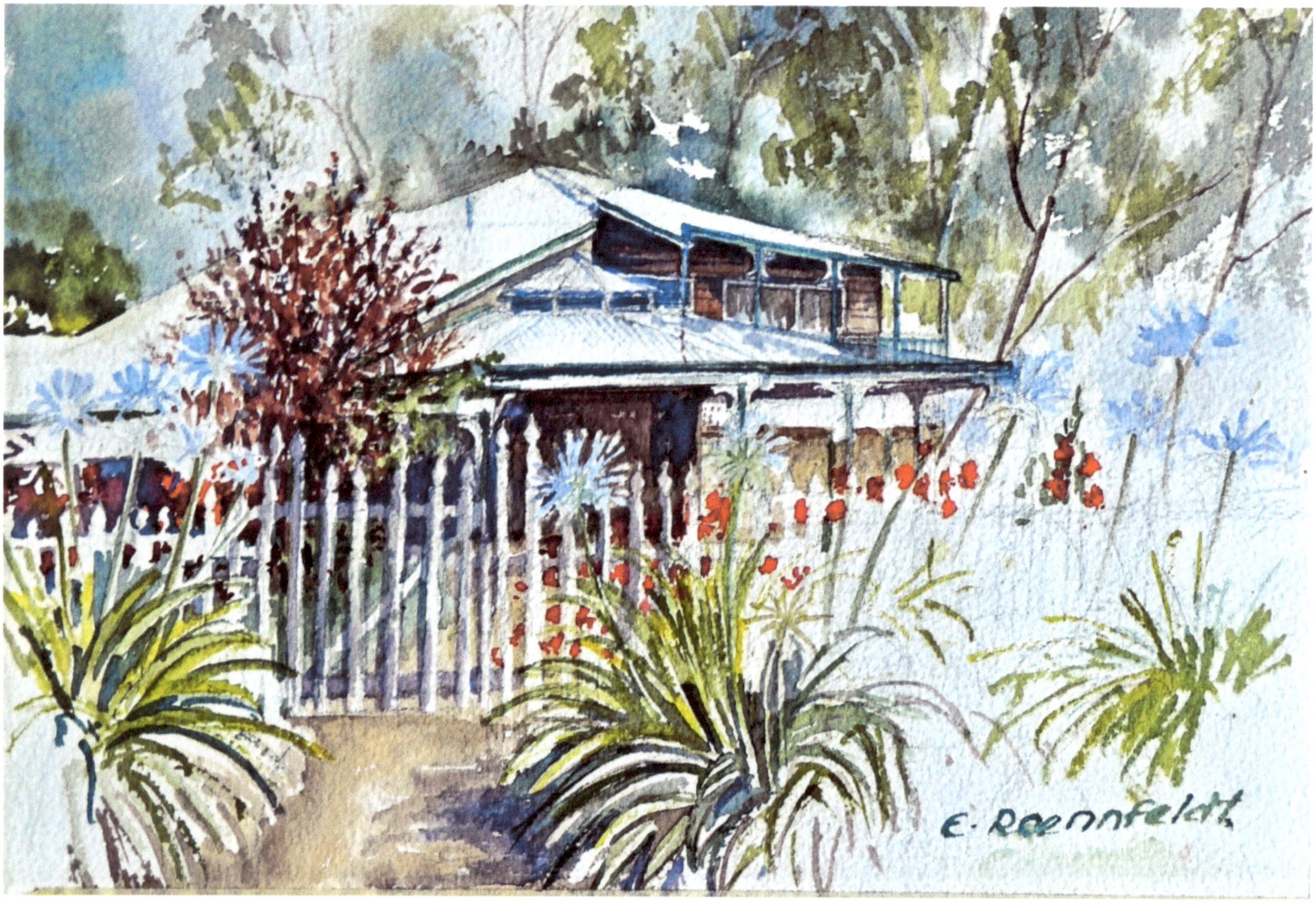

E. Roennfeldt.

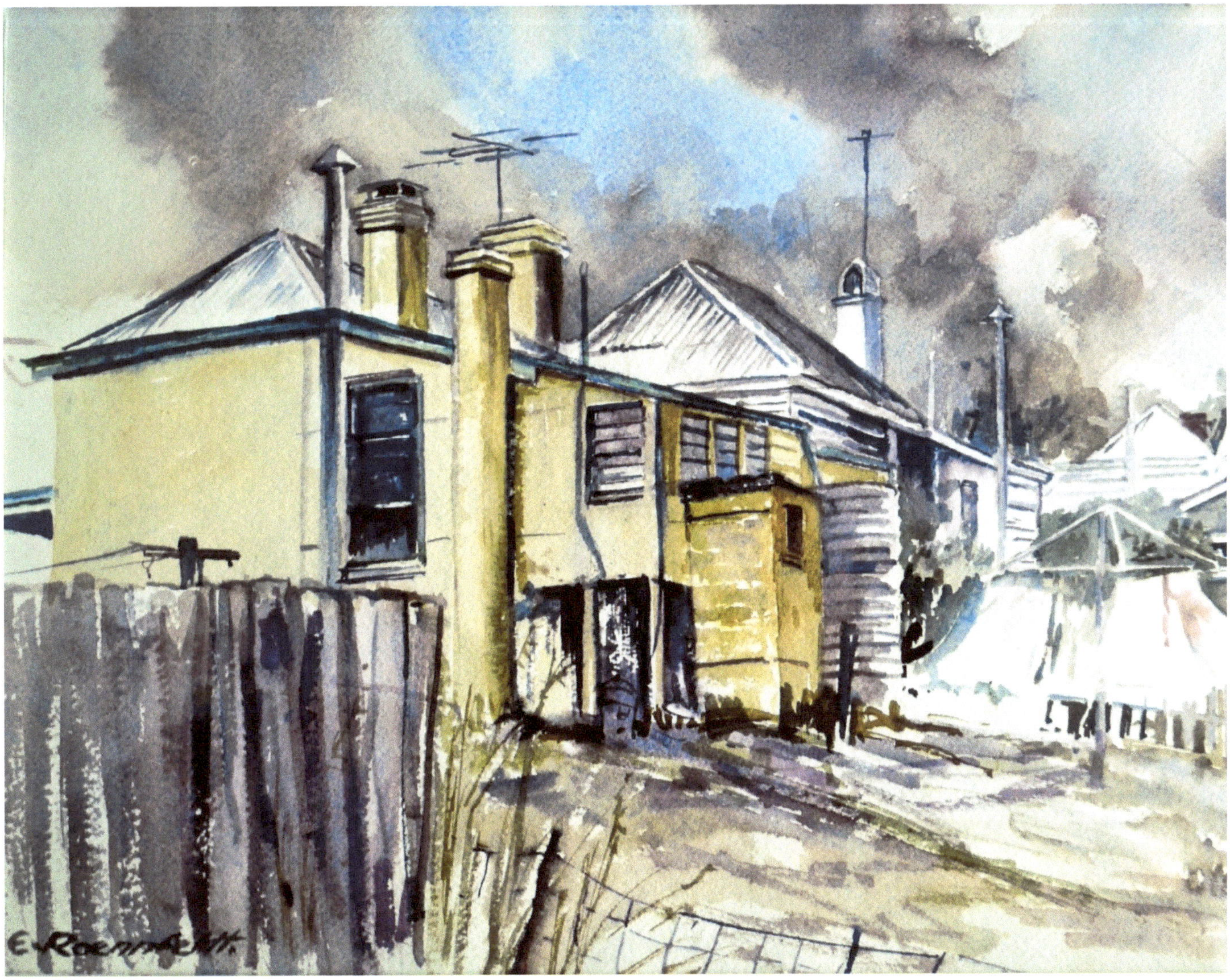

E. Roennfeldt.

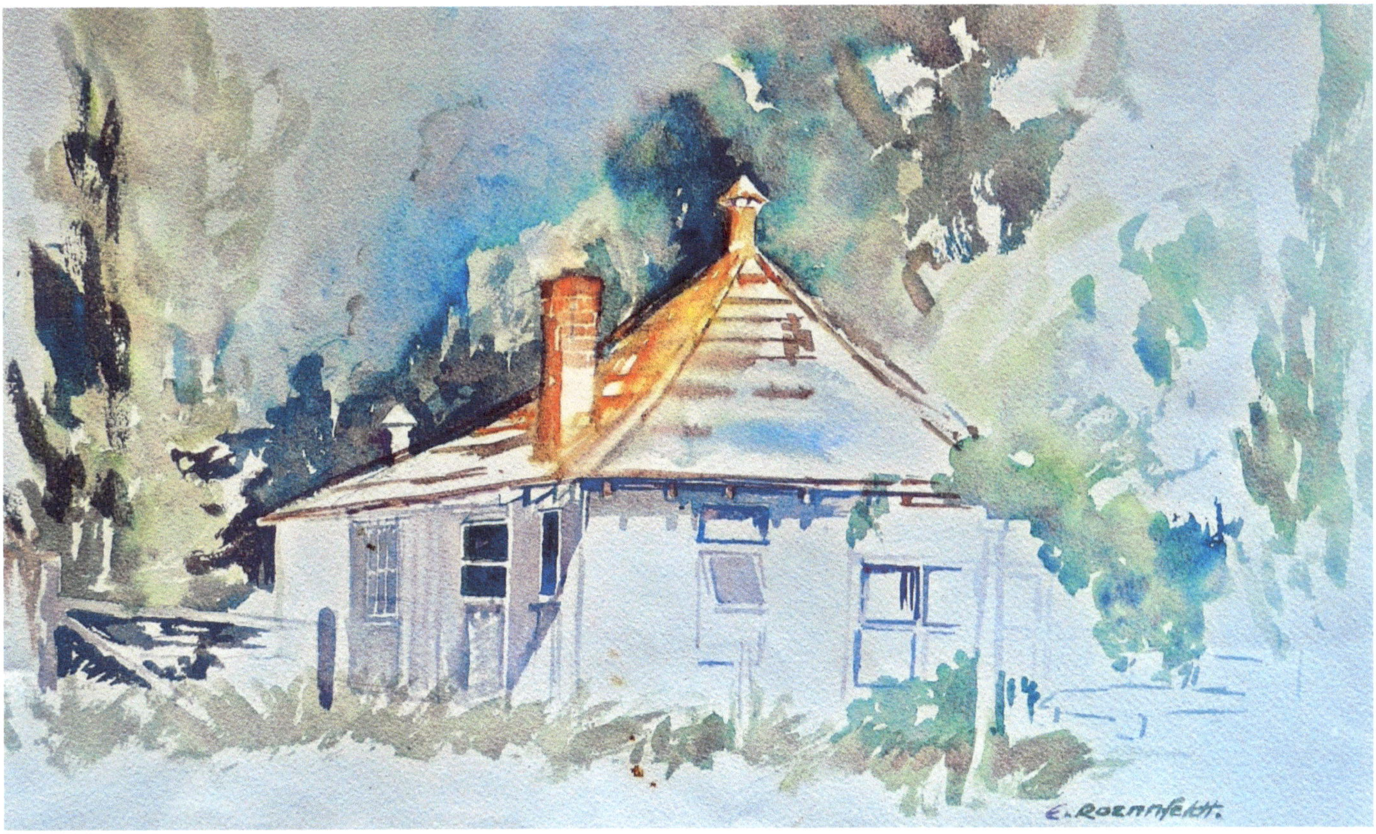

E. Roennfeldt.

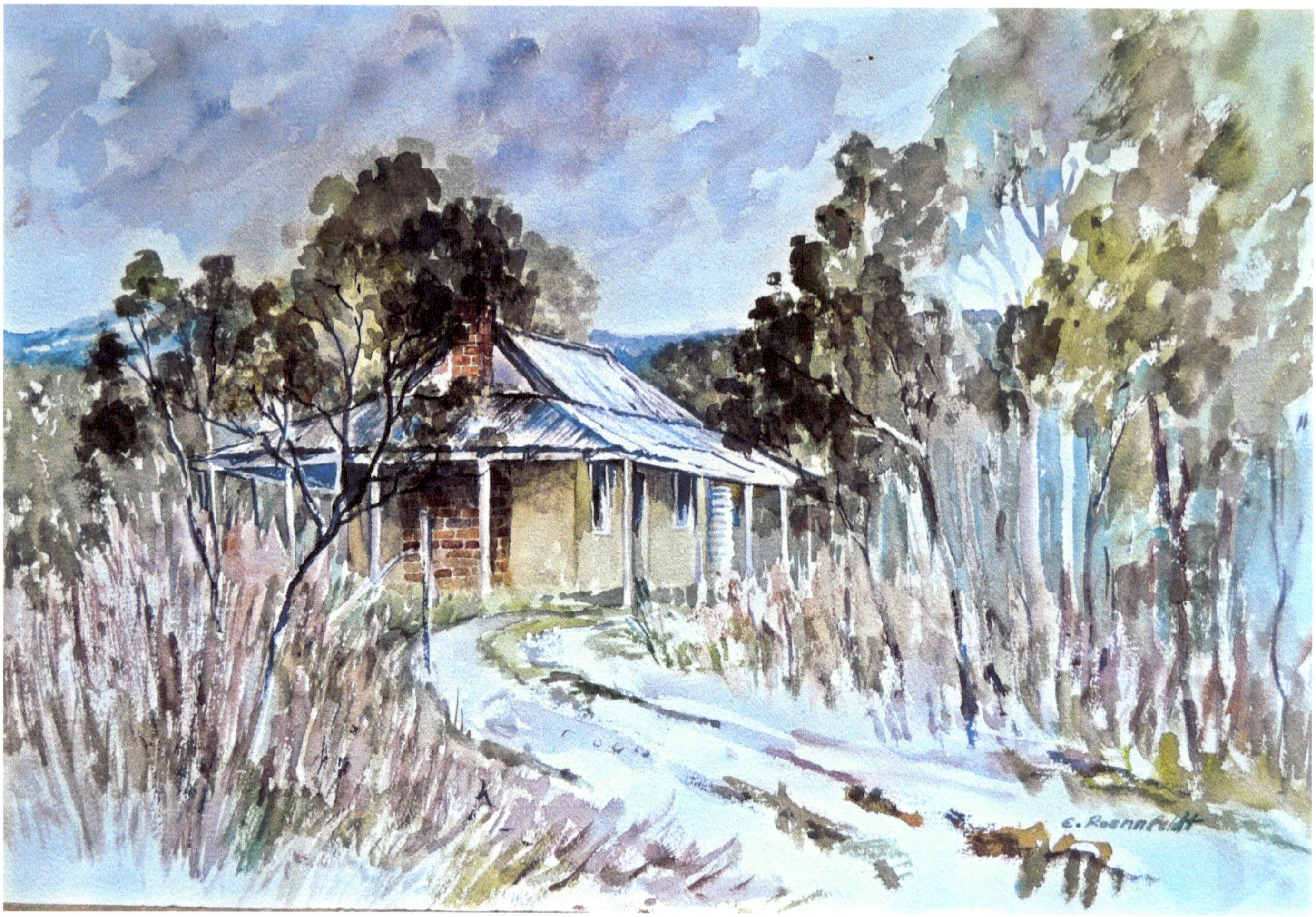

E. Roennfeldt

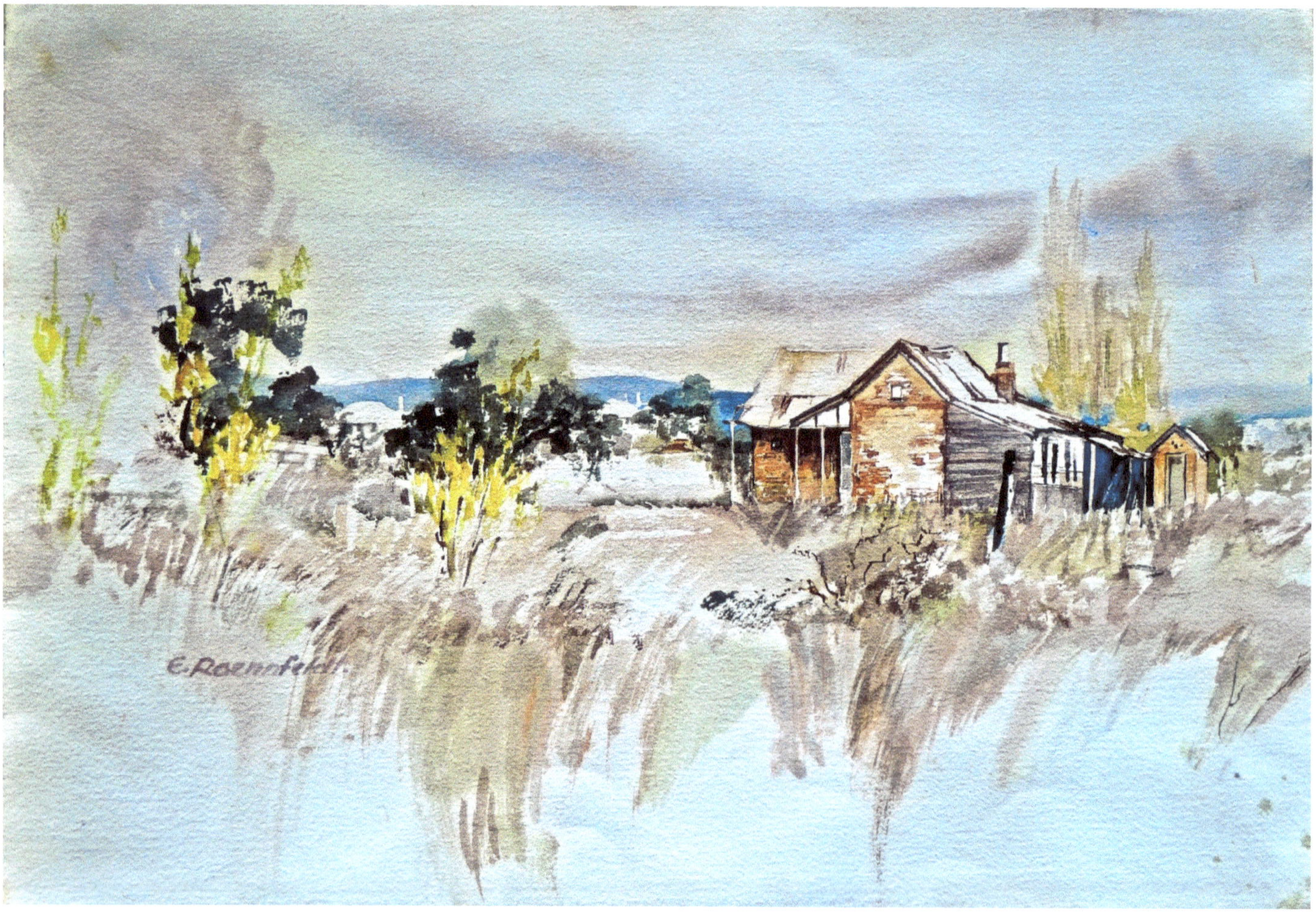

E. Roennfeldt

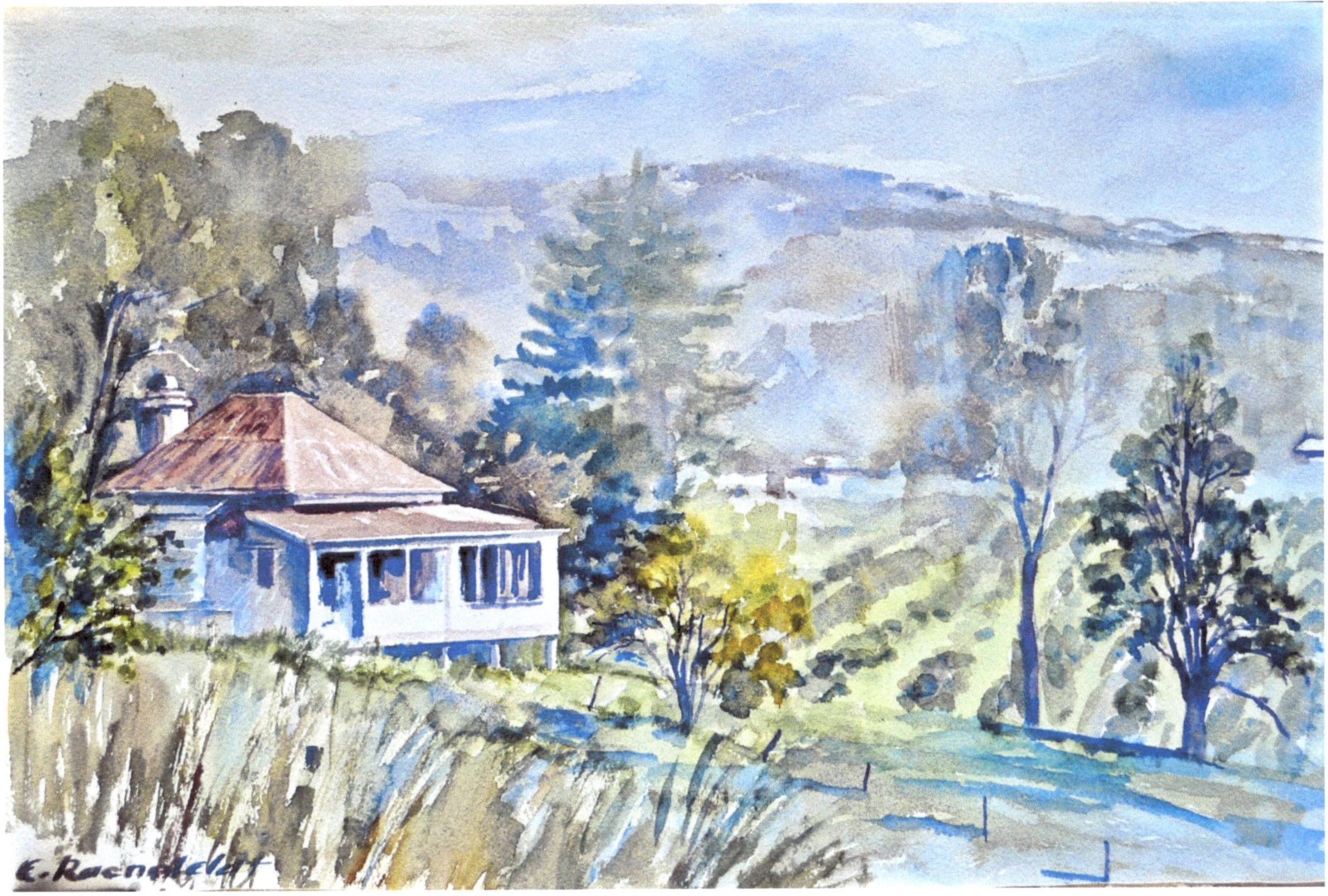

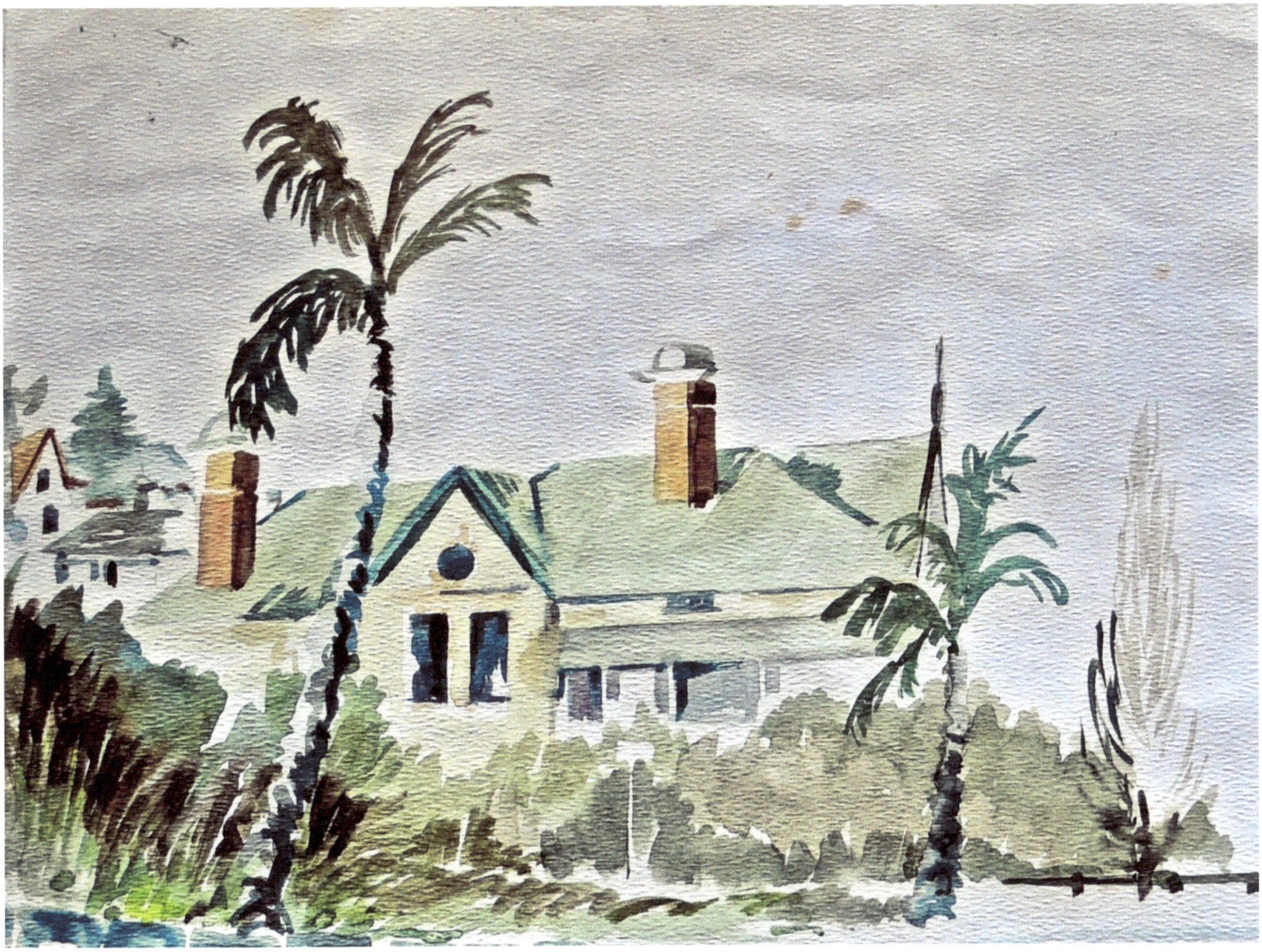

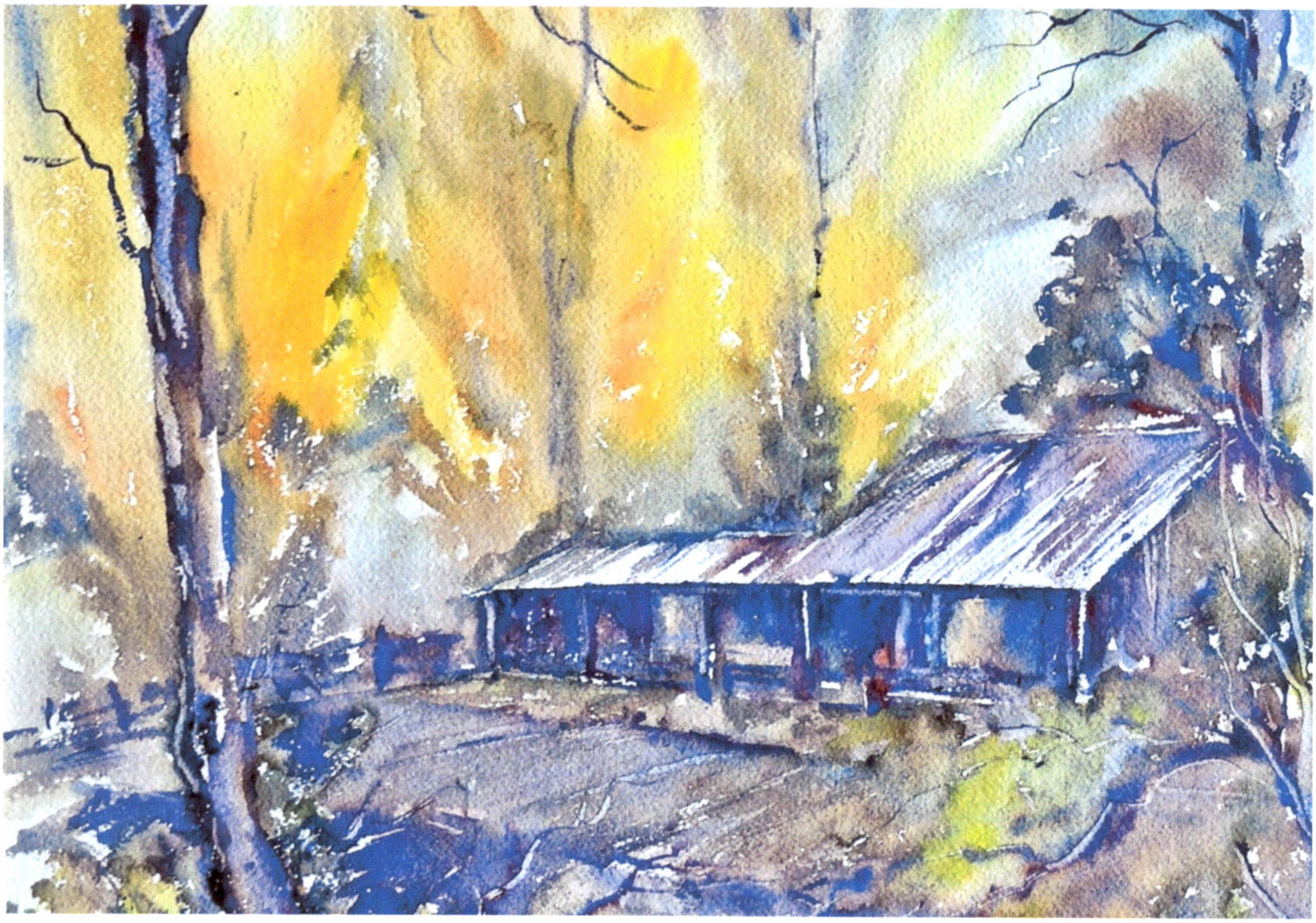

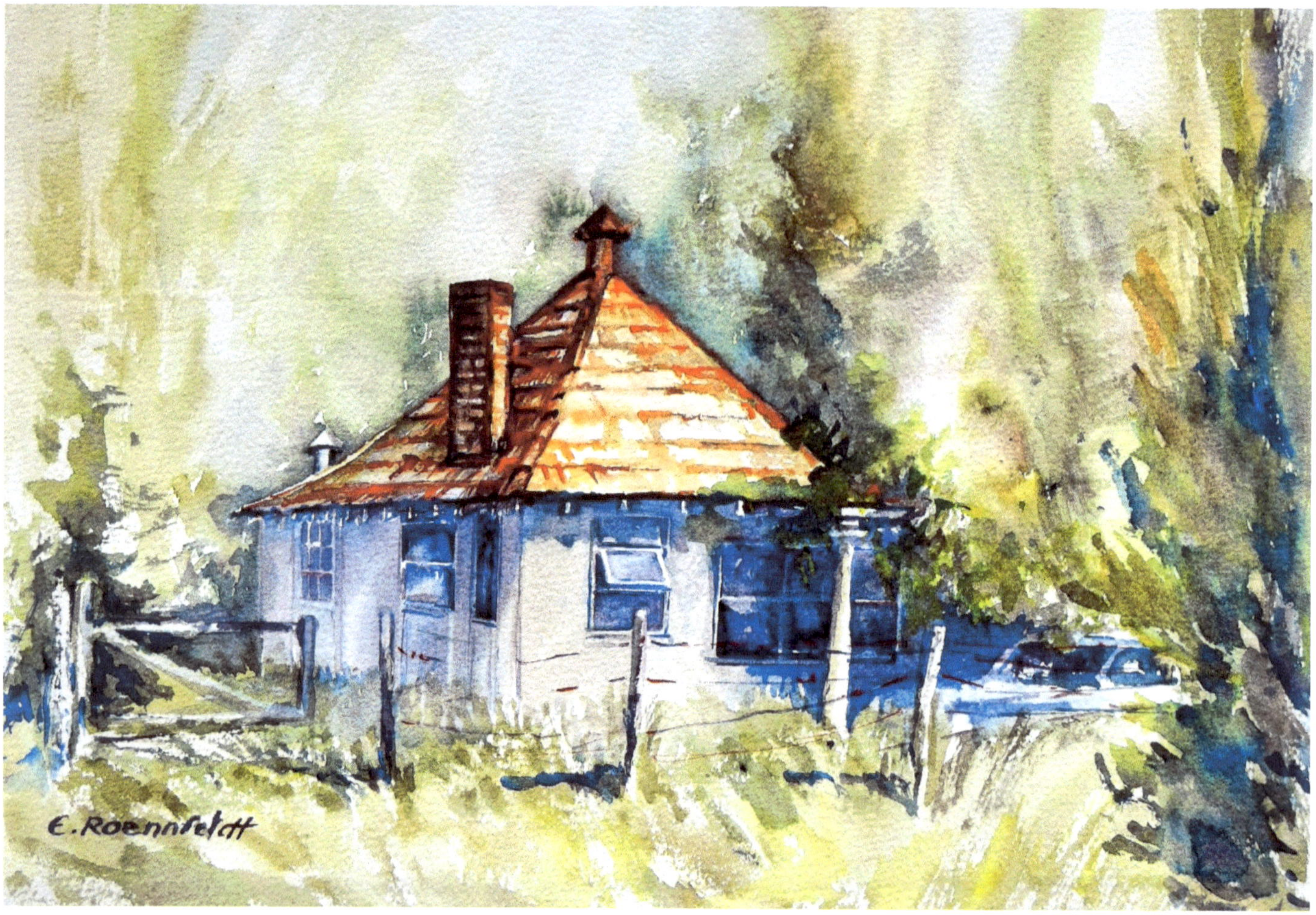

E. Roennfeldt

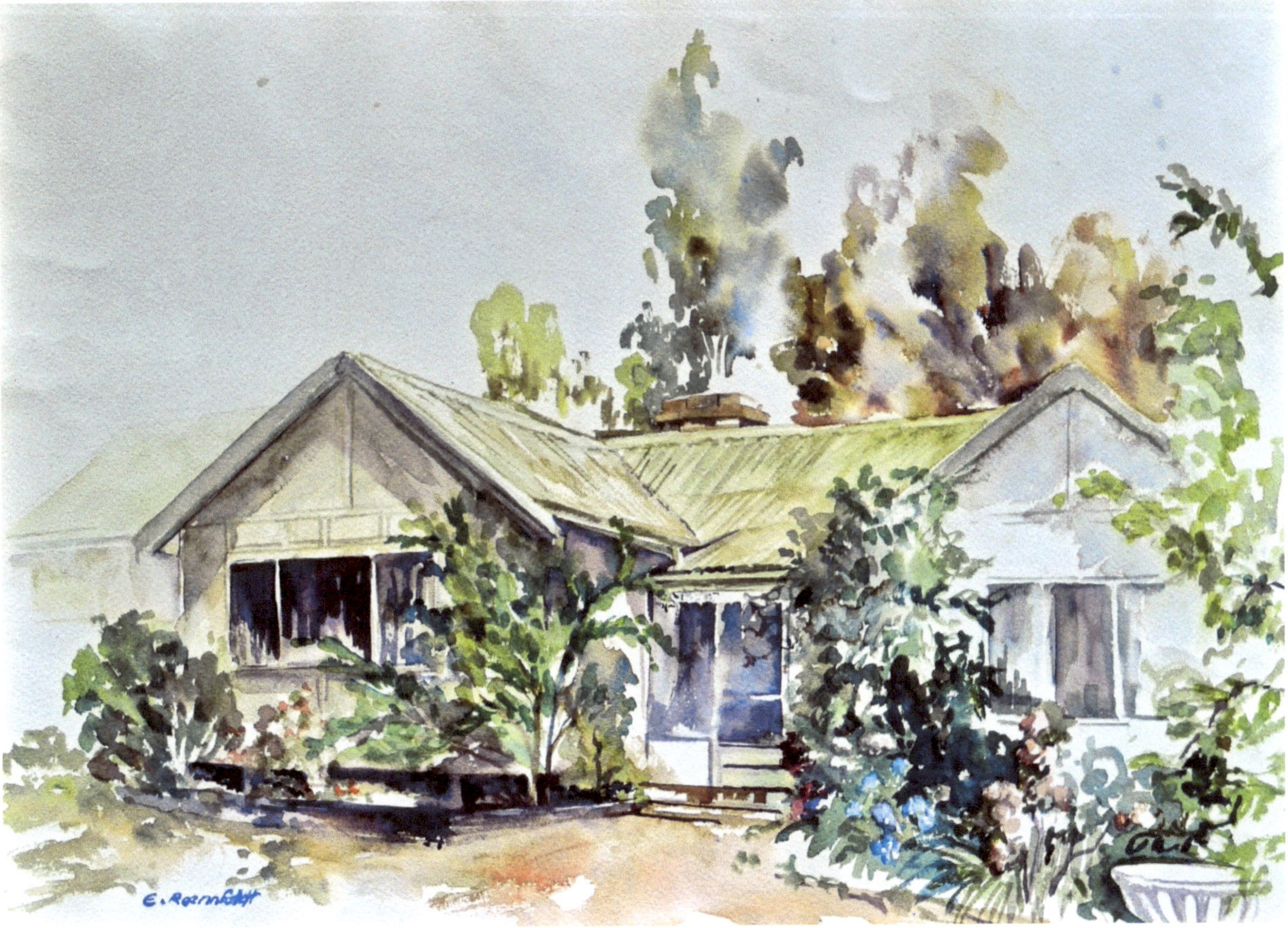

E. Roennfeldt

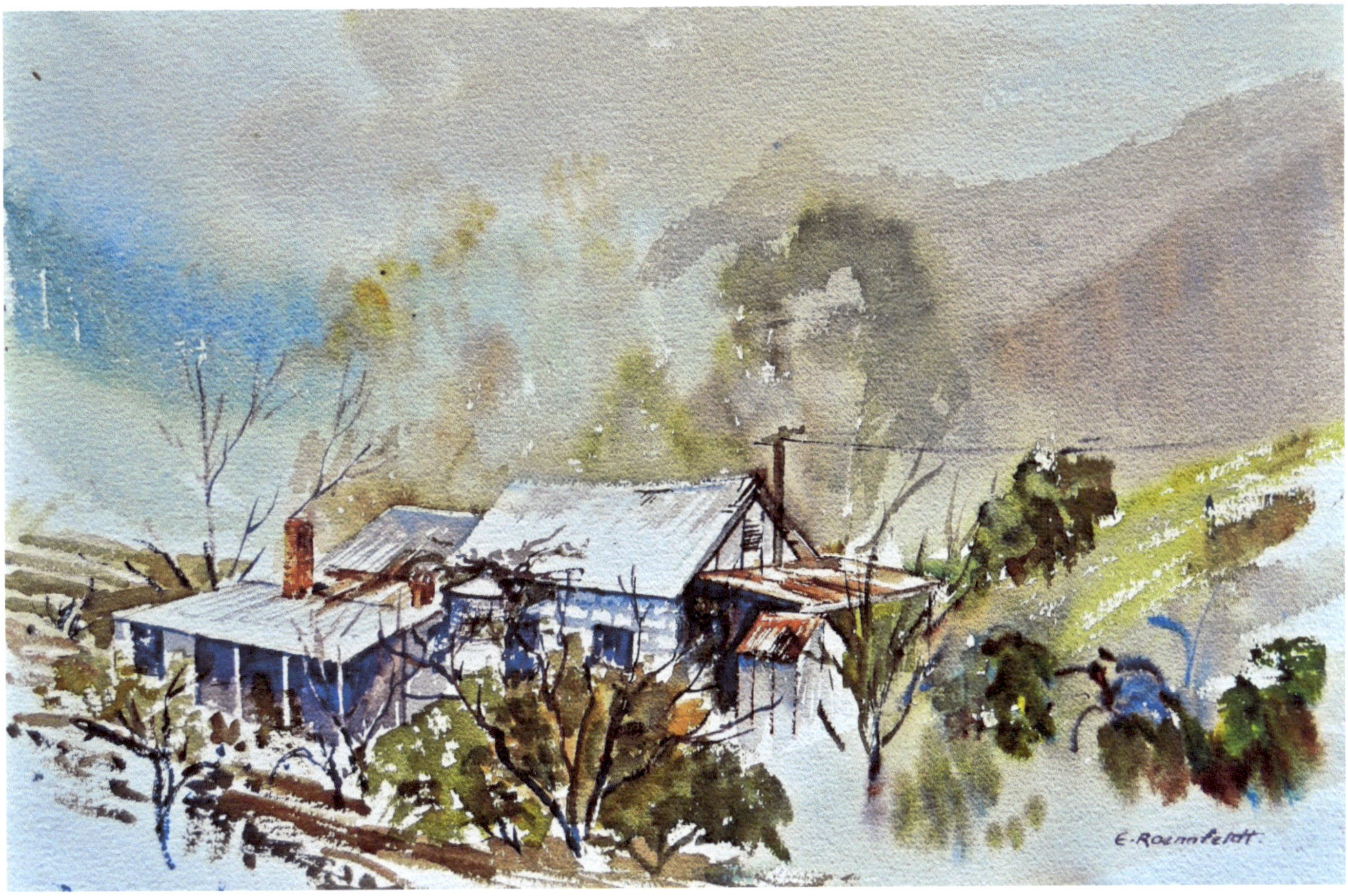

E. Roennfeldt

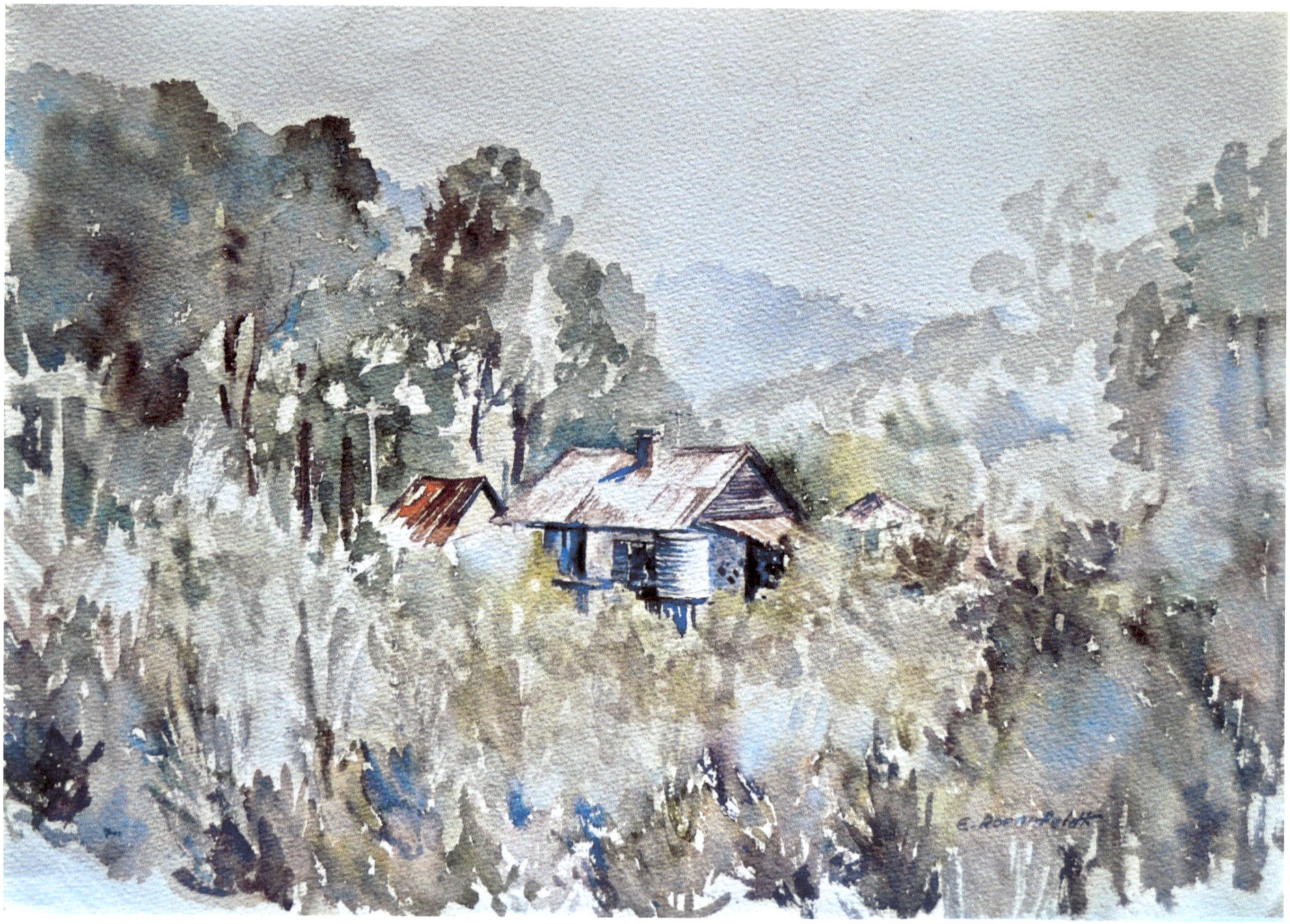

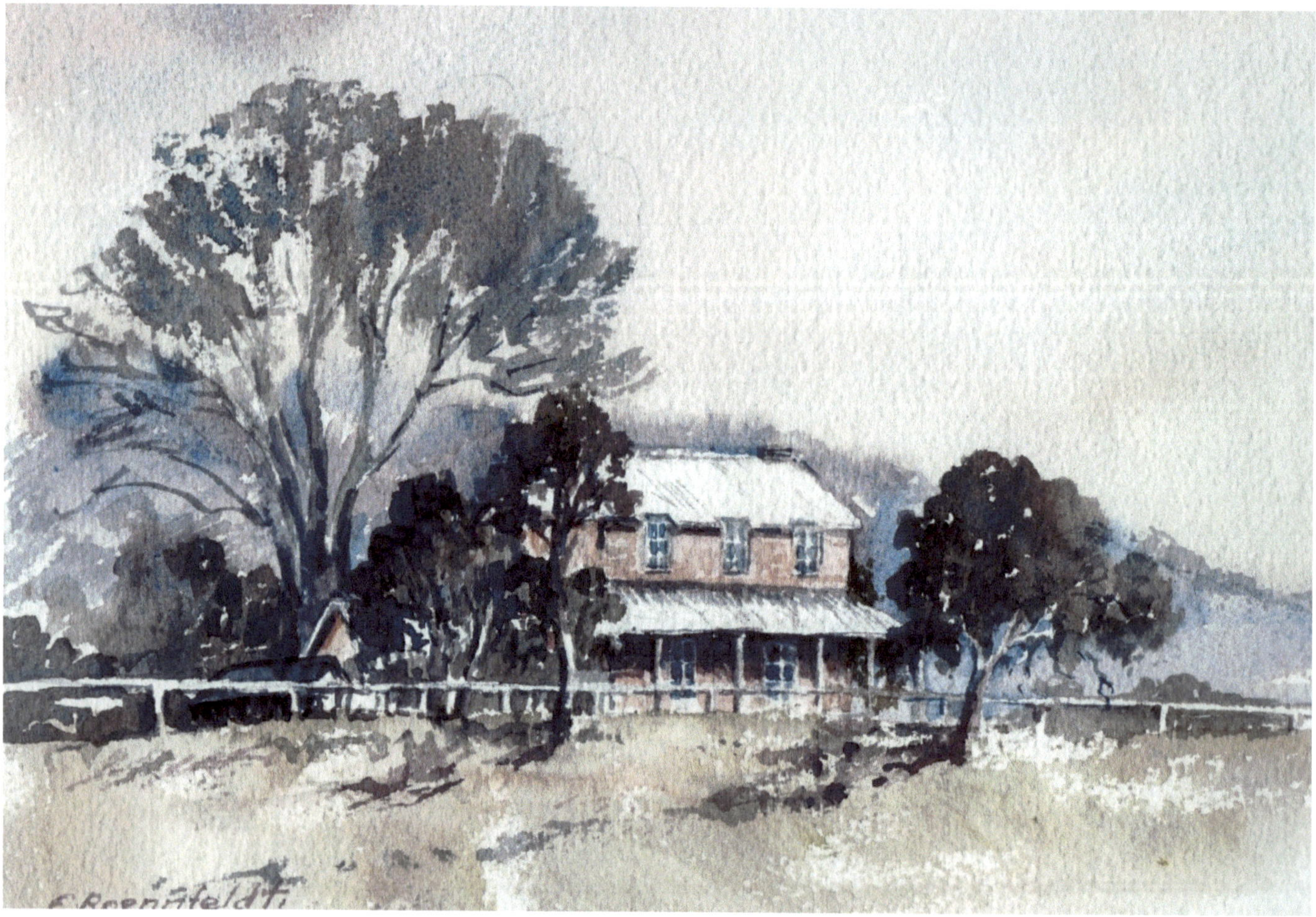

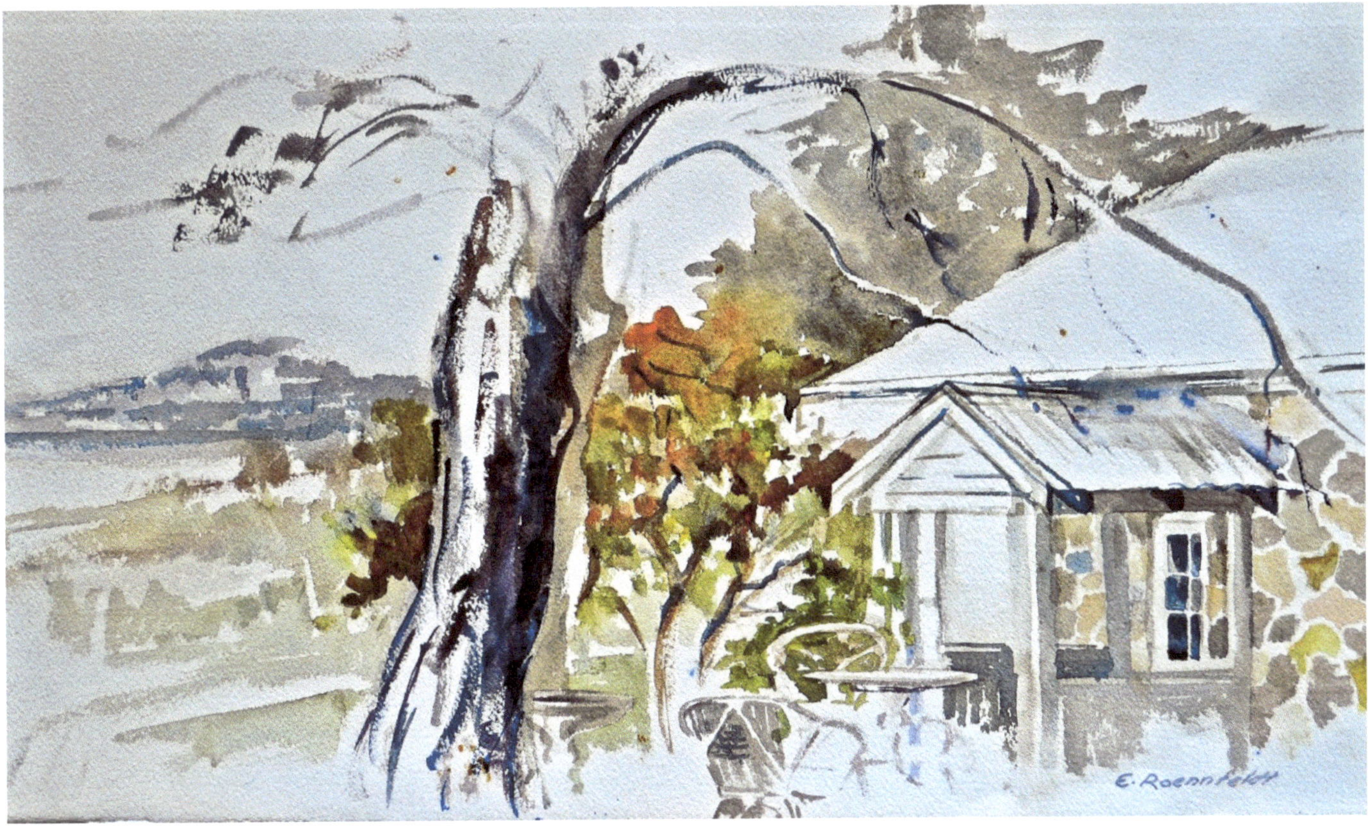
E. Roennfeldt

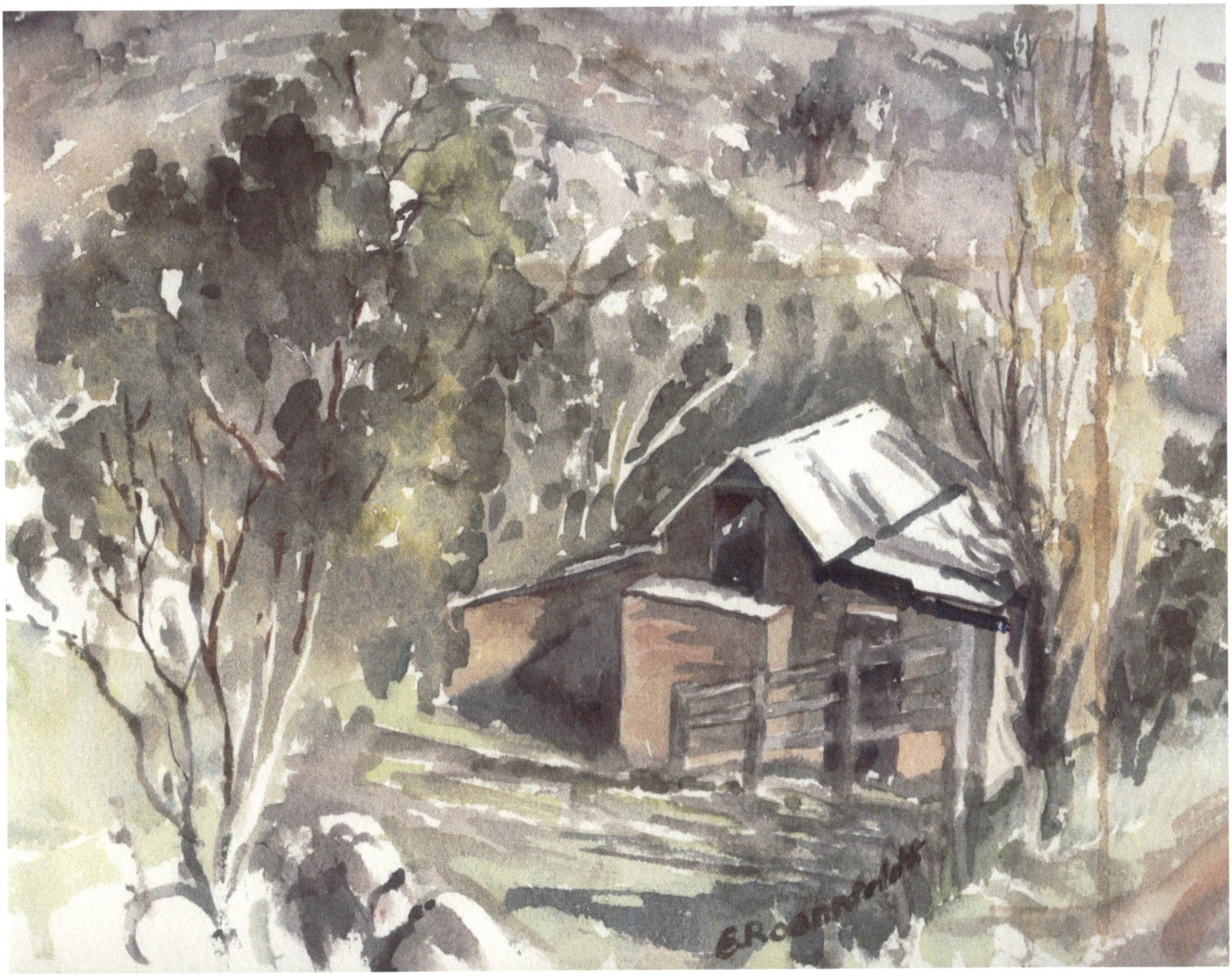
E.Roennfeldt

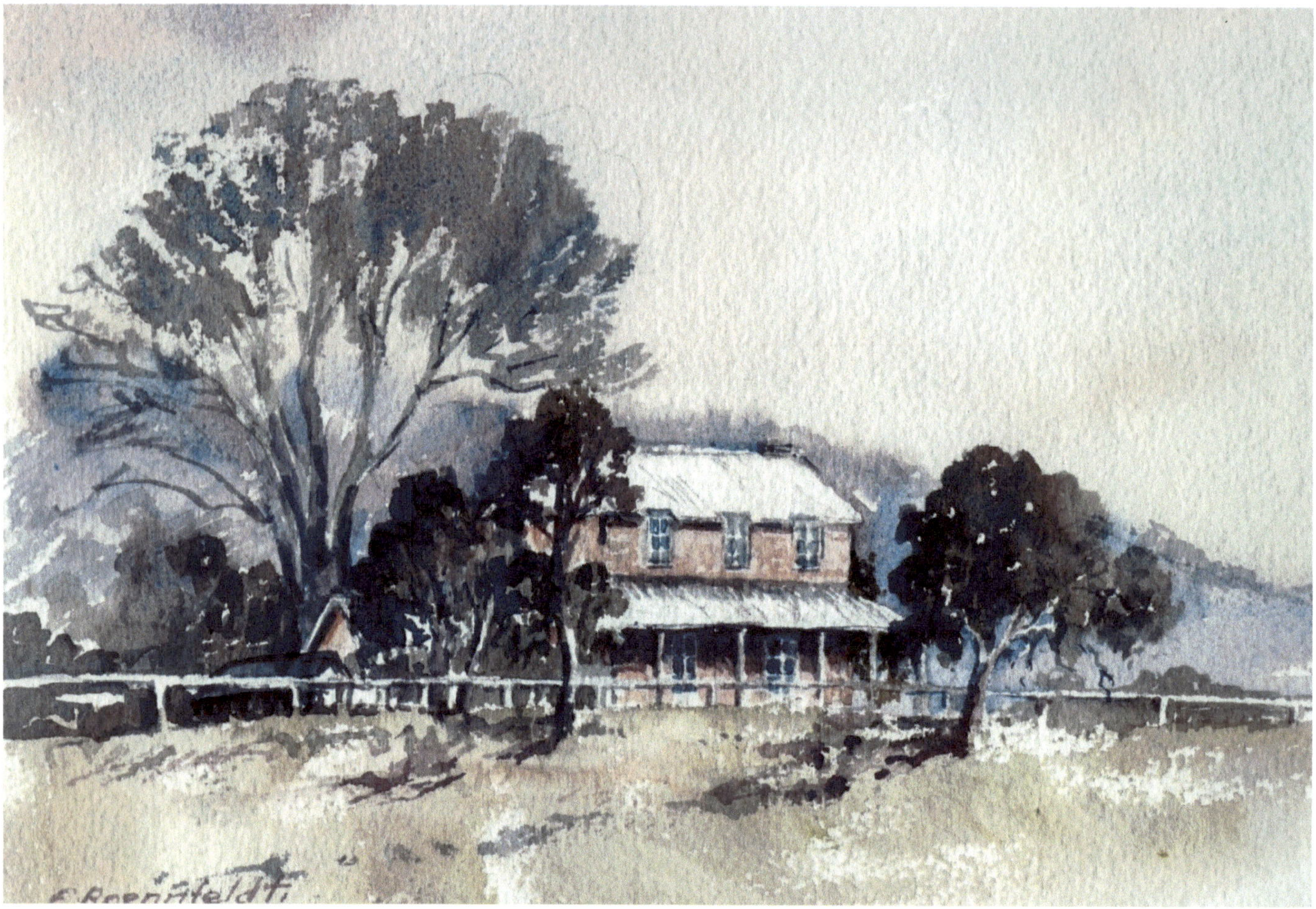

E.Roennfeldt.

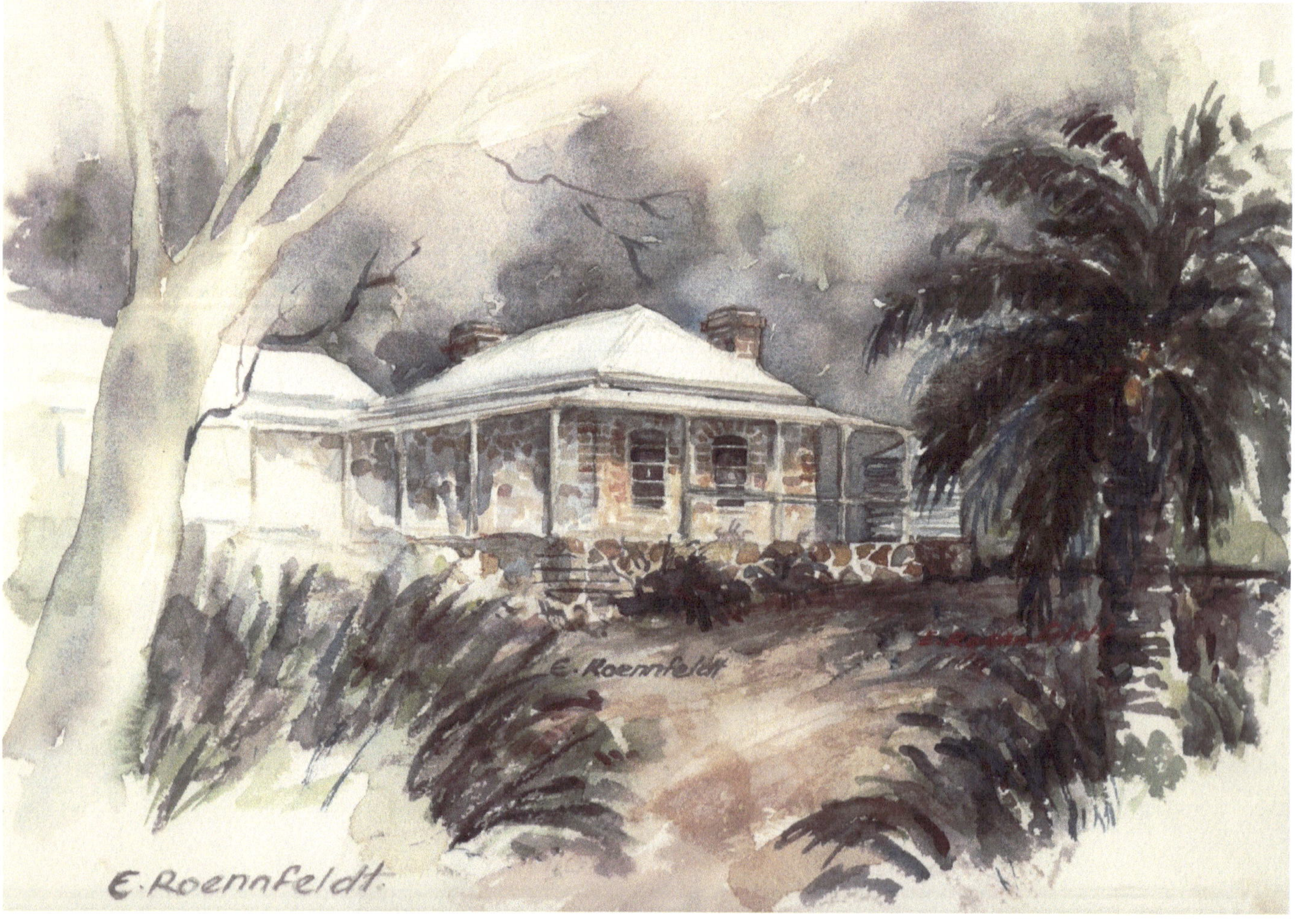

E.Roennfeldt

E.Roennfeldt.

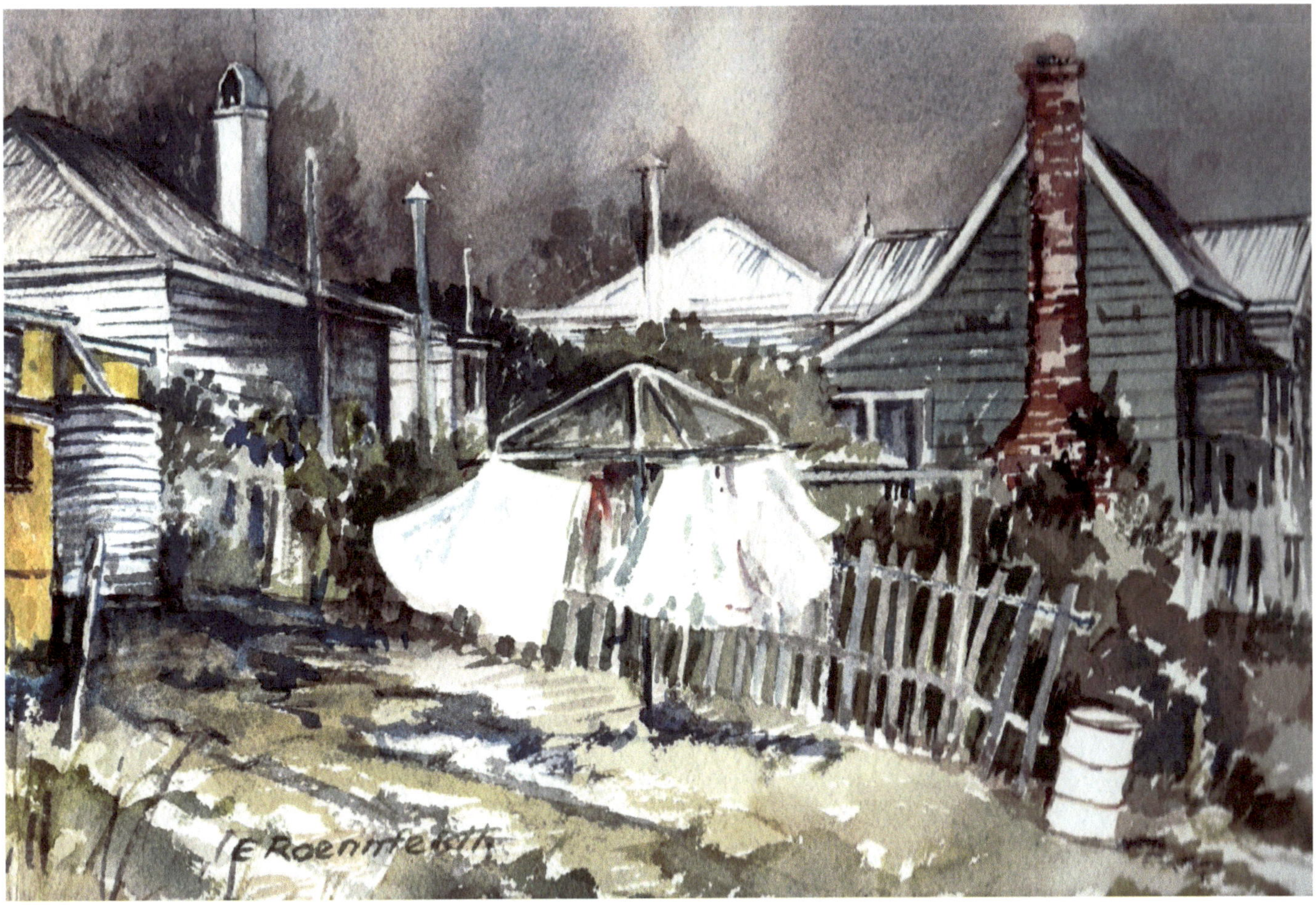

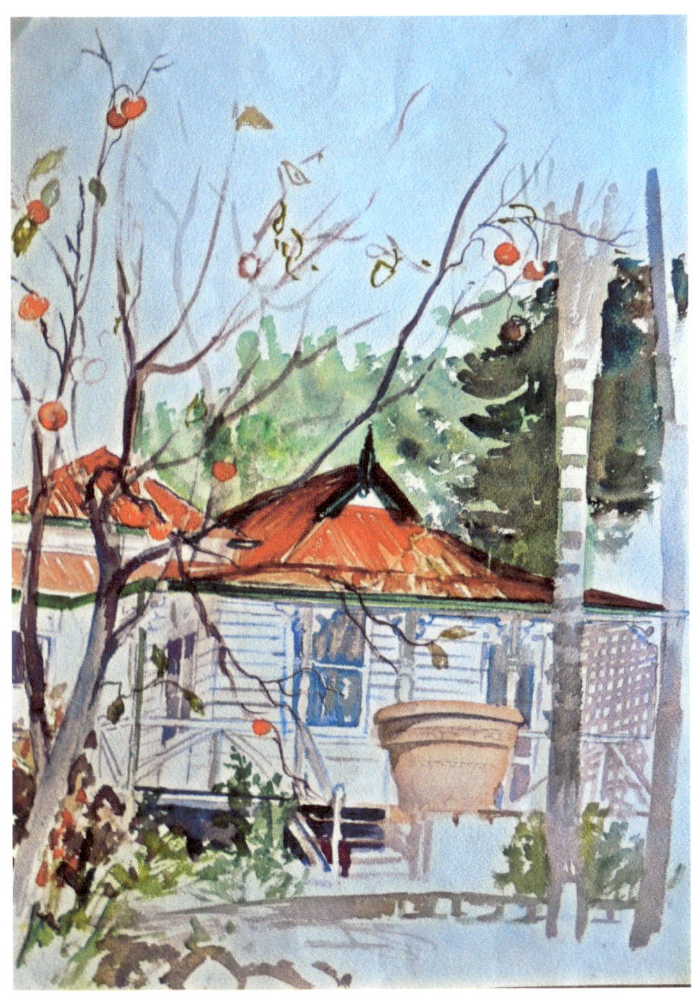

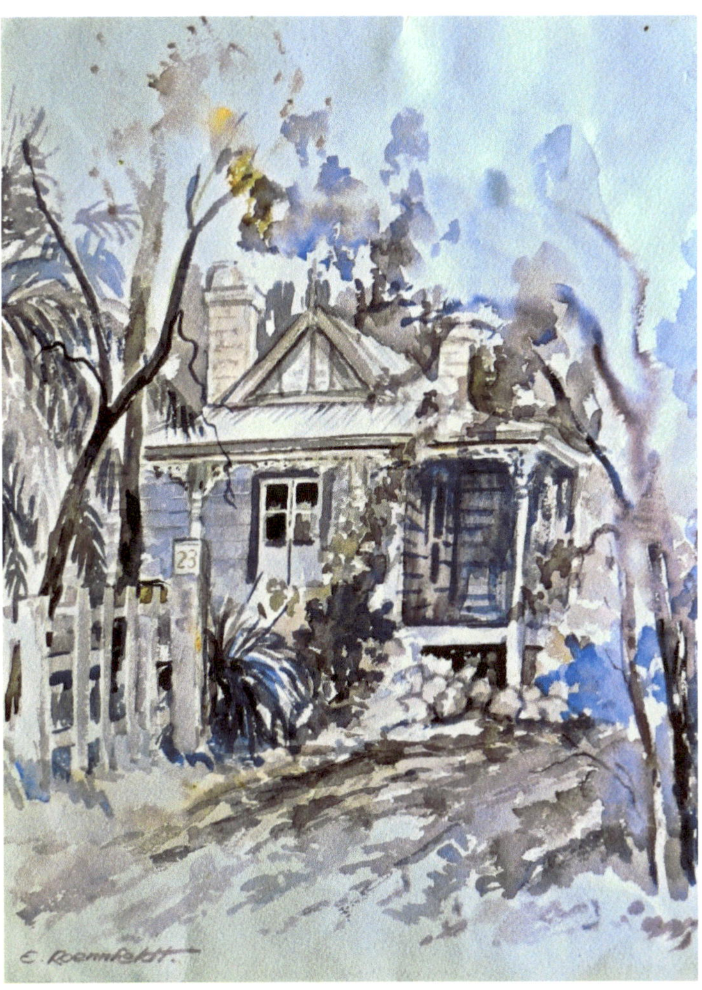
23

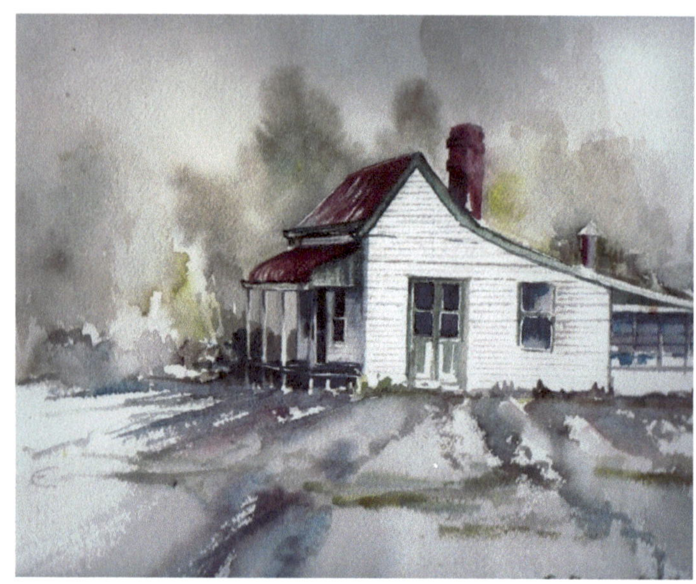

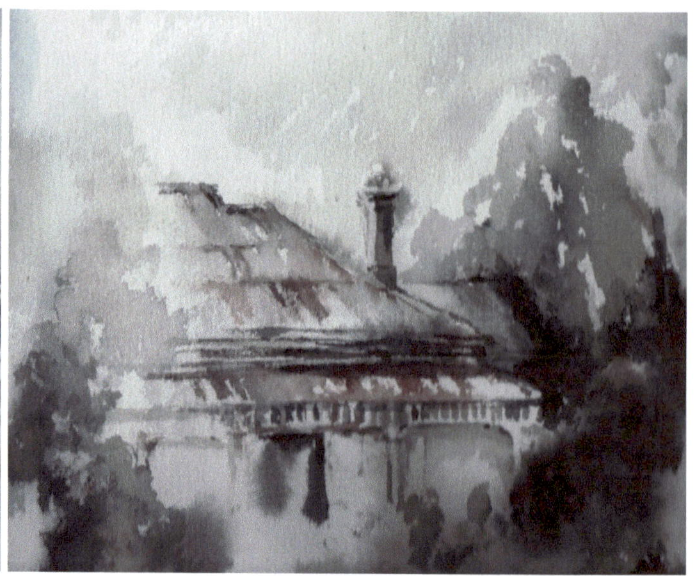

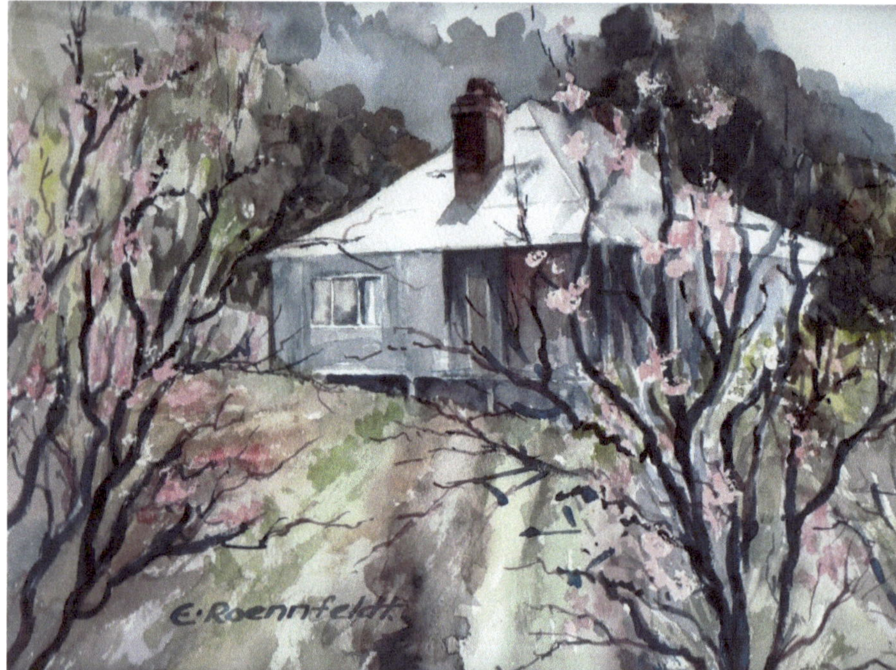
E.Roennfeldt

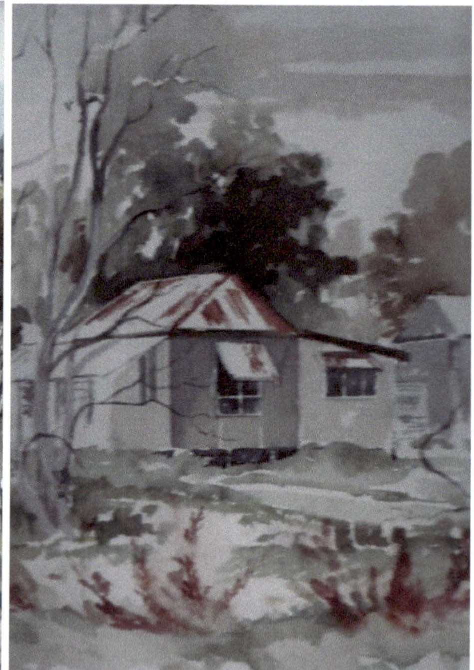

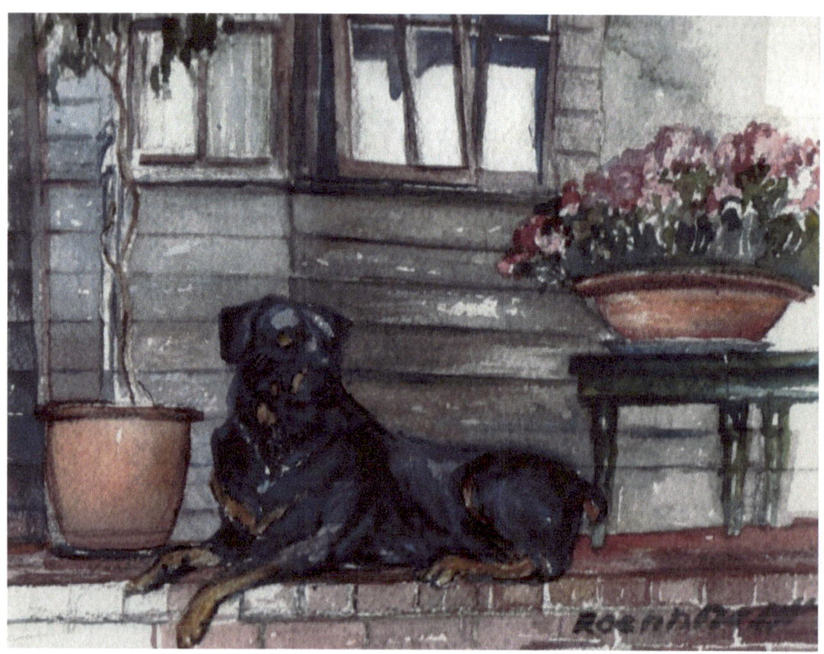

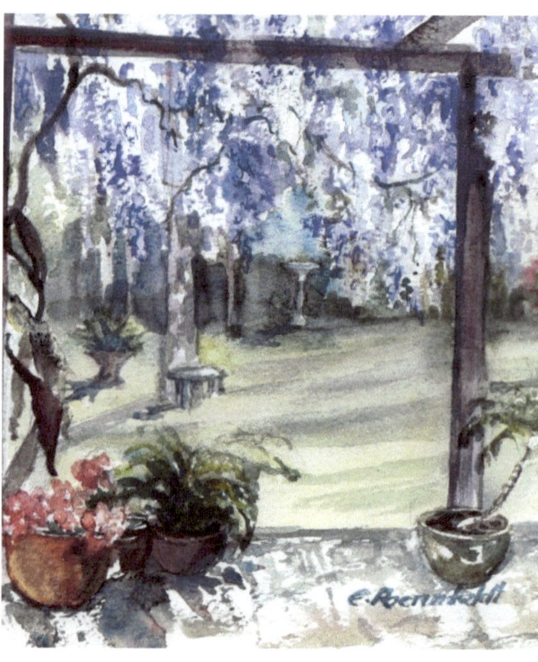
E.Roennfeldt

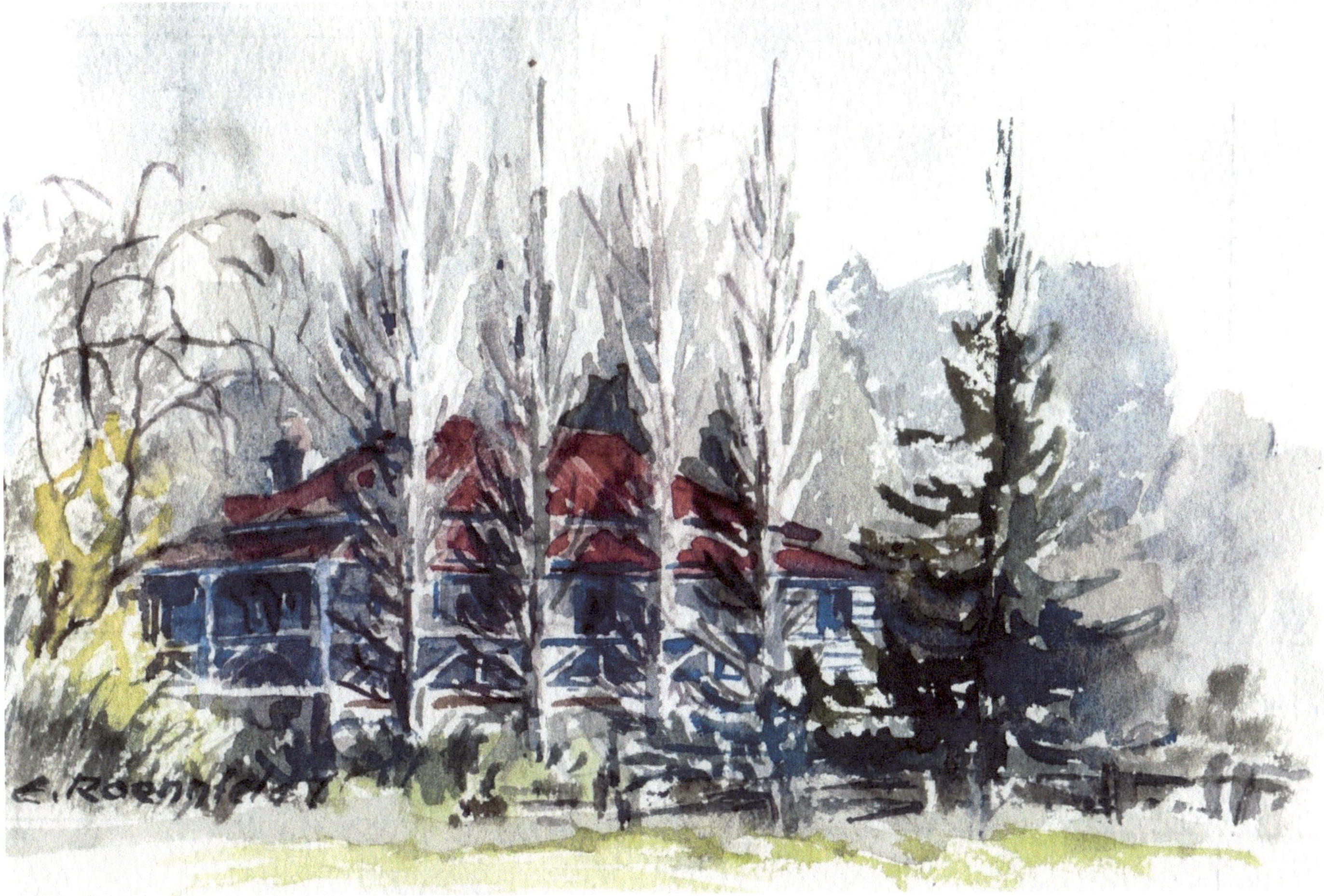

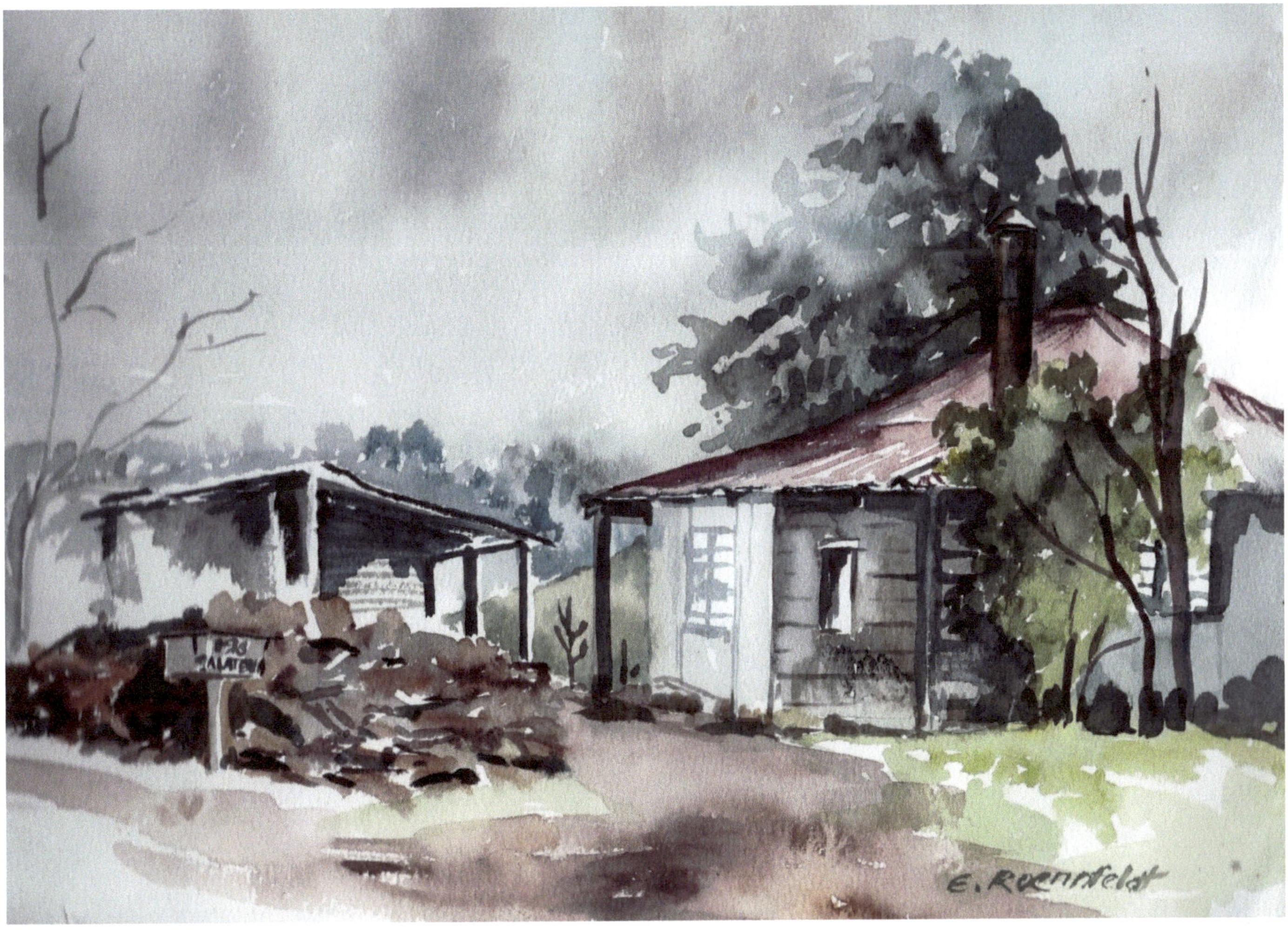

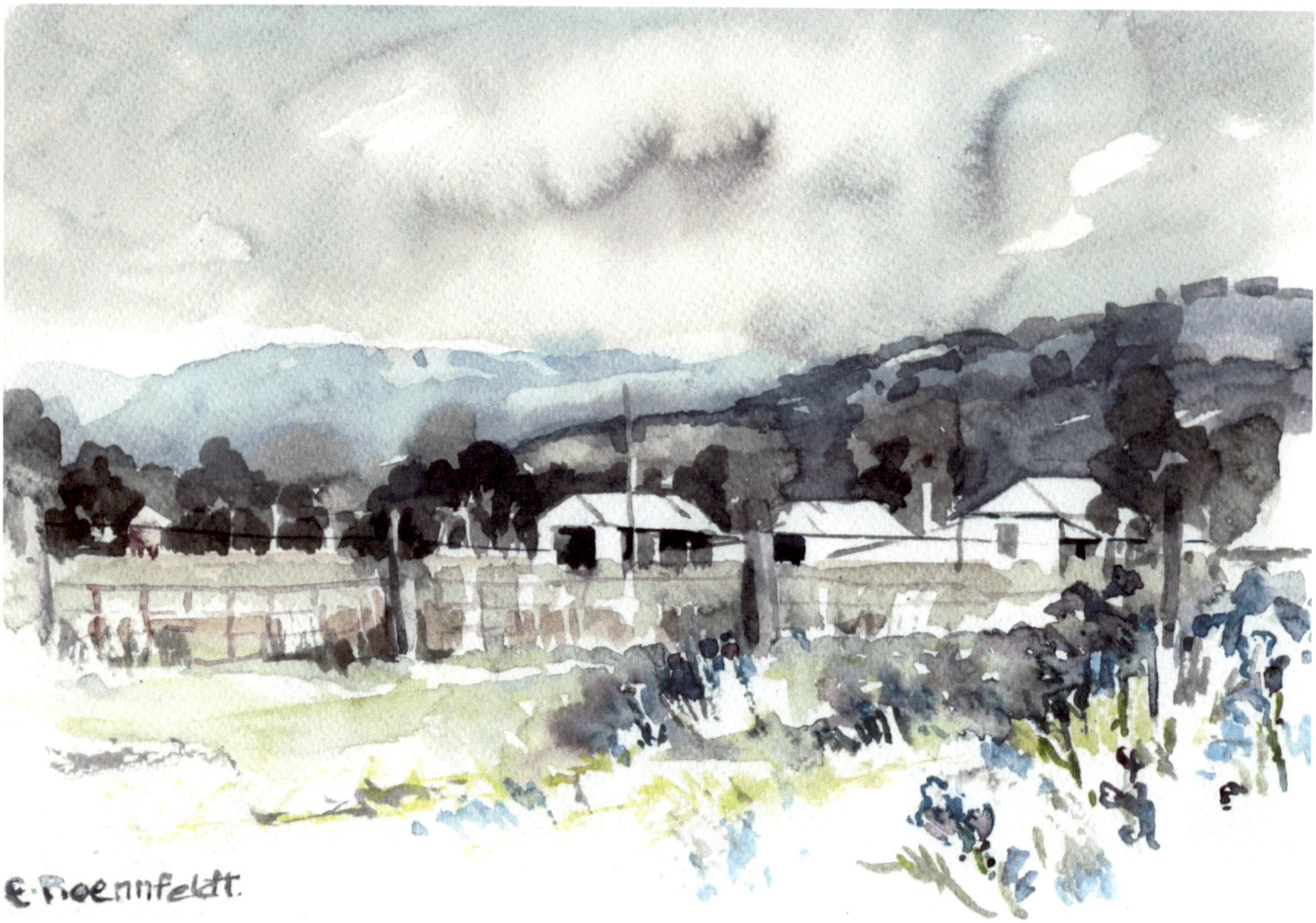

E. Roennfeldt.

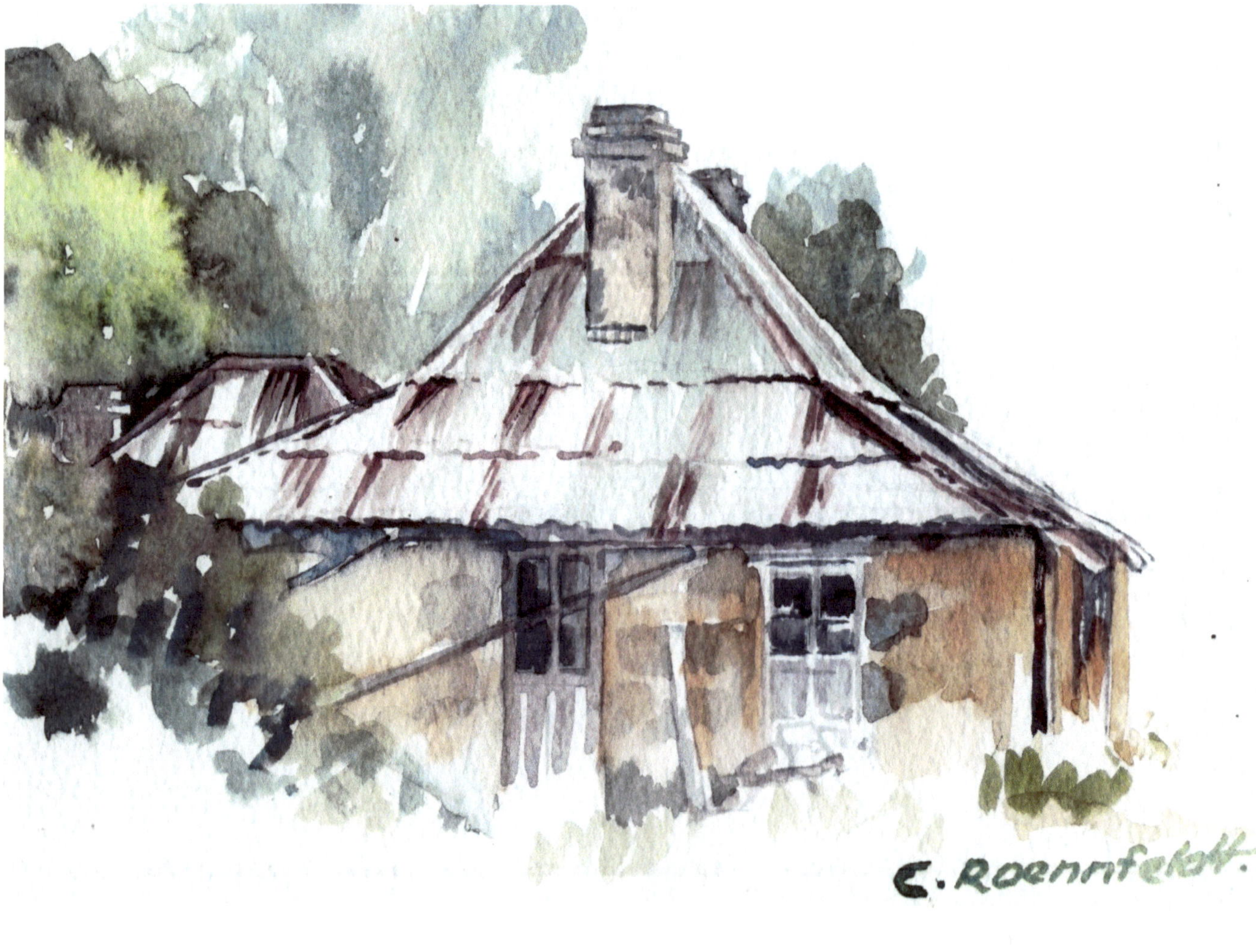

C. Roennfeldt.

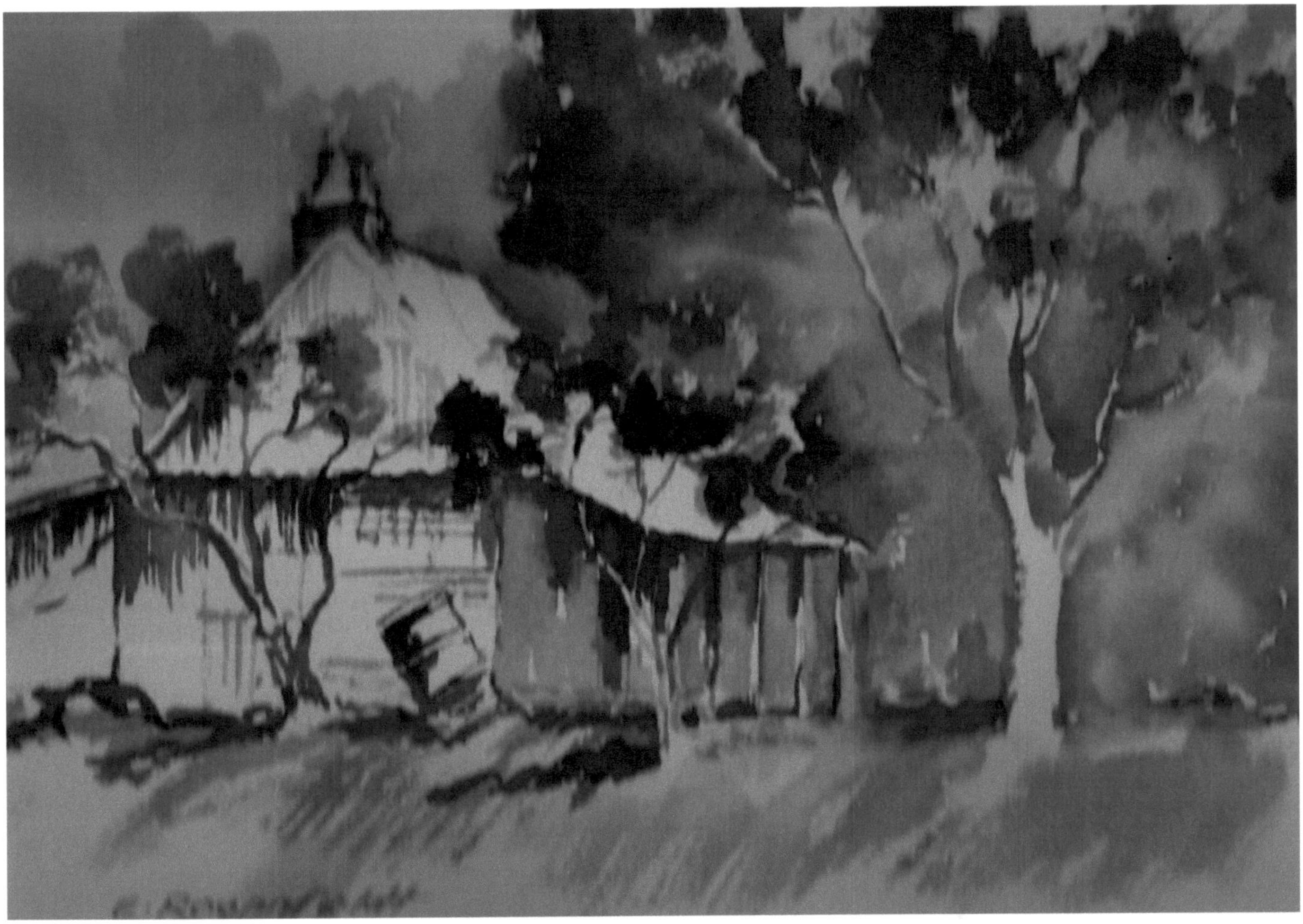

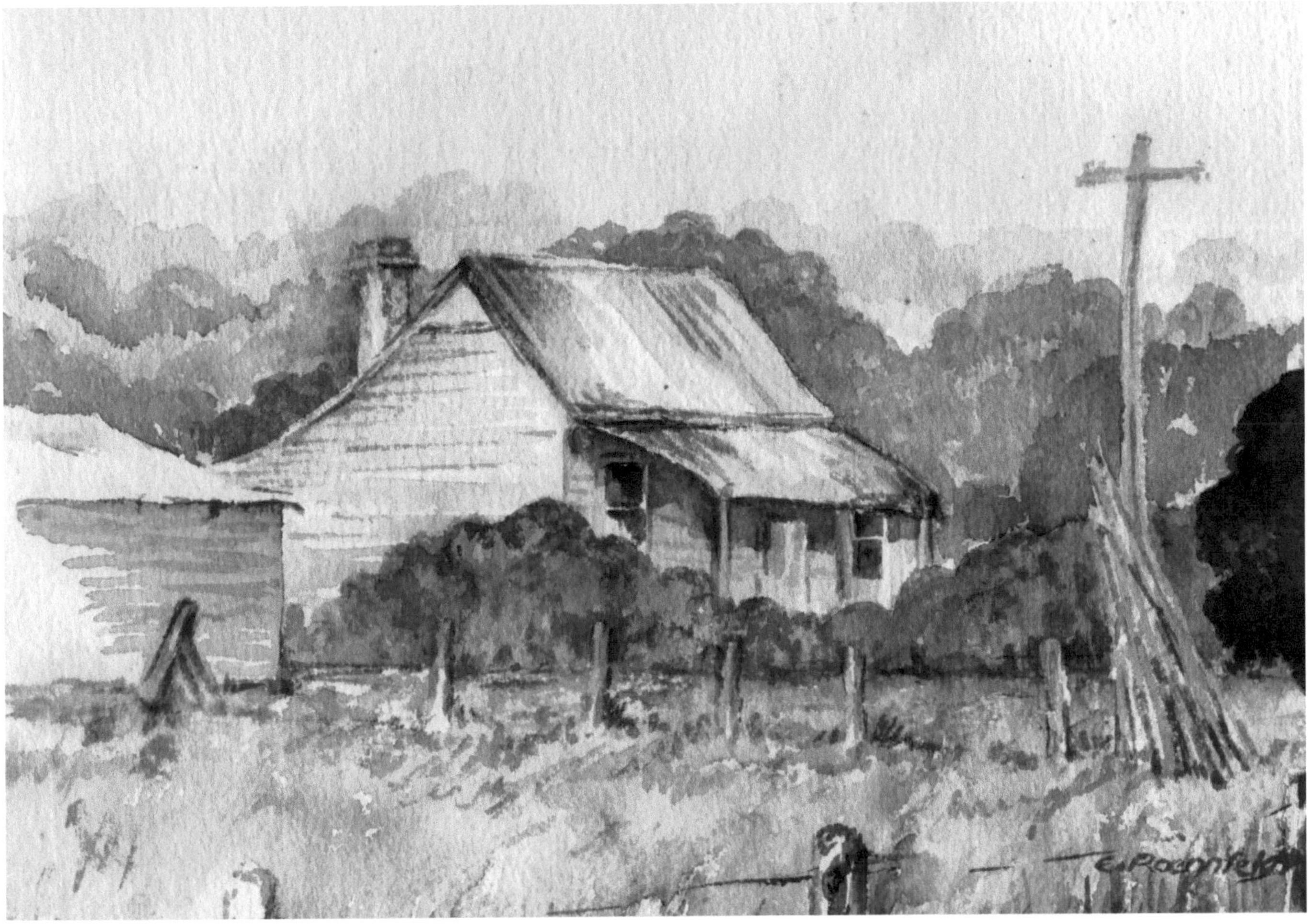

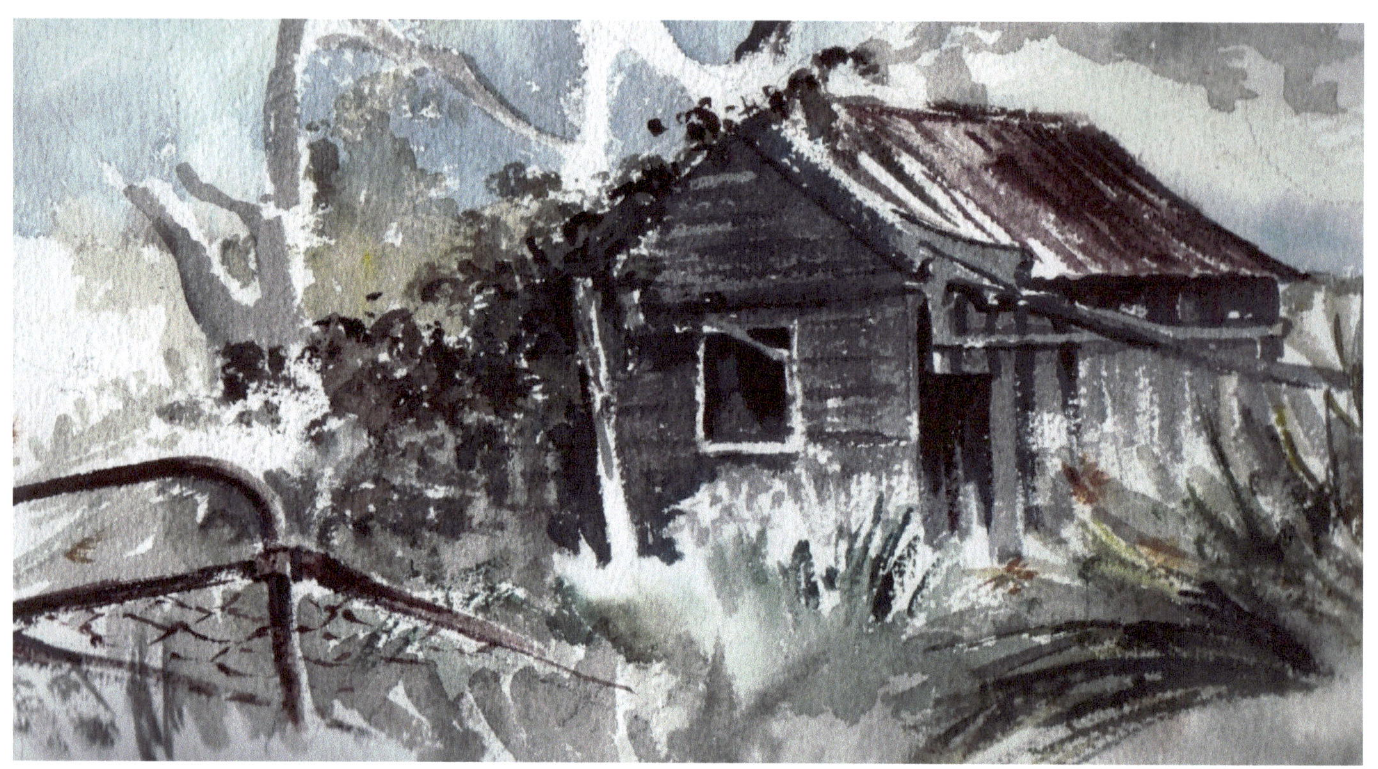

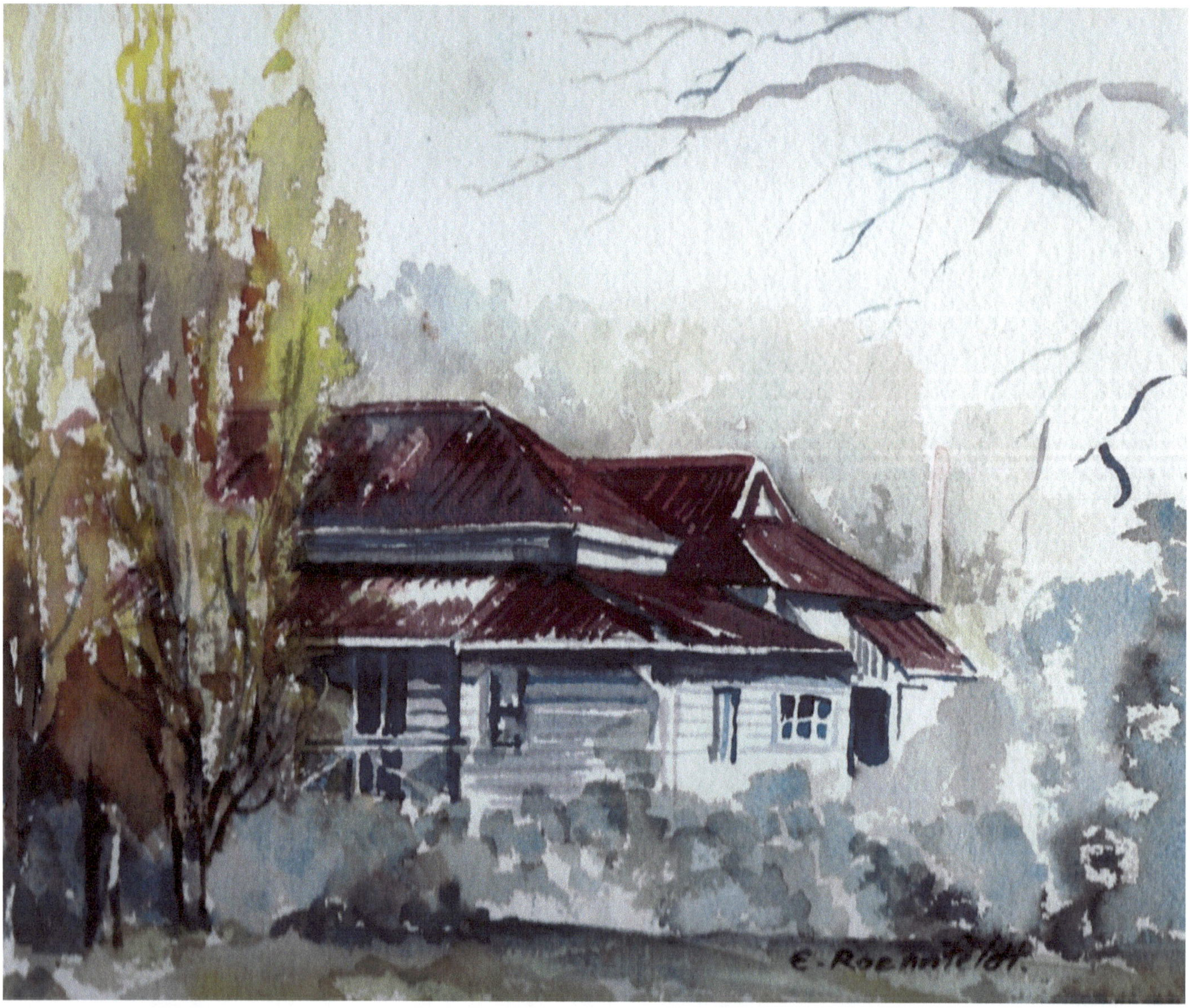

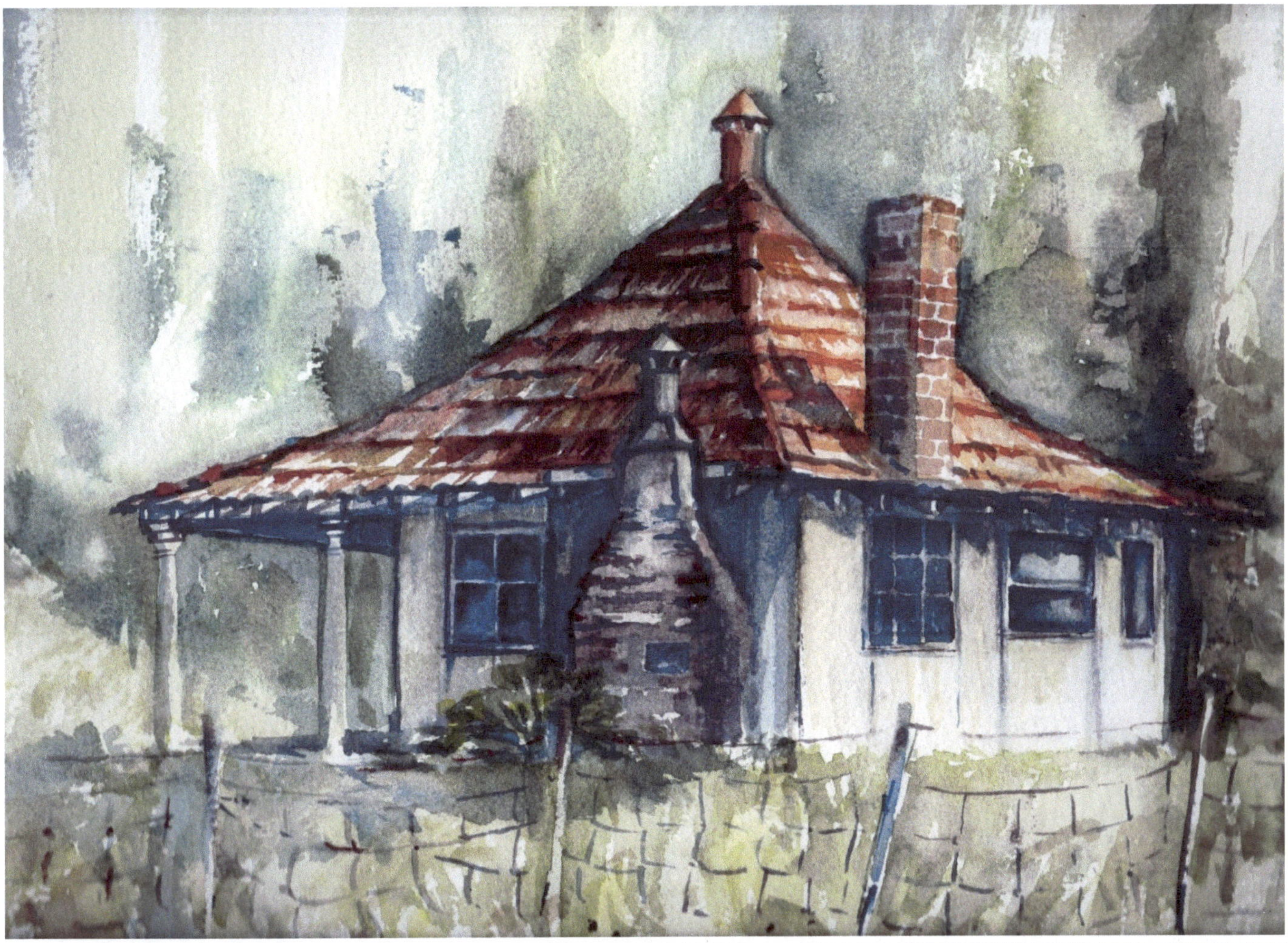

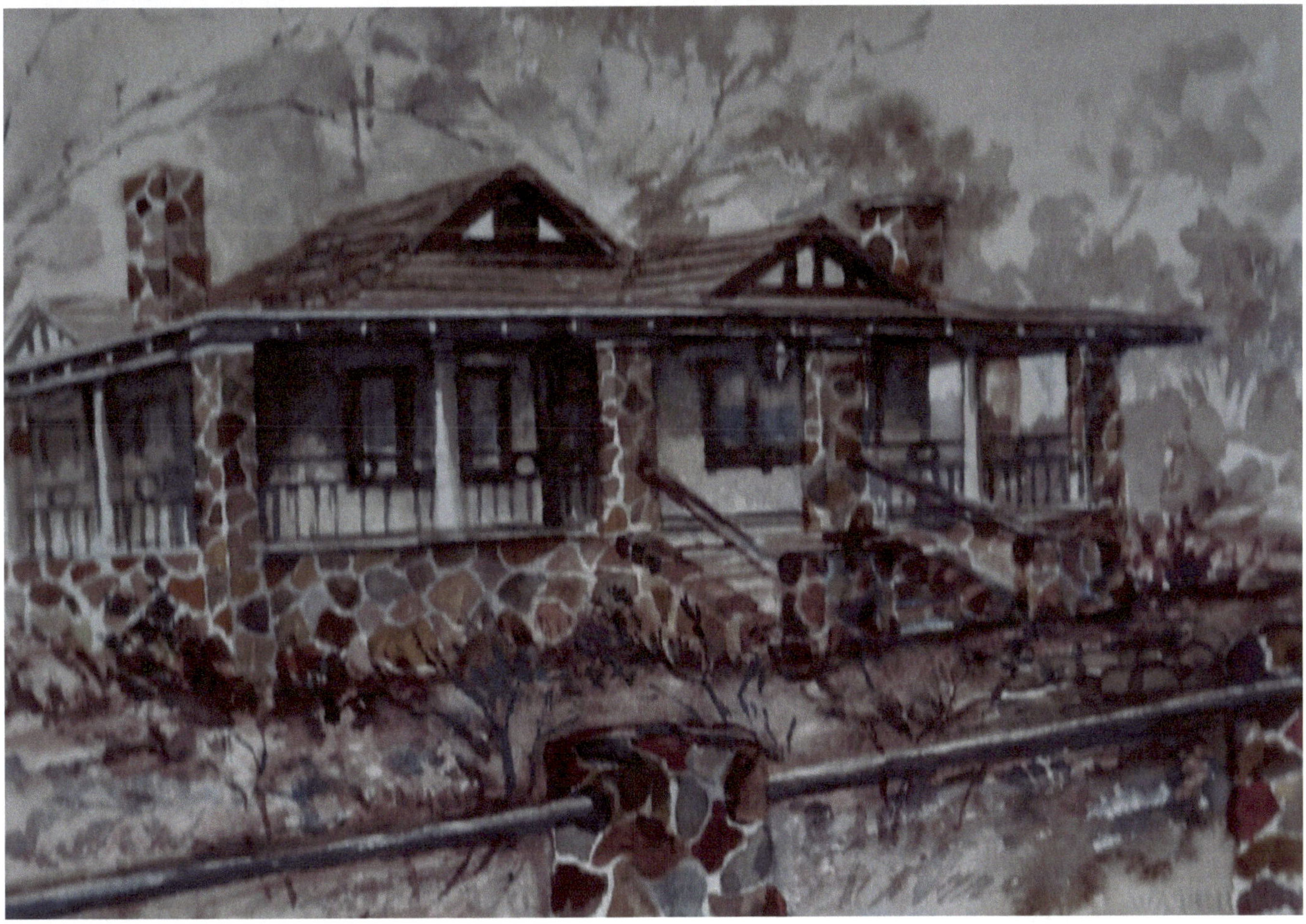

Historical and old buildings

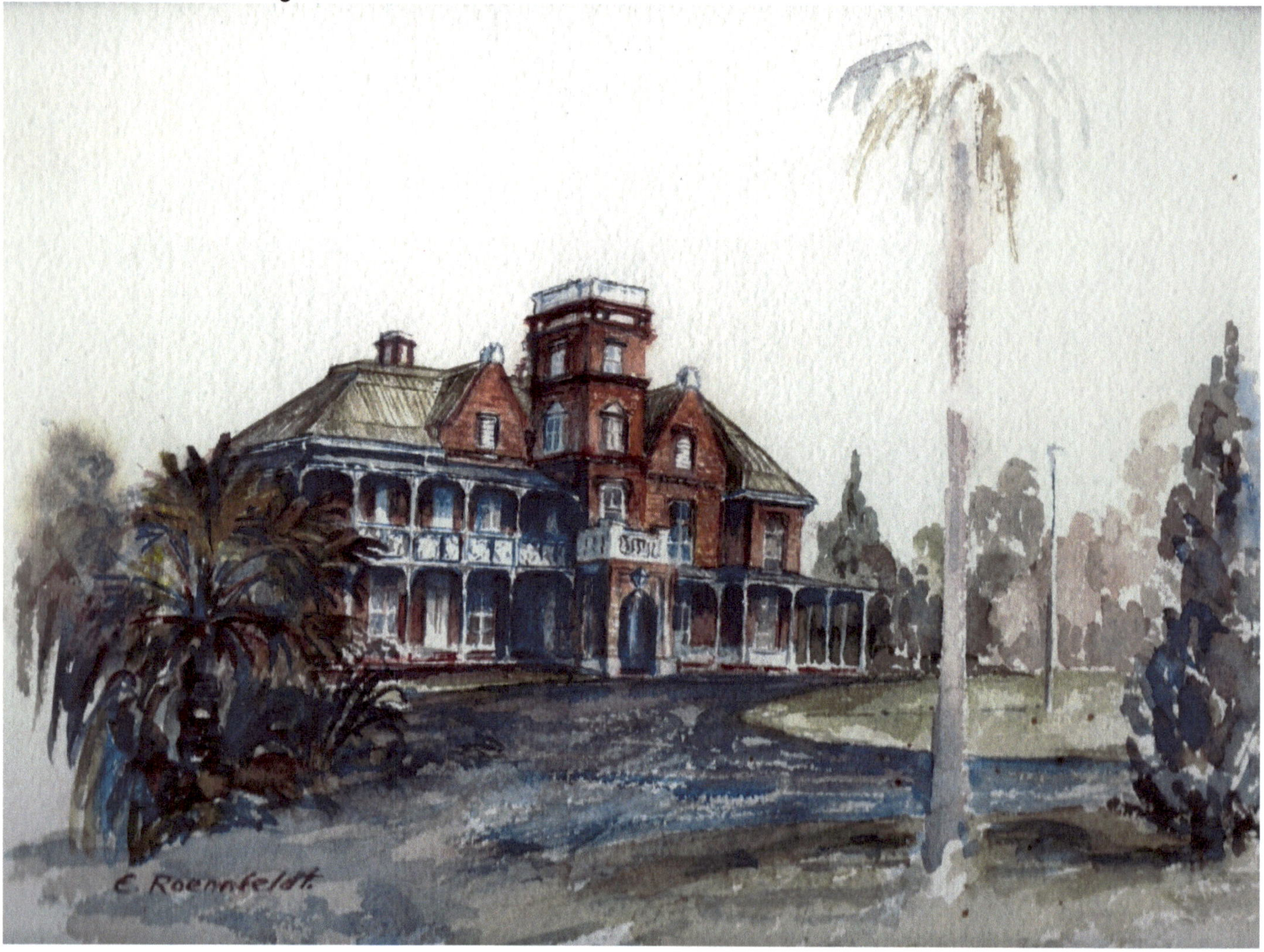

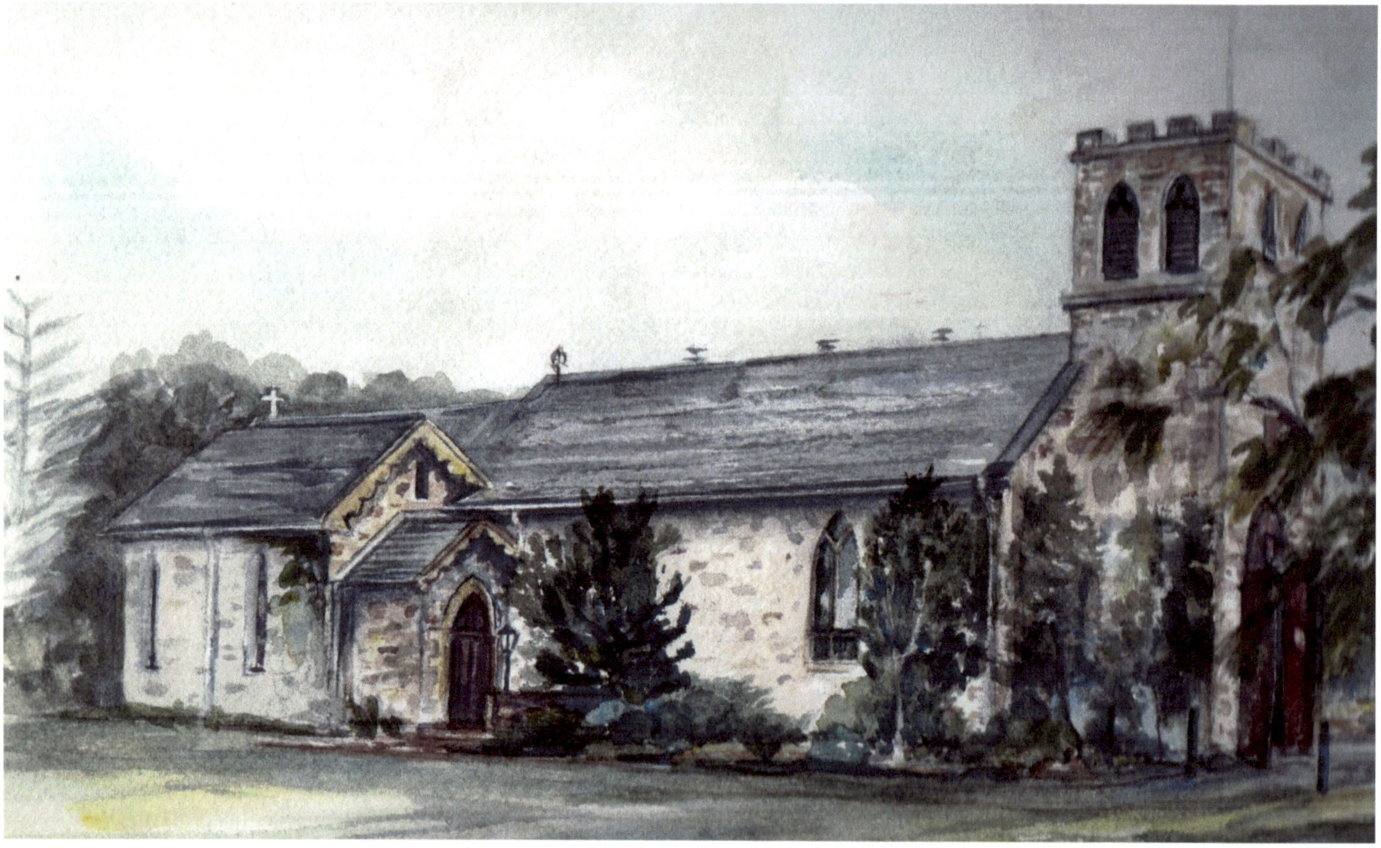

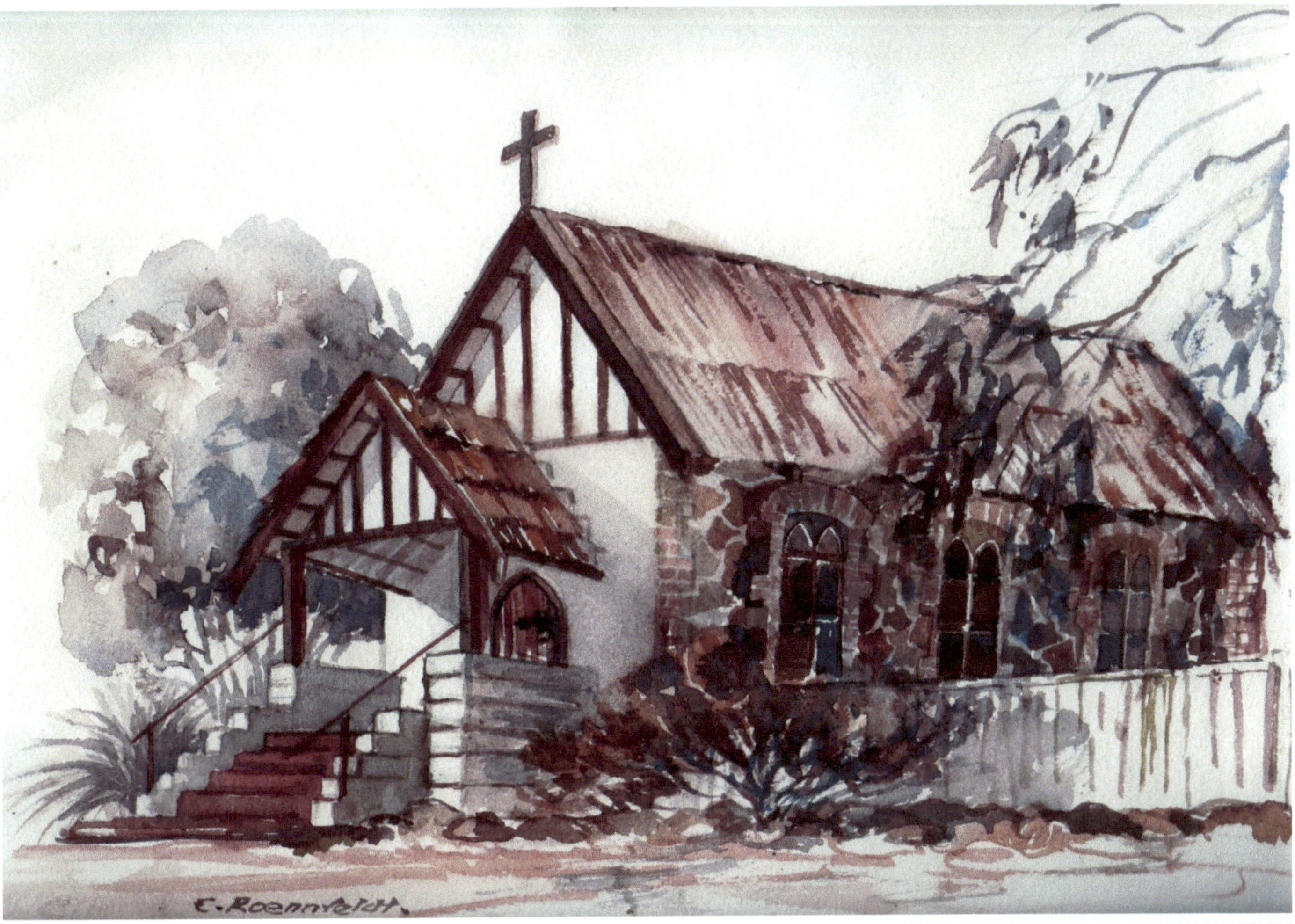

C. Roennfeldt.

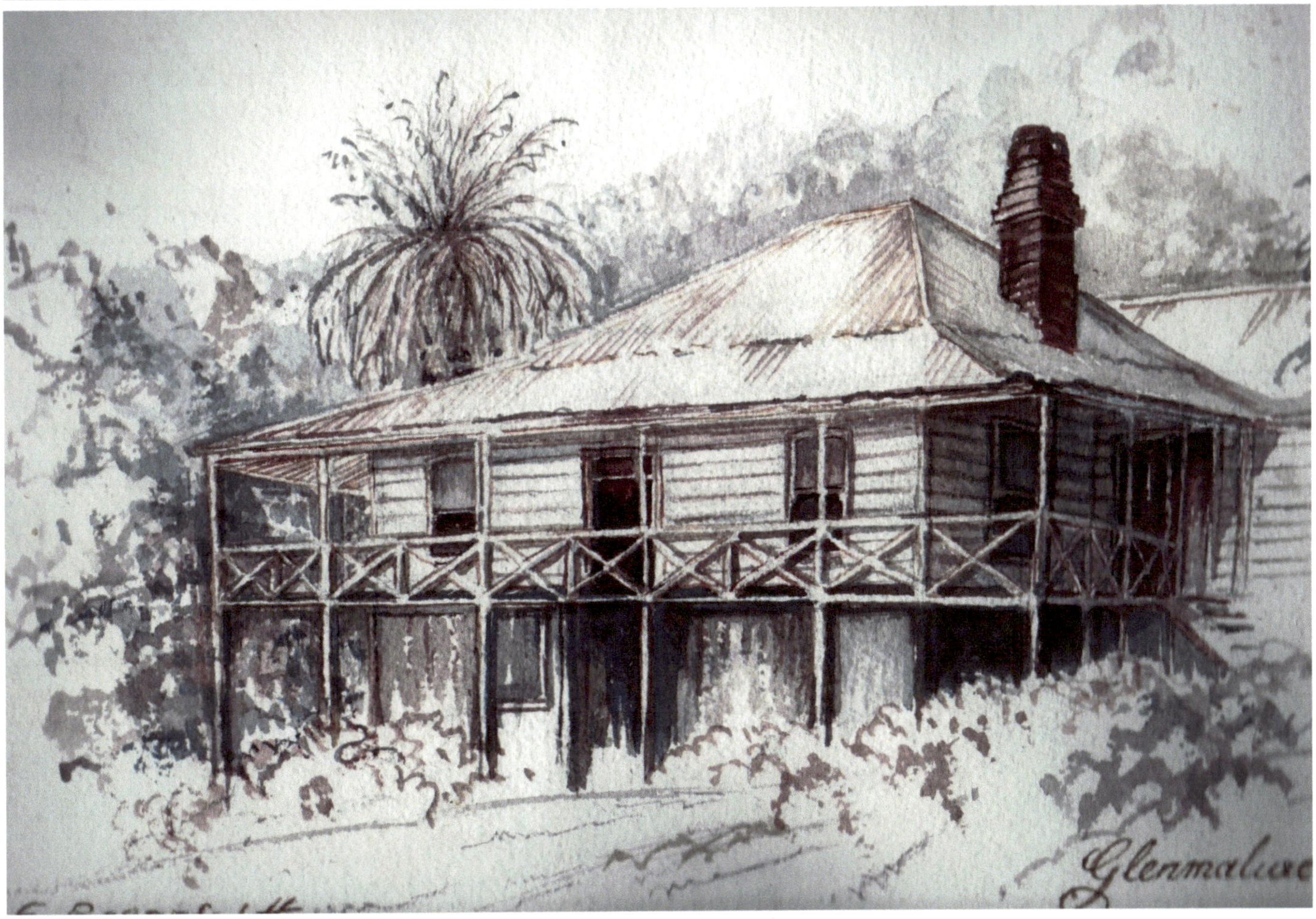

Glenmalure

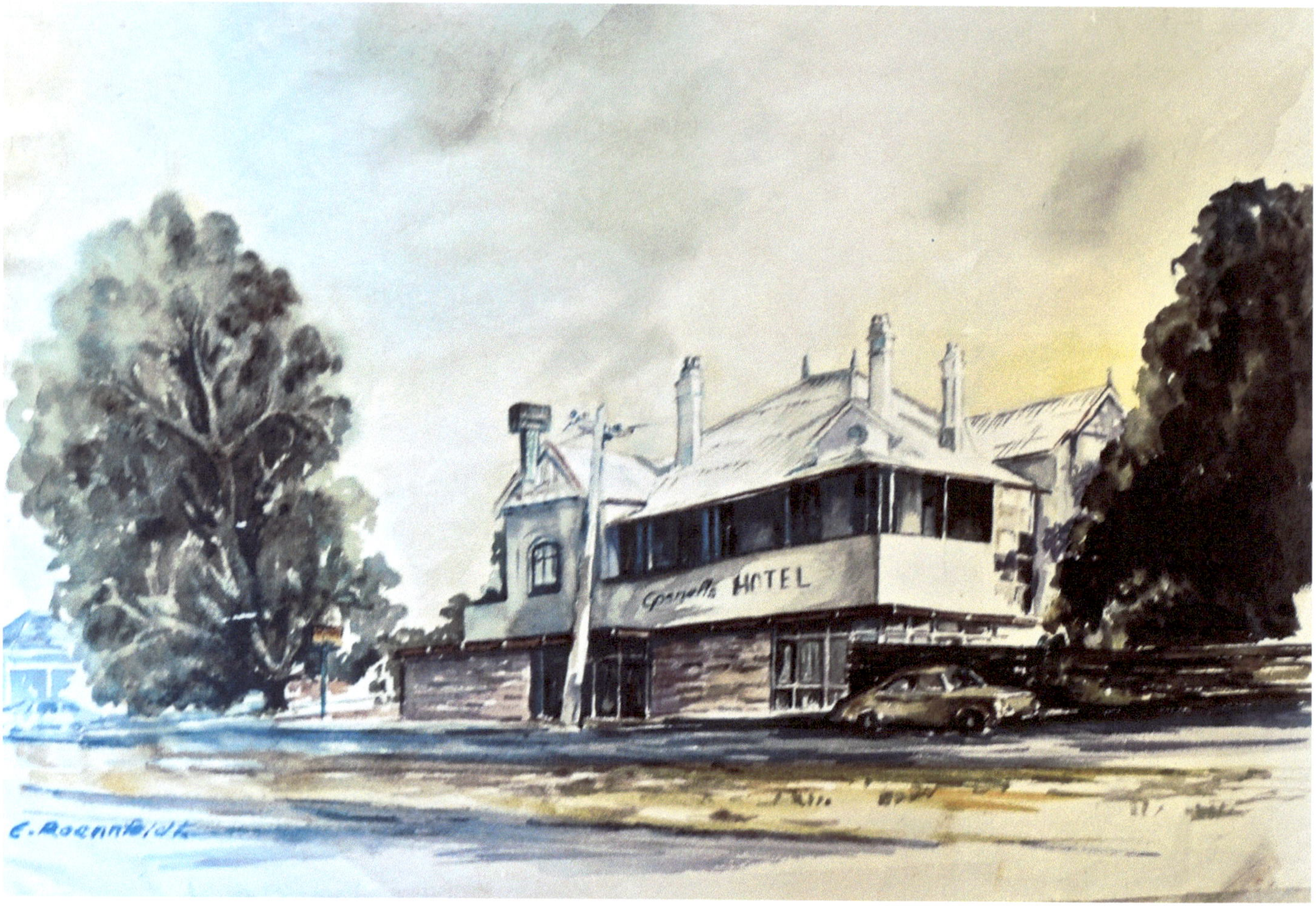

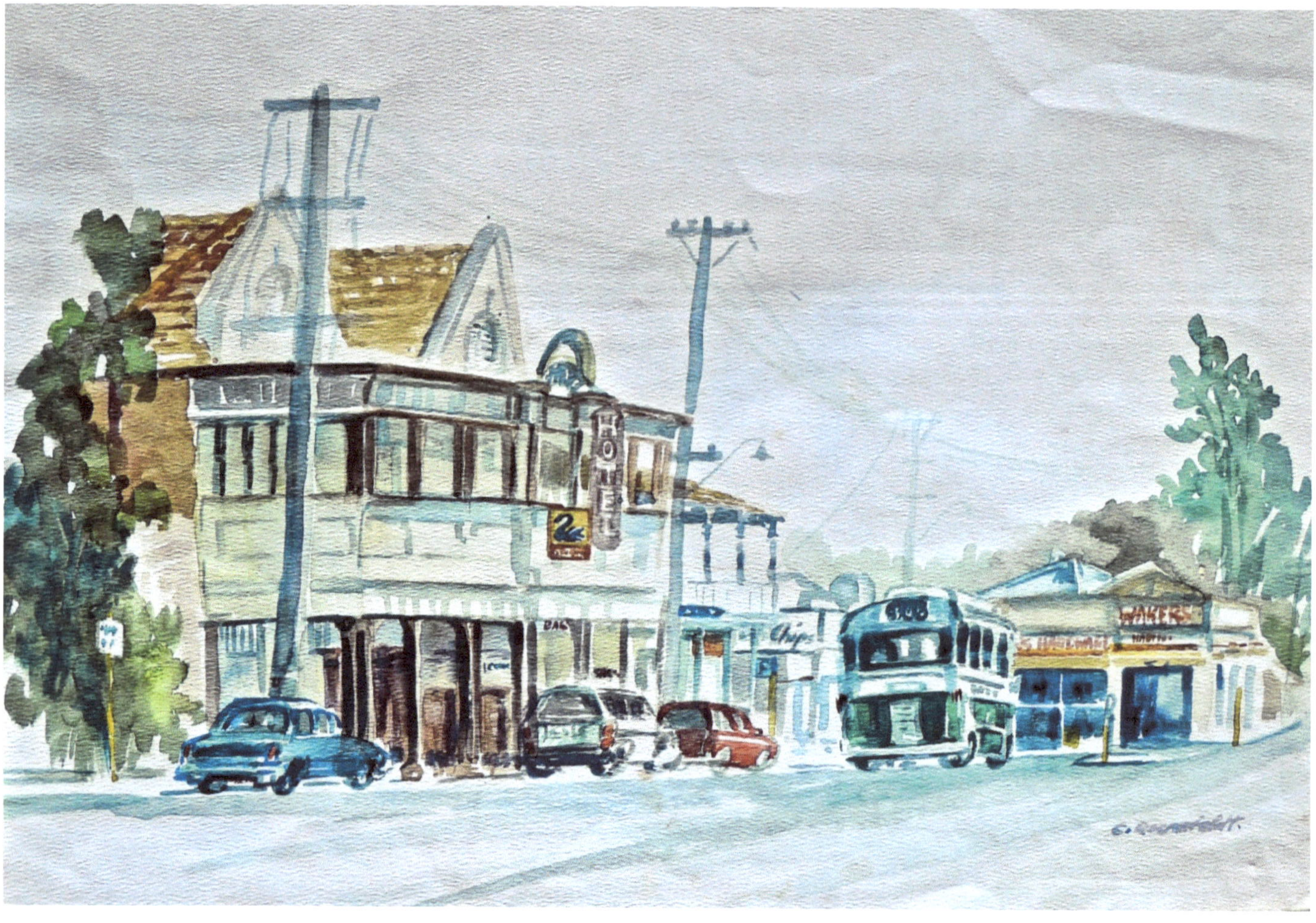

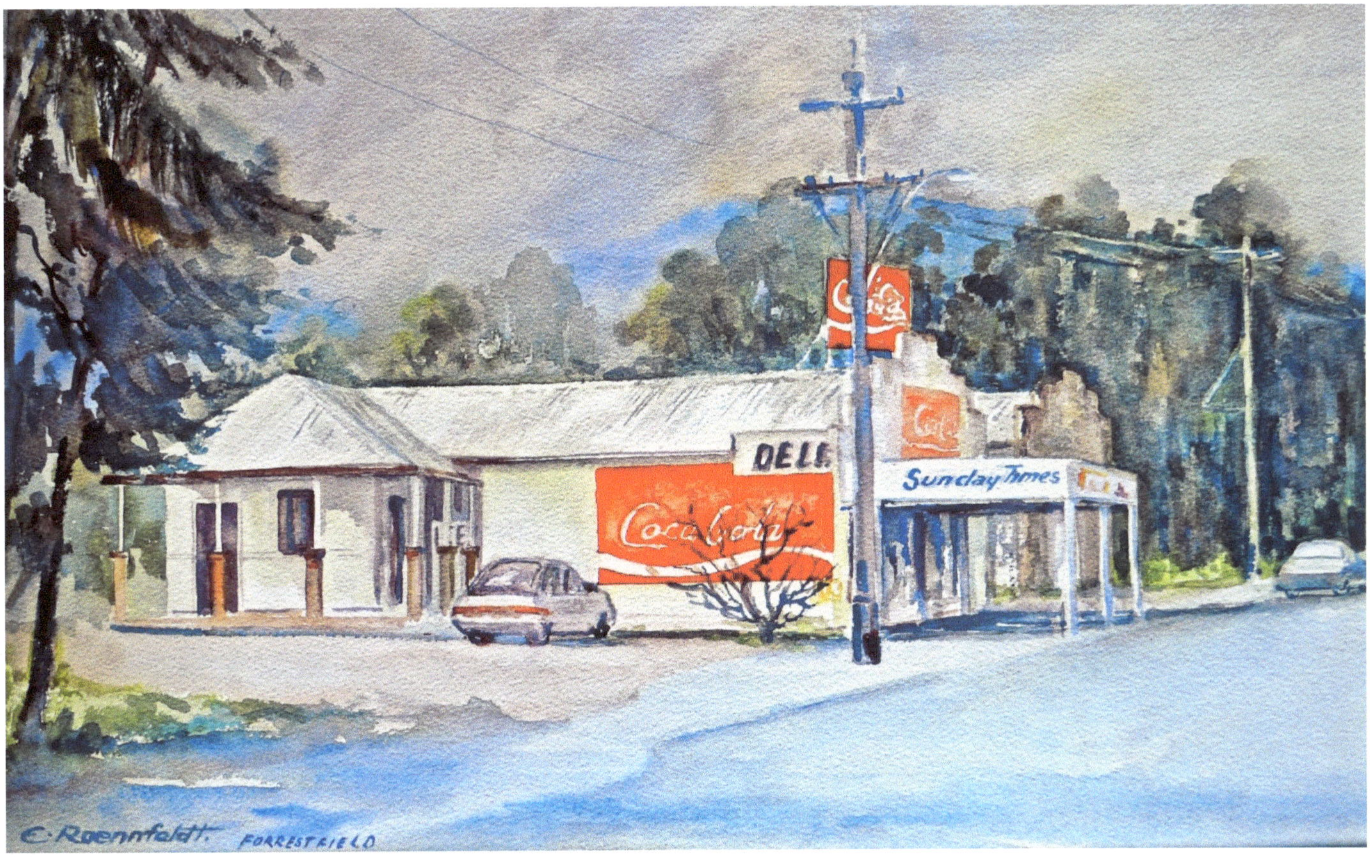

DELI
Coca-Cola
Sunday Times
E.Roennfeldt. FORRESTFIELD

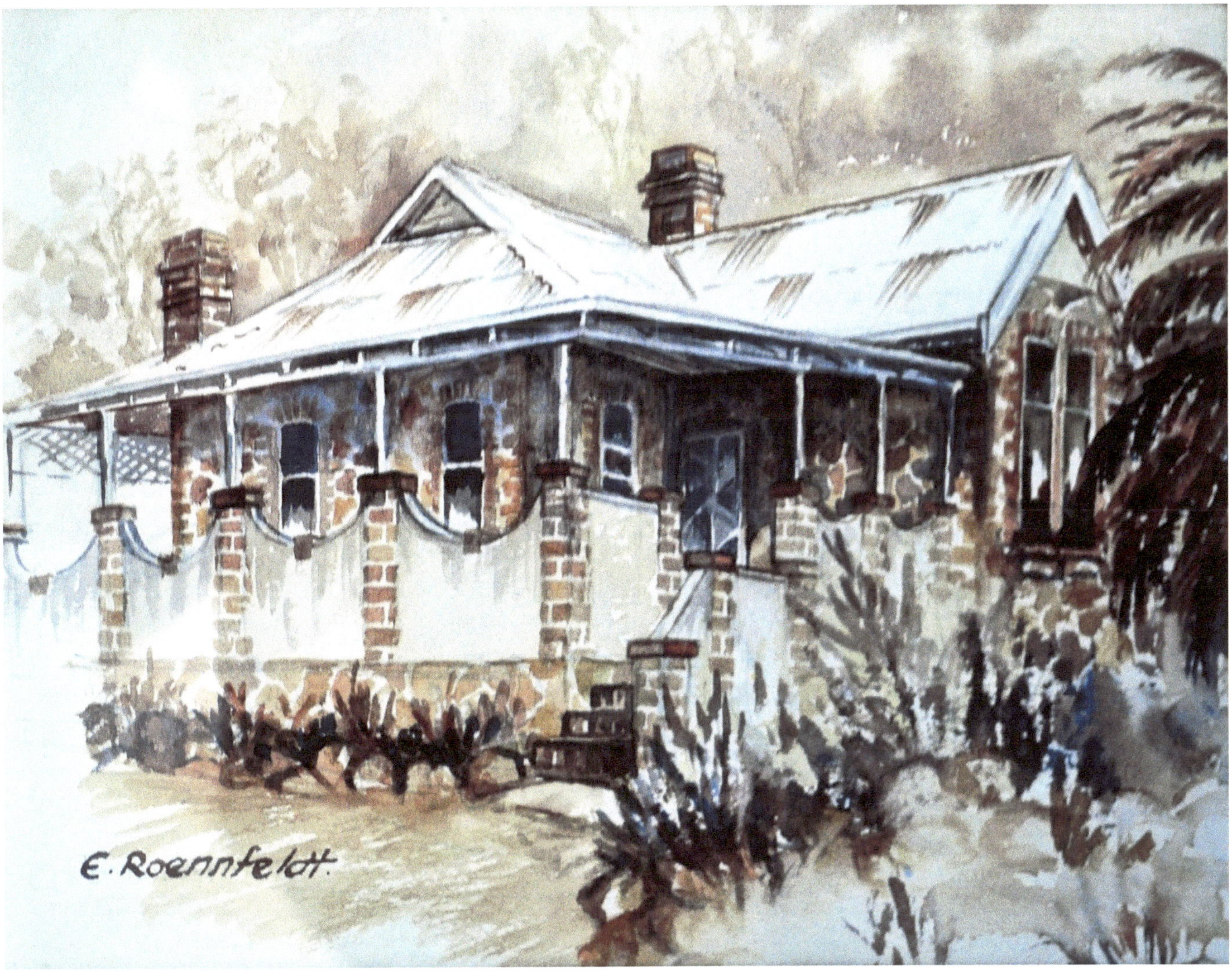

E.Roennfeldt.

Swan Valley

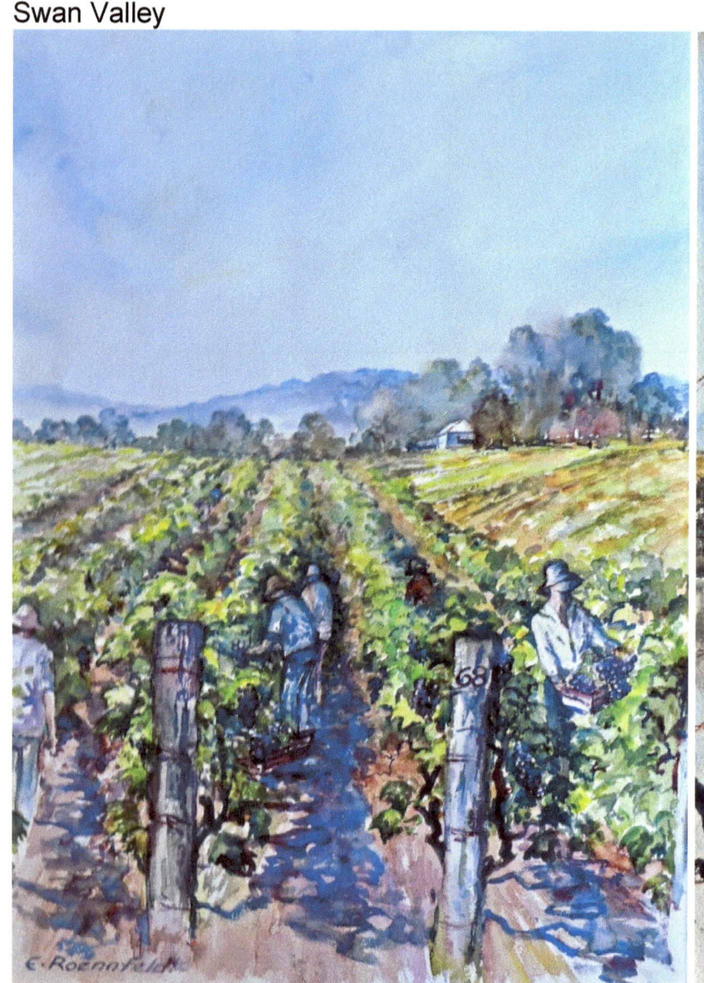

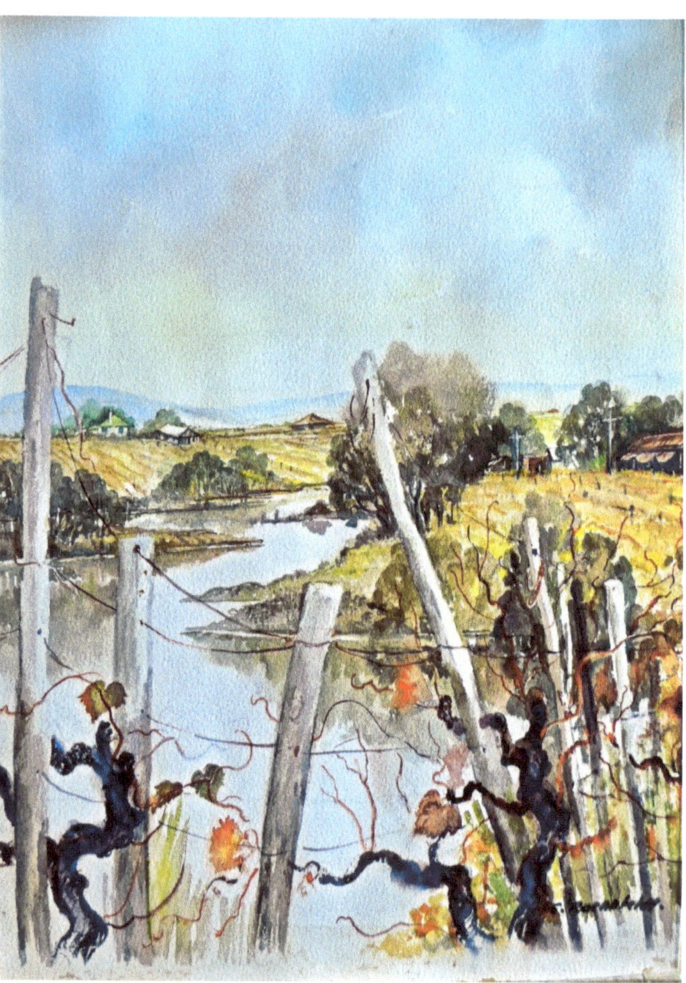

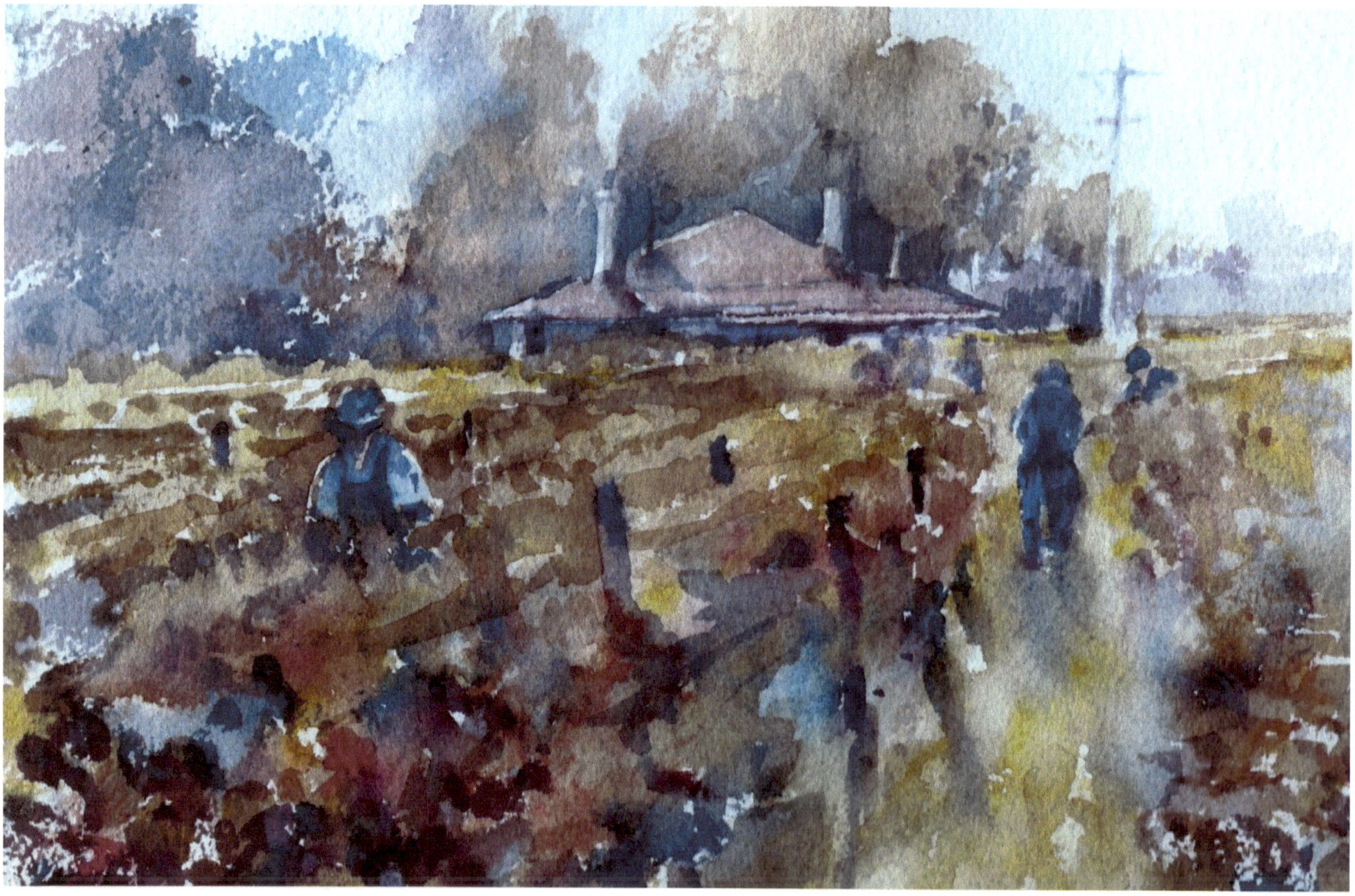

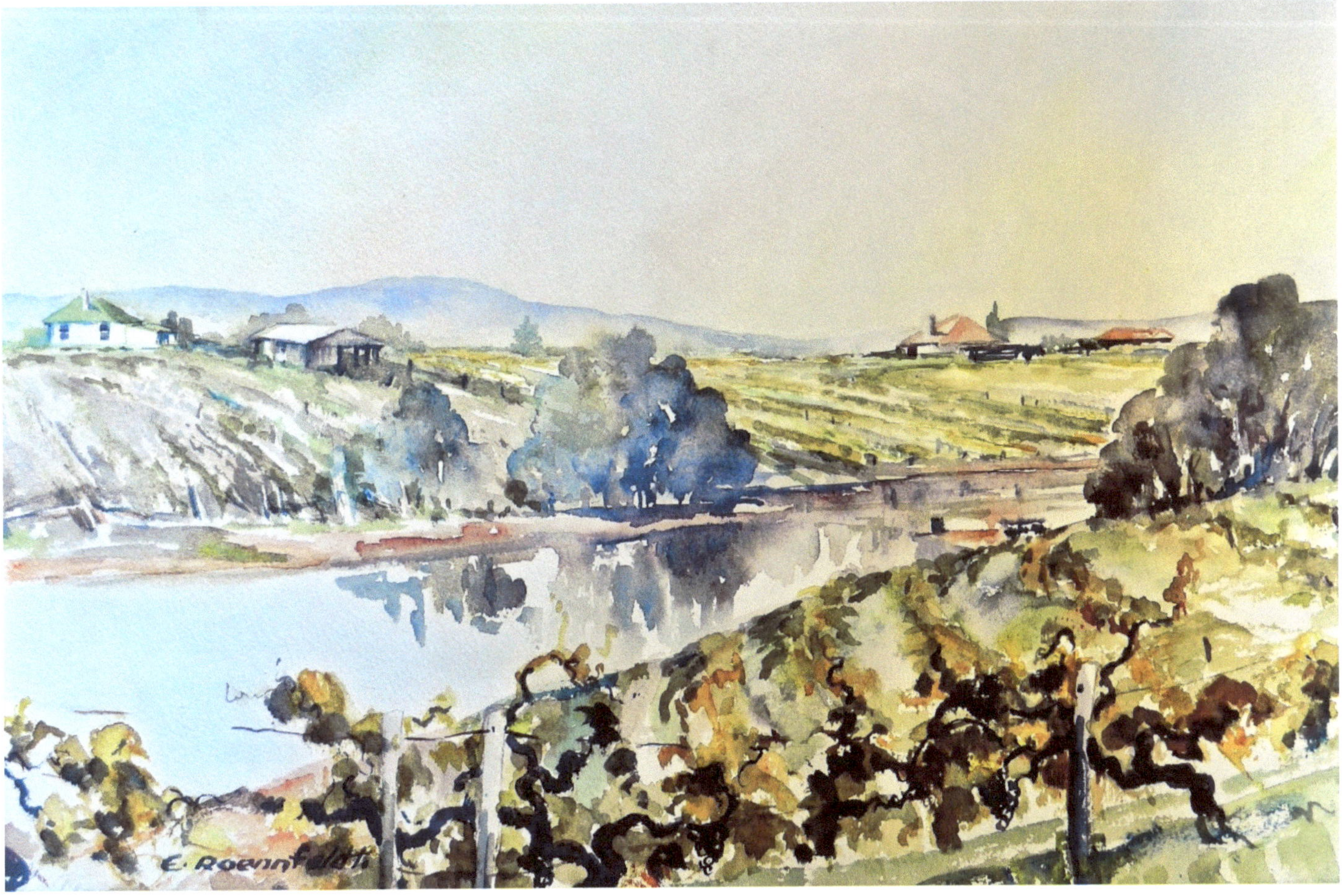

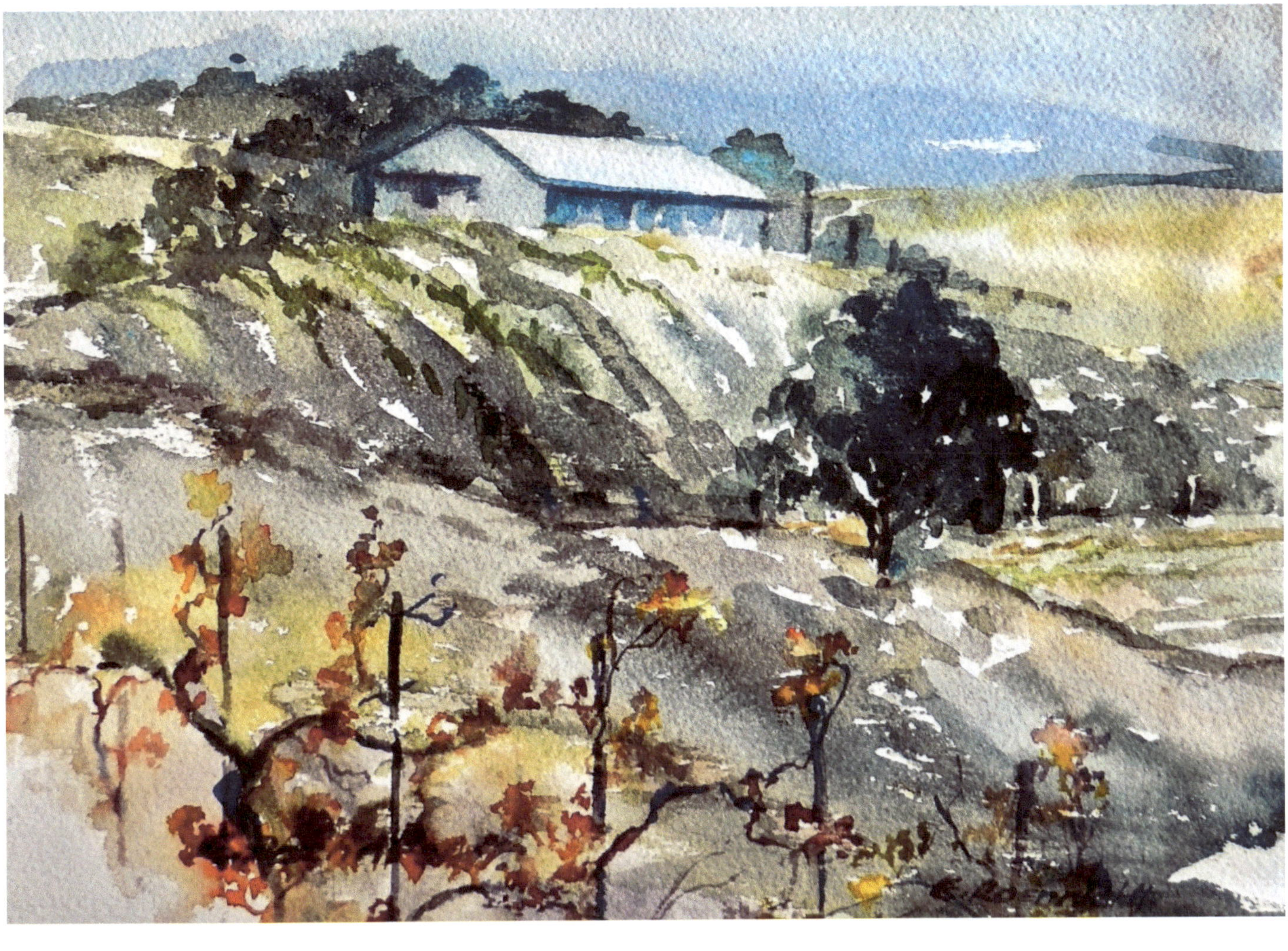

Trees and the bush

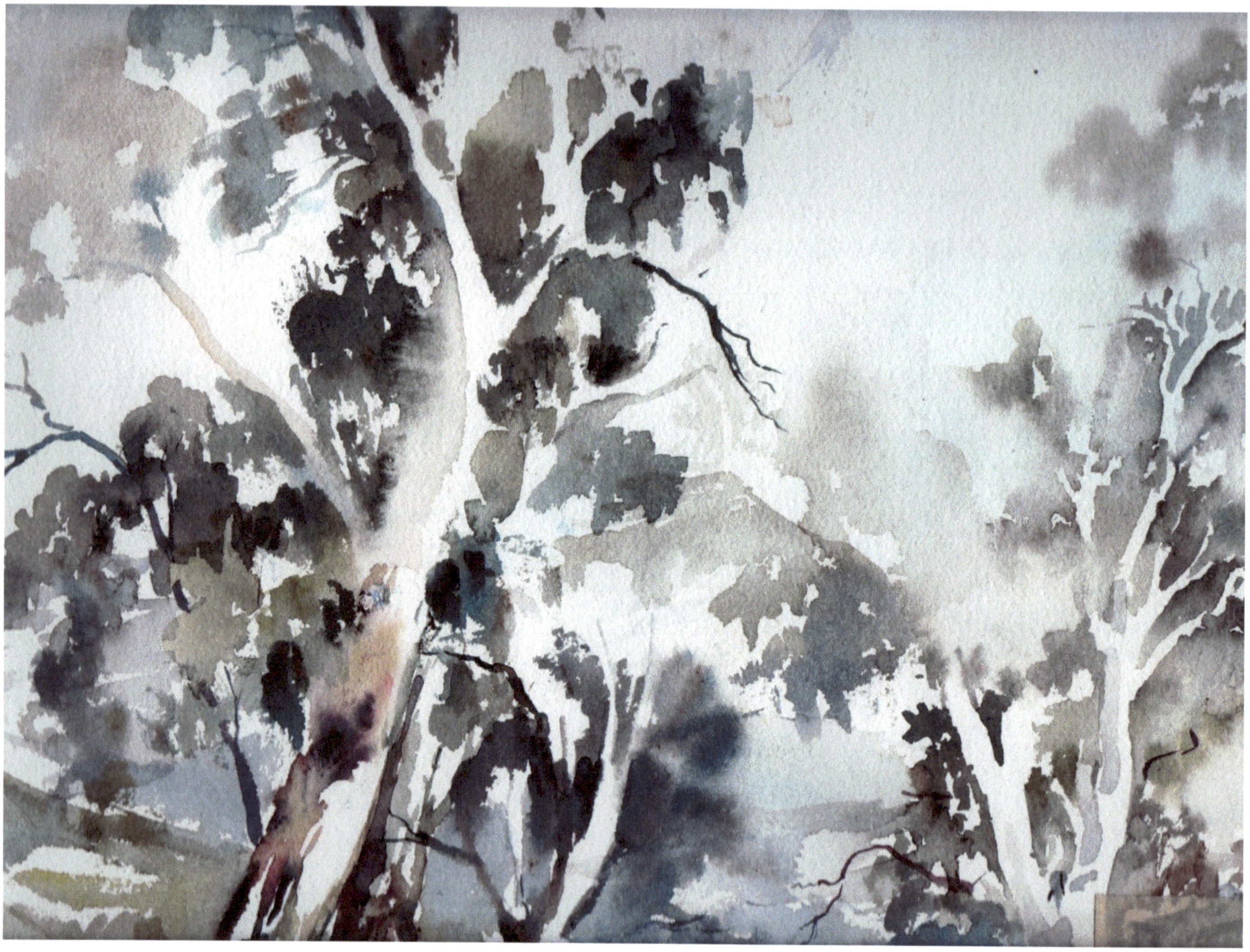

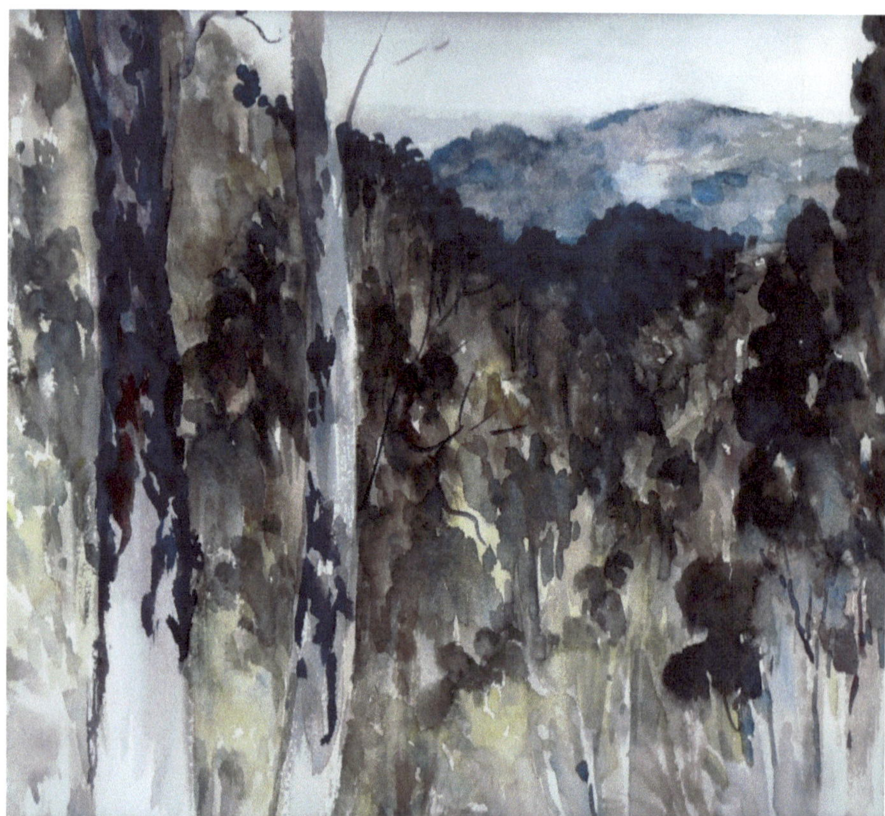

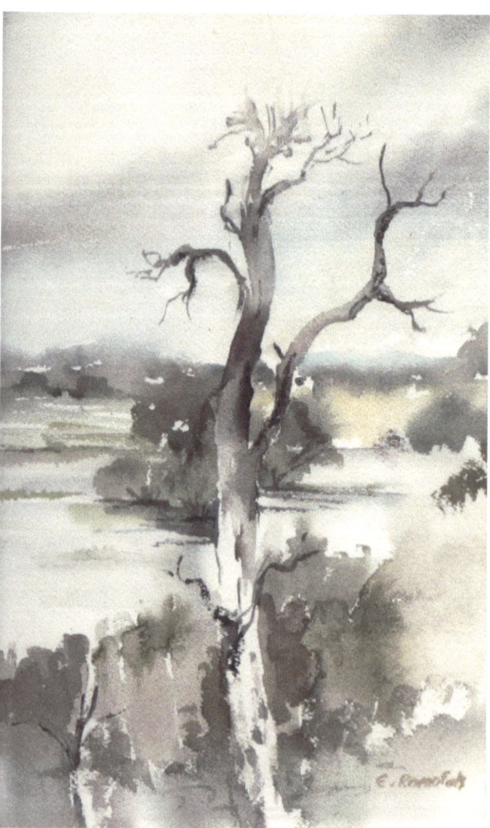

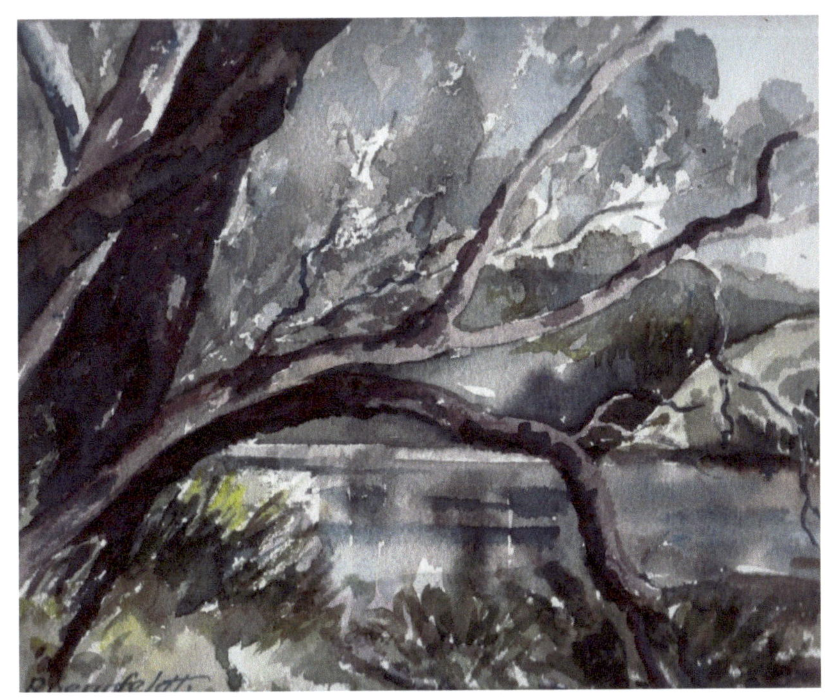

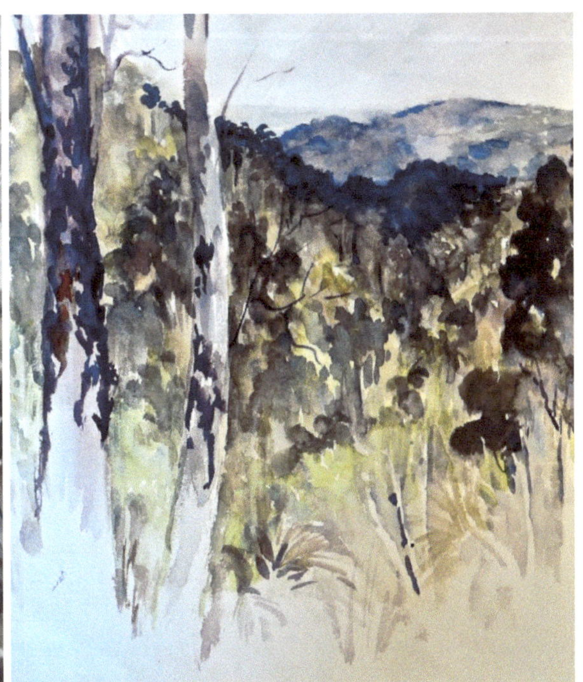

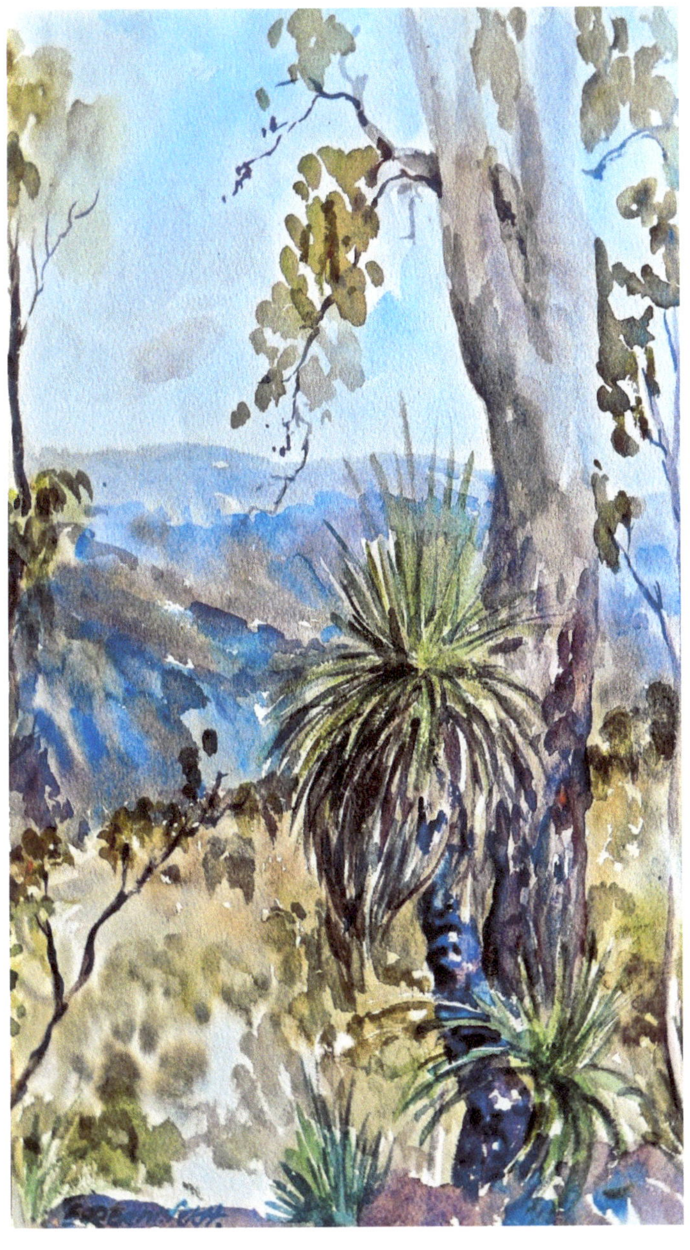

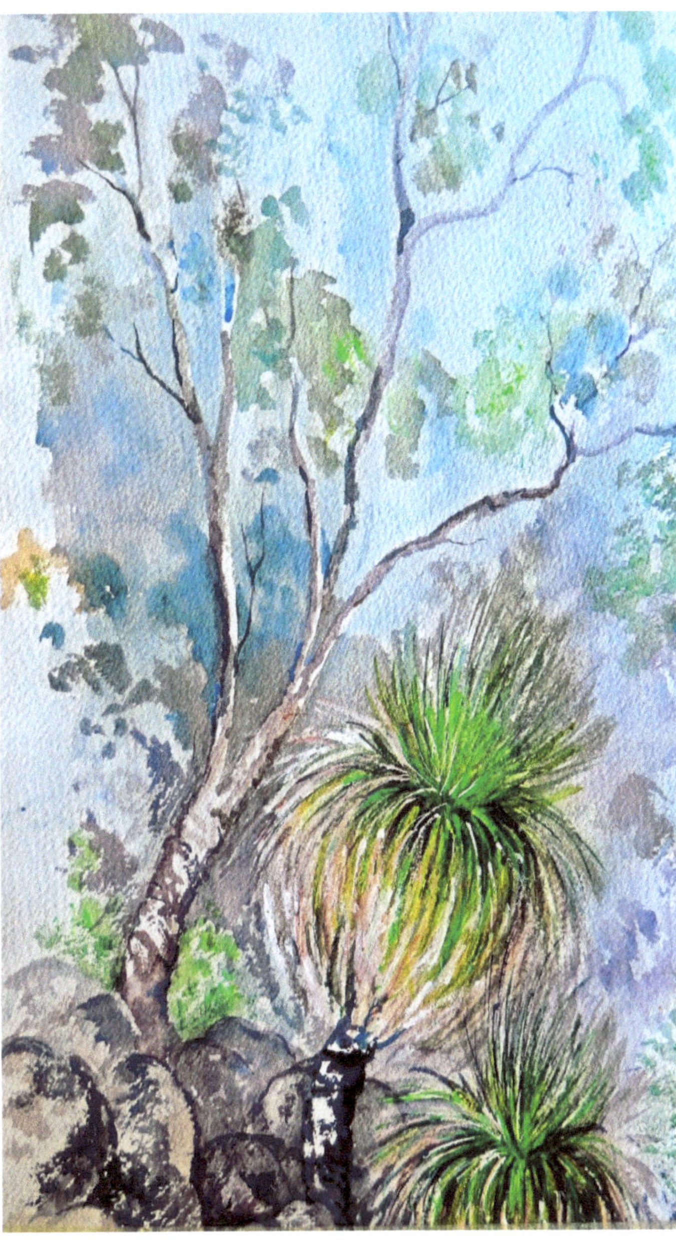

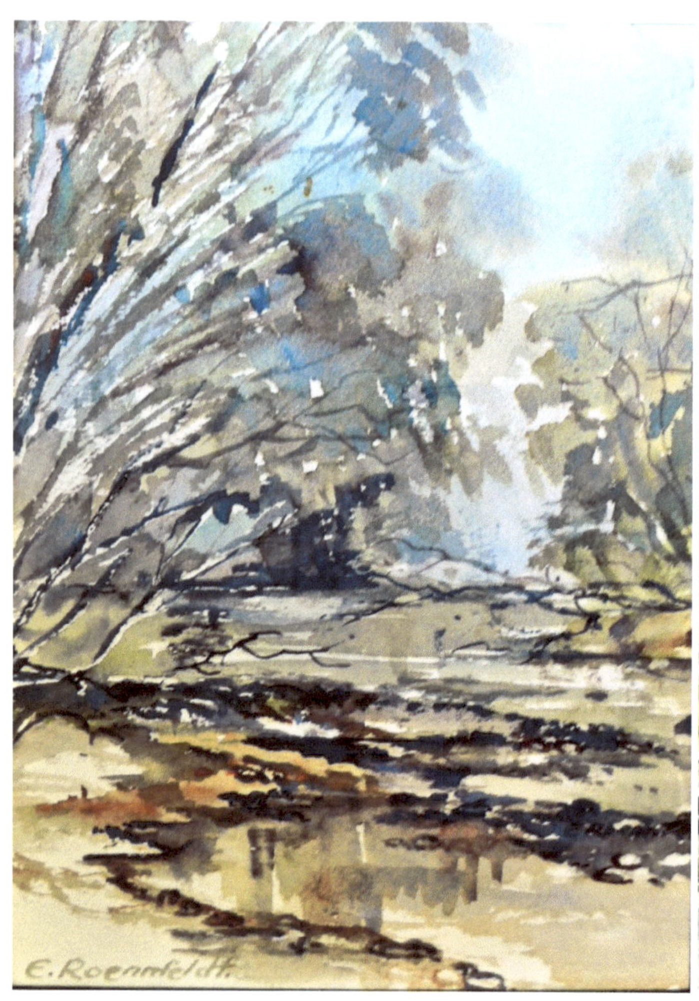
E.Roennfeldt

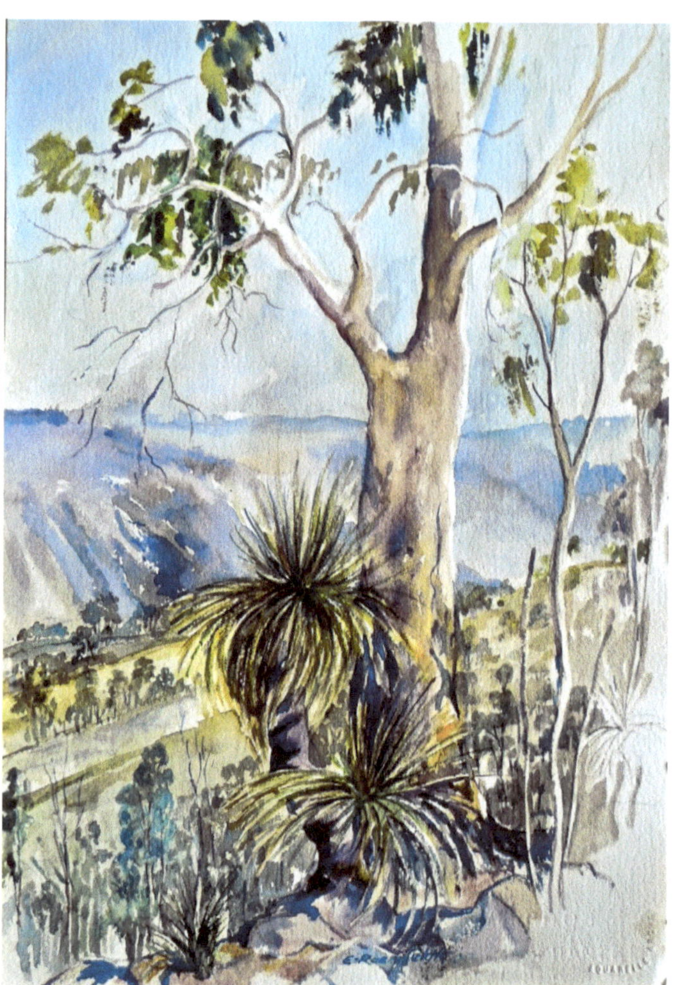

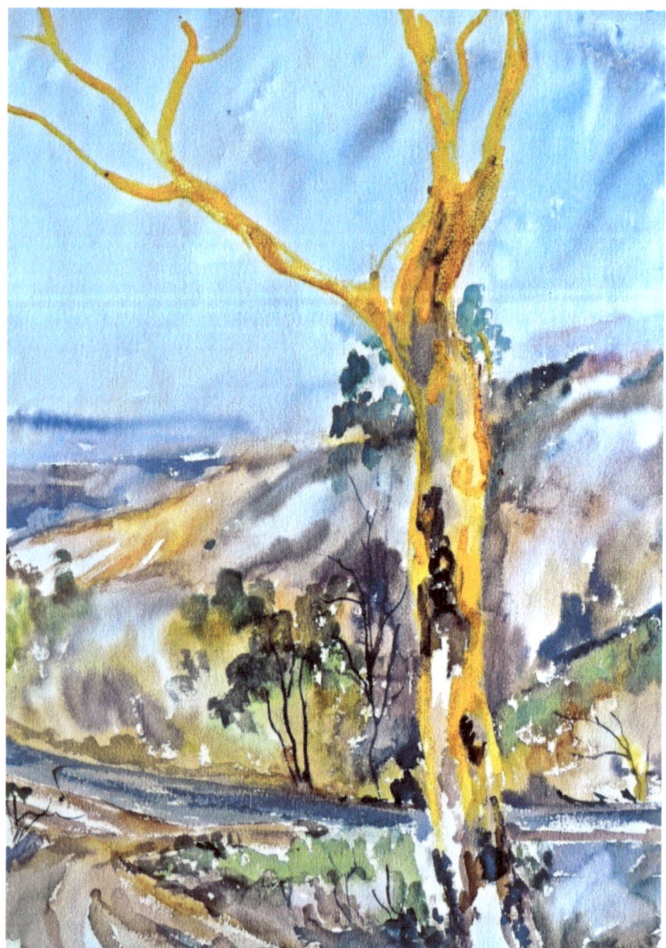

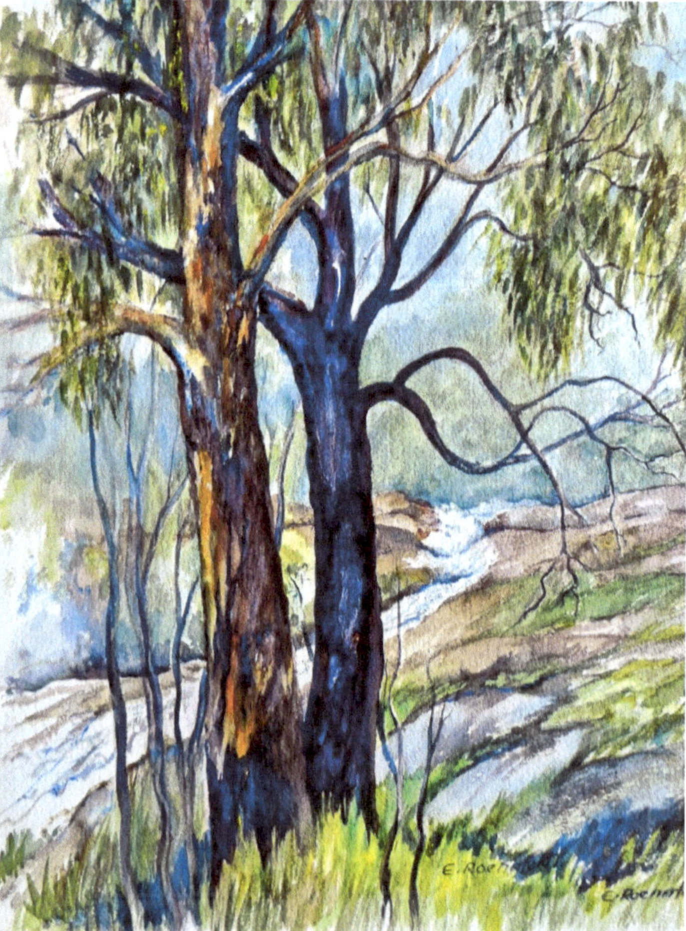

Flowers

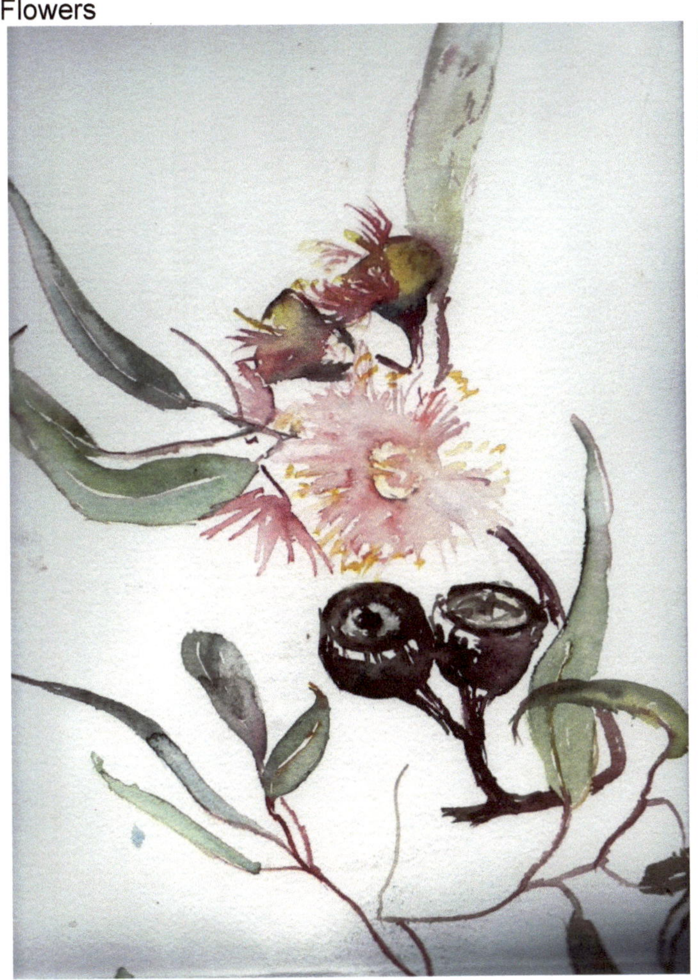

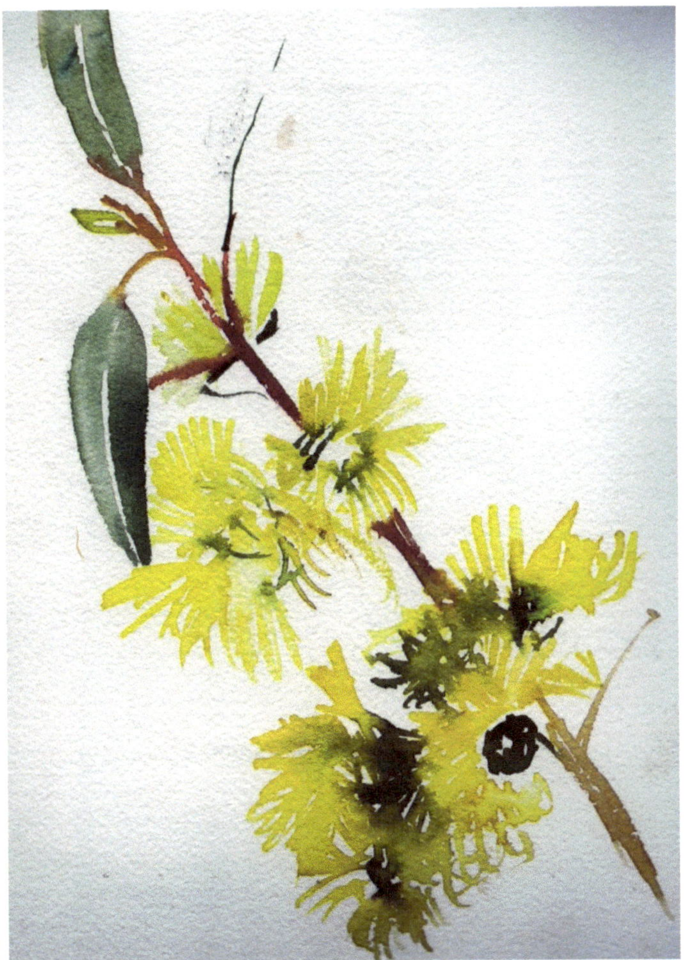

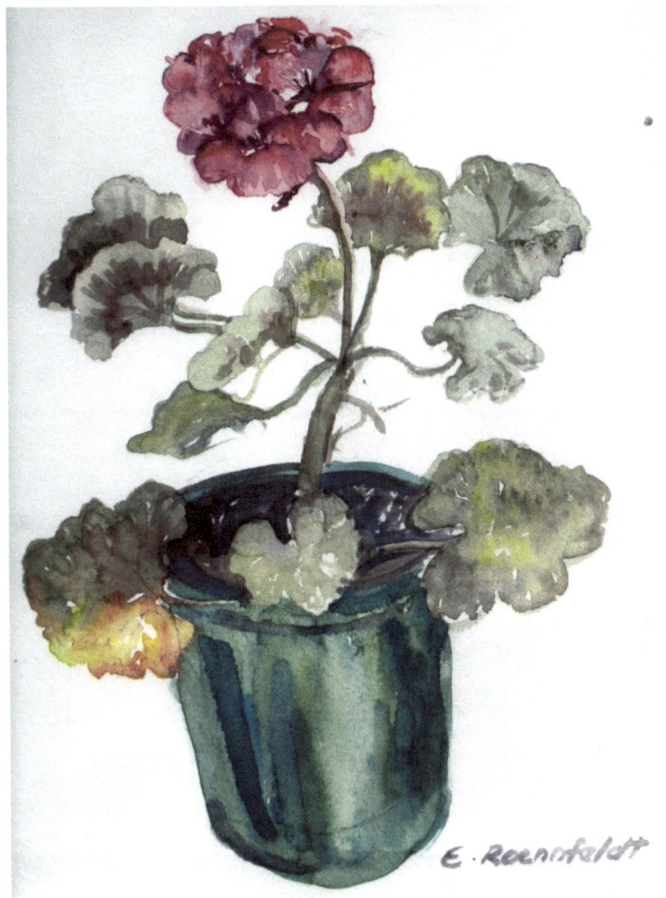

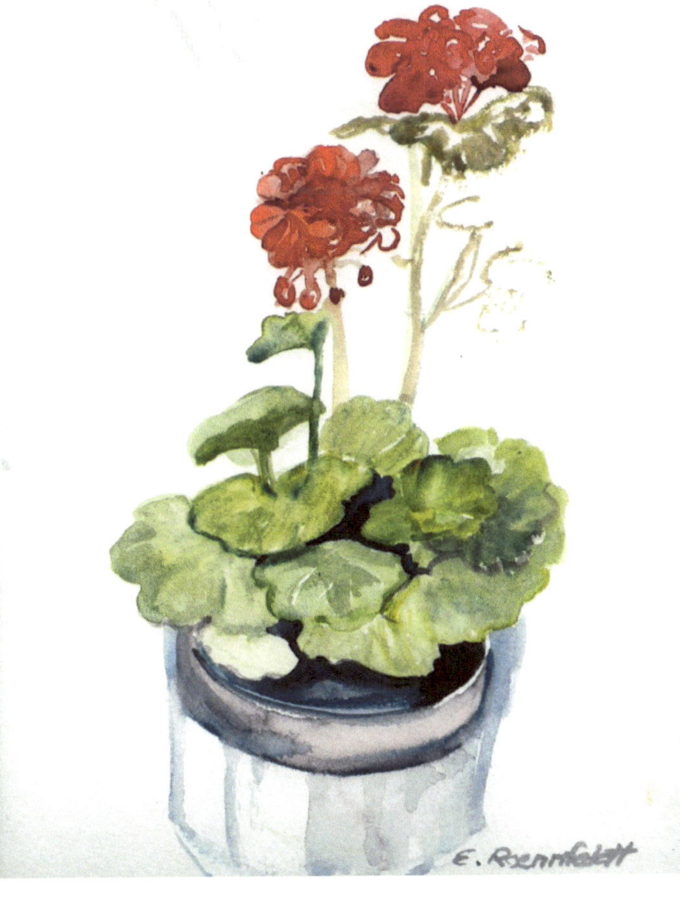

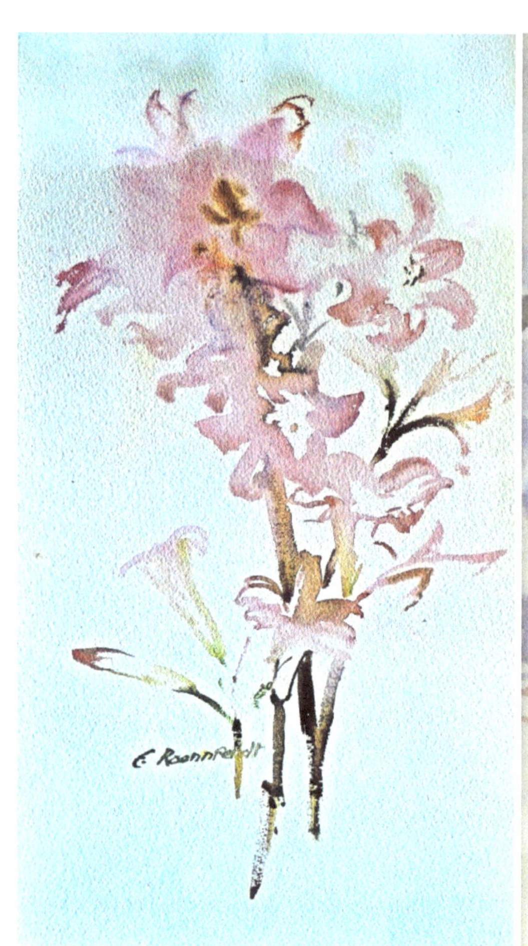
E. Roennfeldt

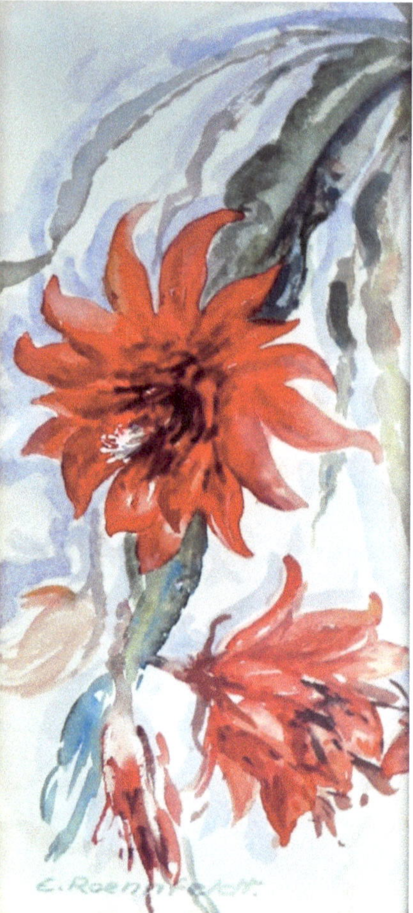
E. Roennfeldt

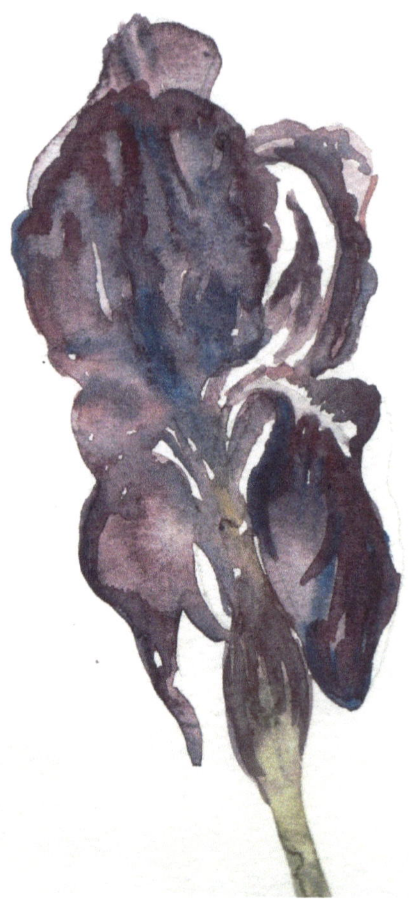

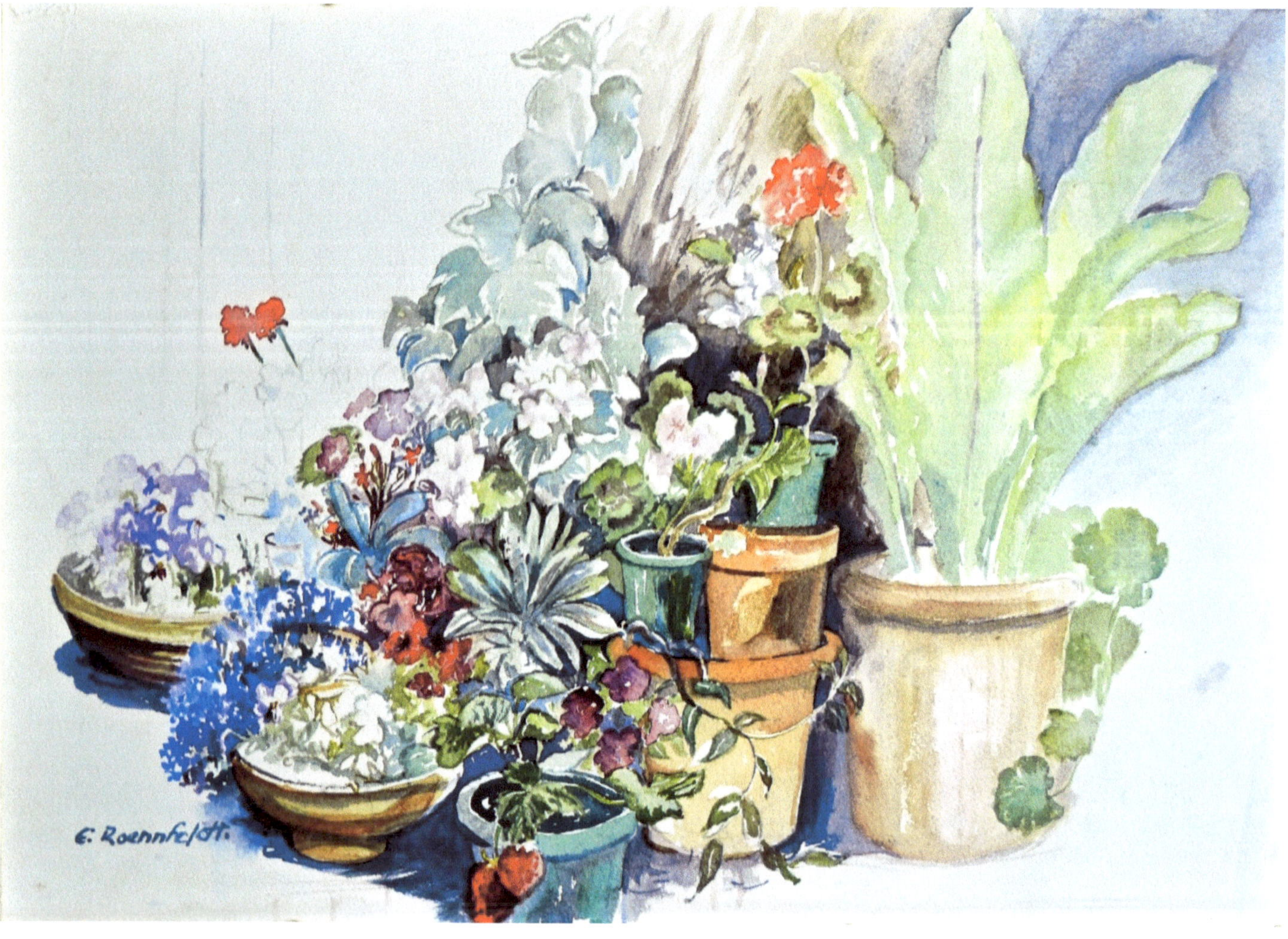

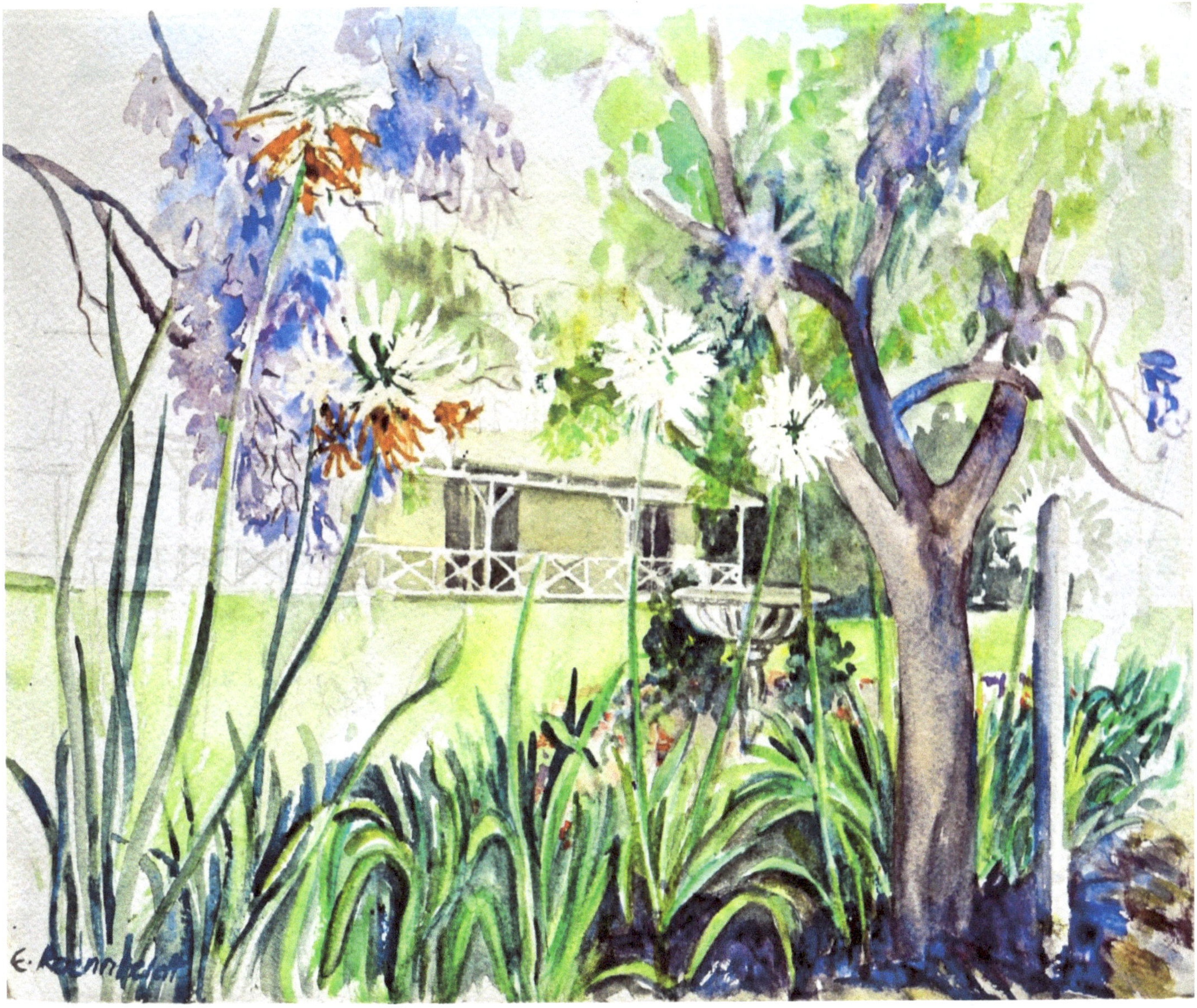

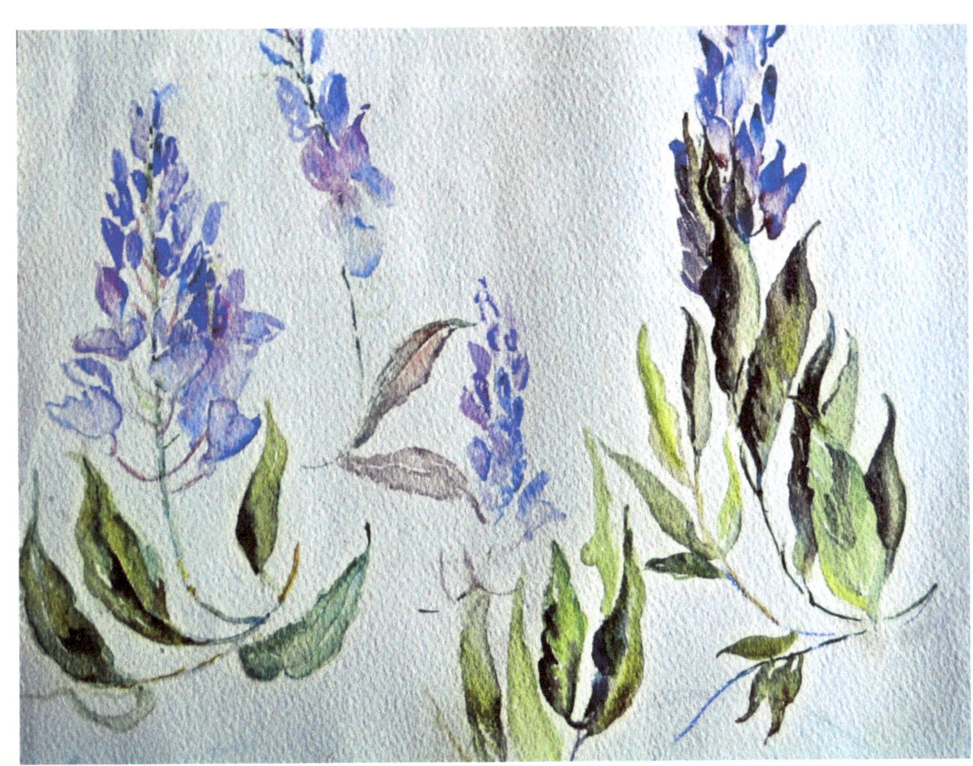

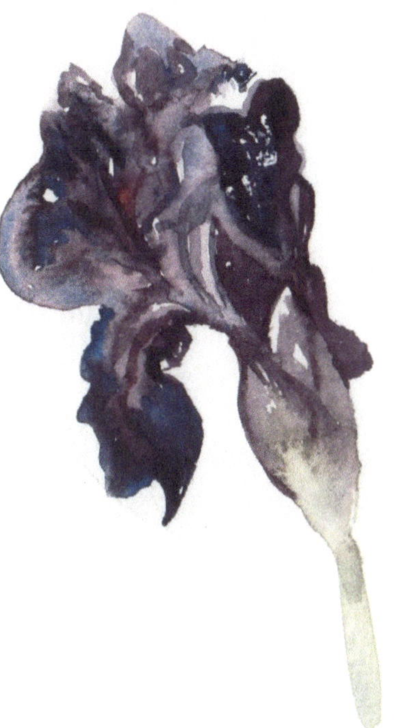

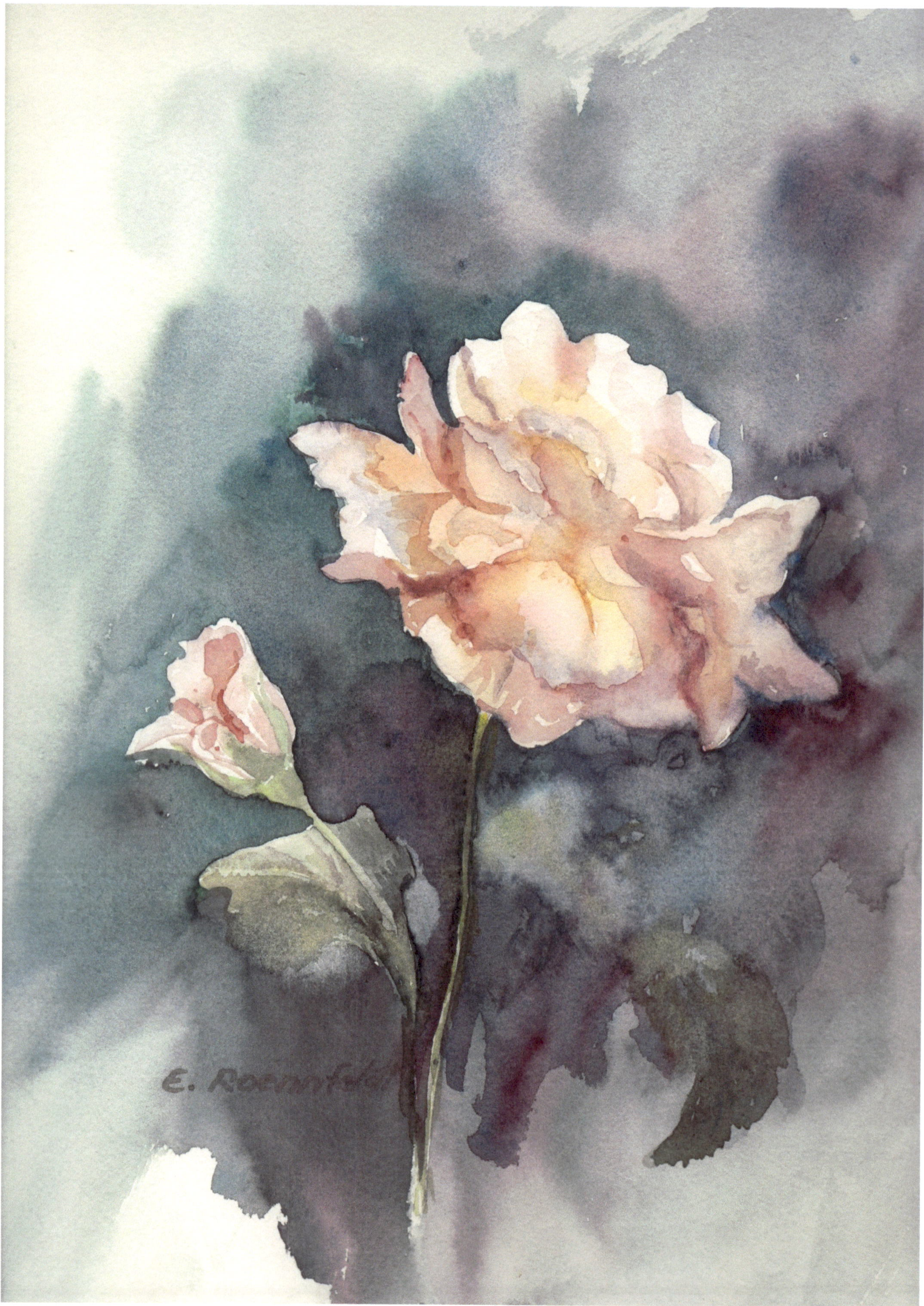

Miniature Landscapes

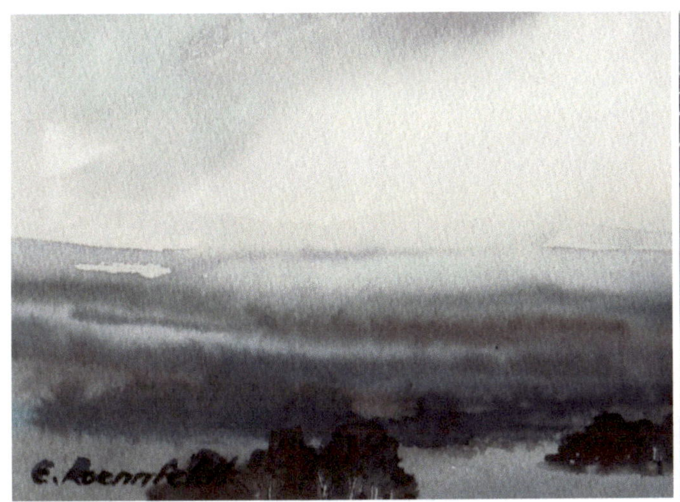

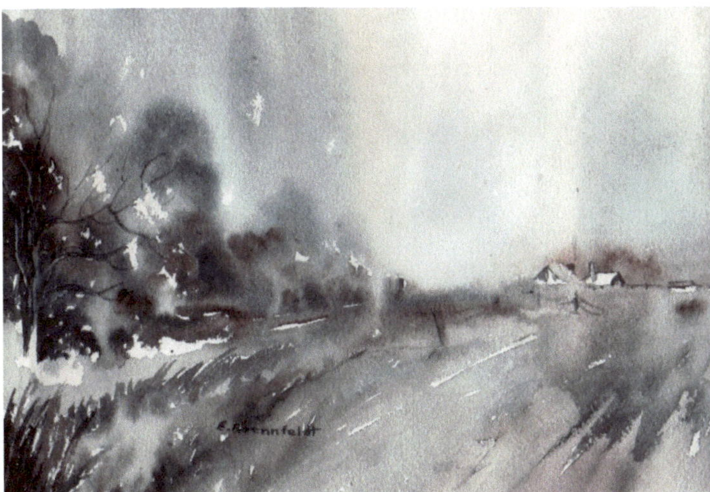

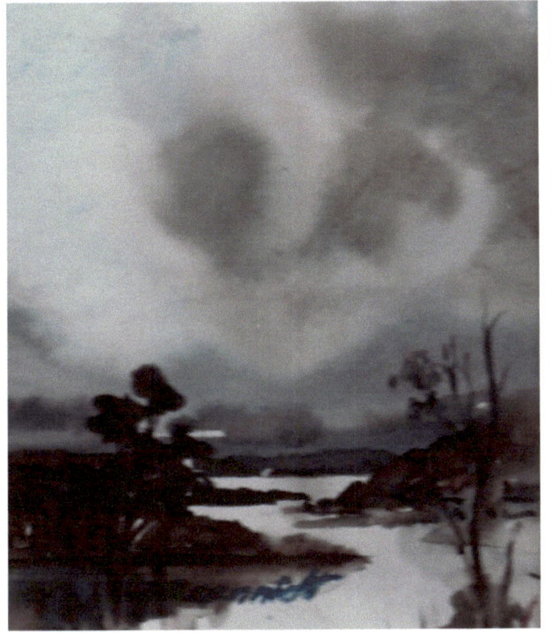

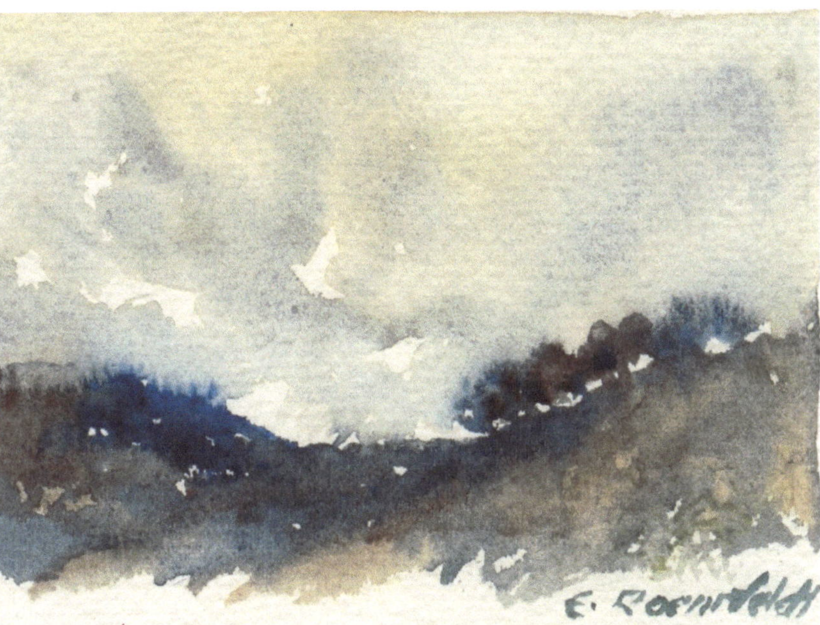

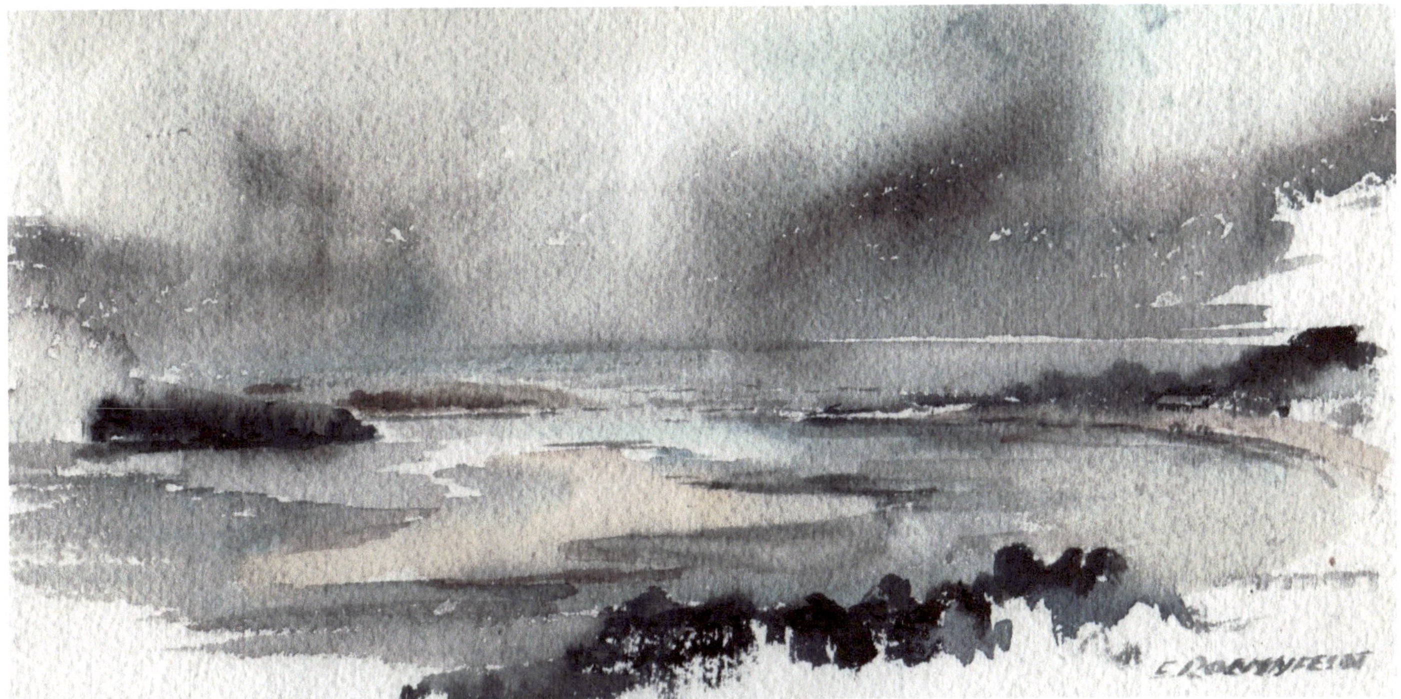

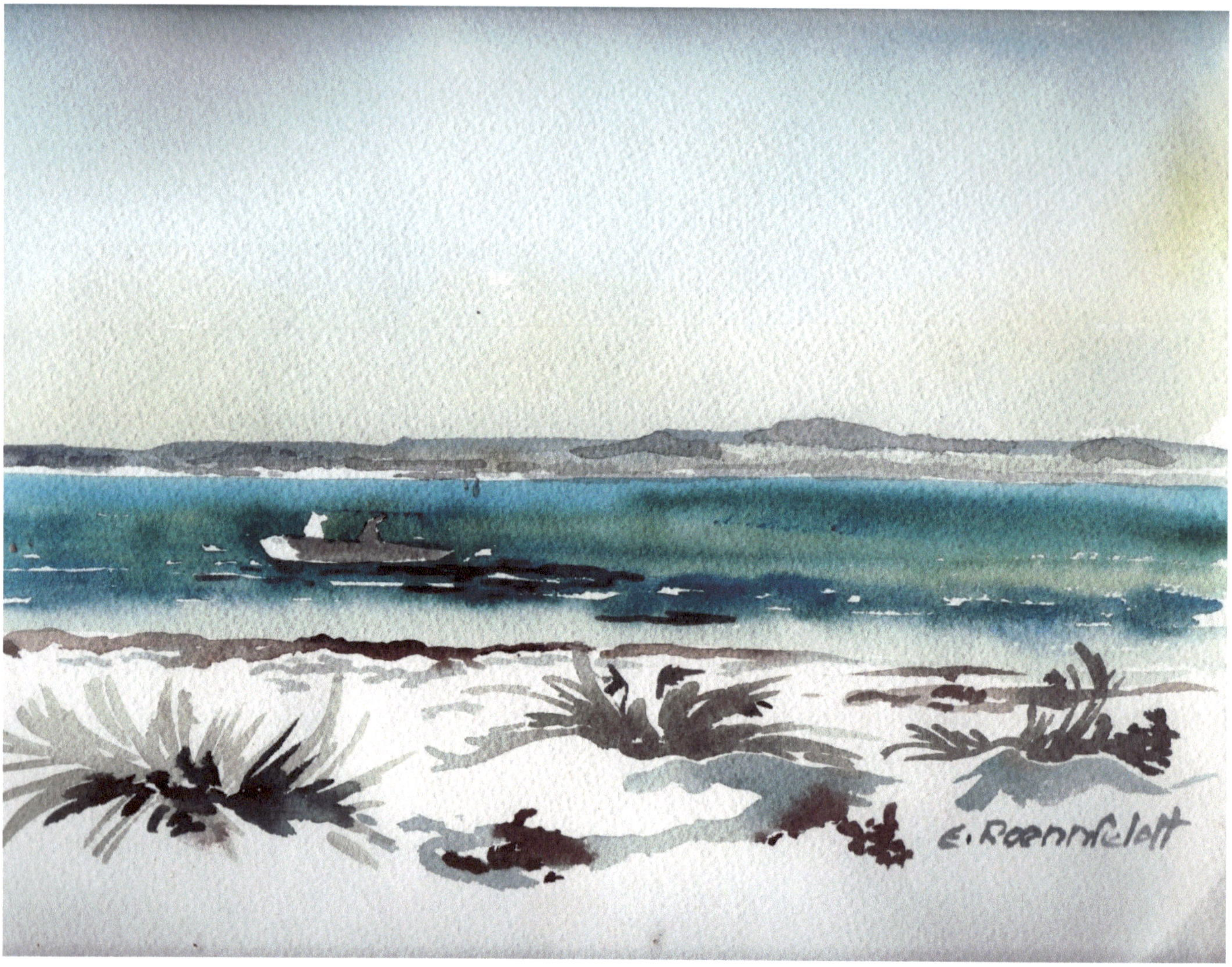

E. Roennfeldt

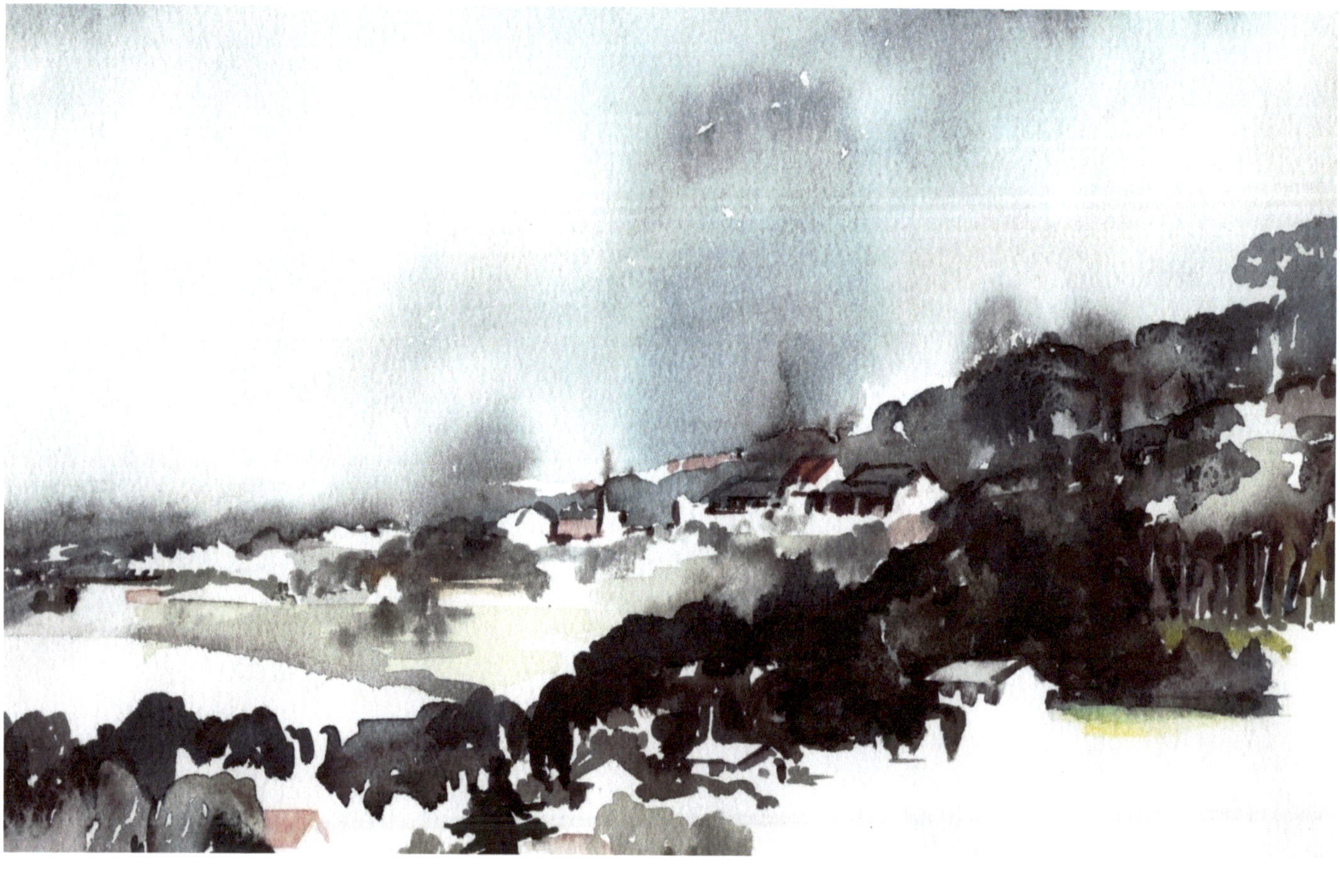

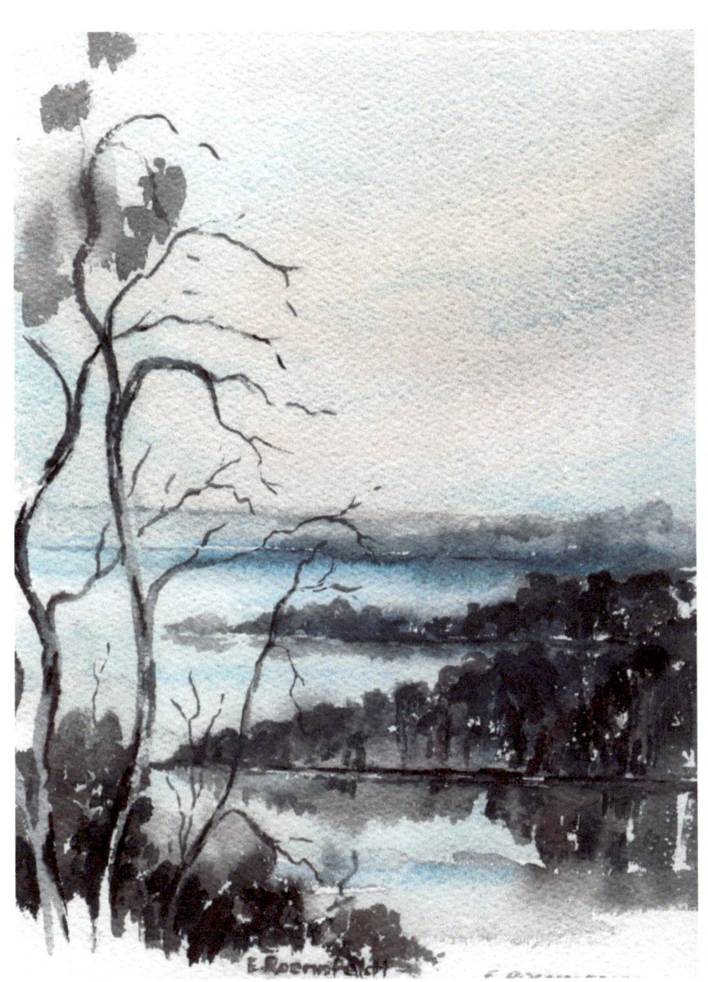

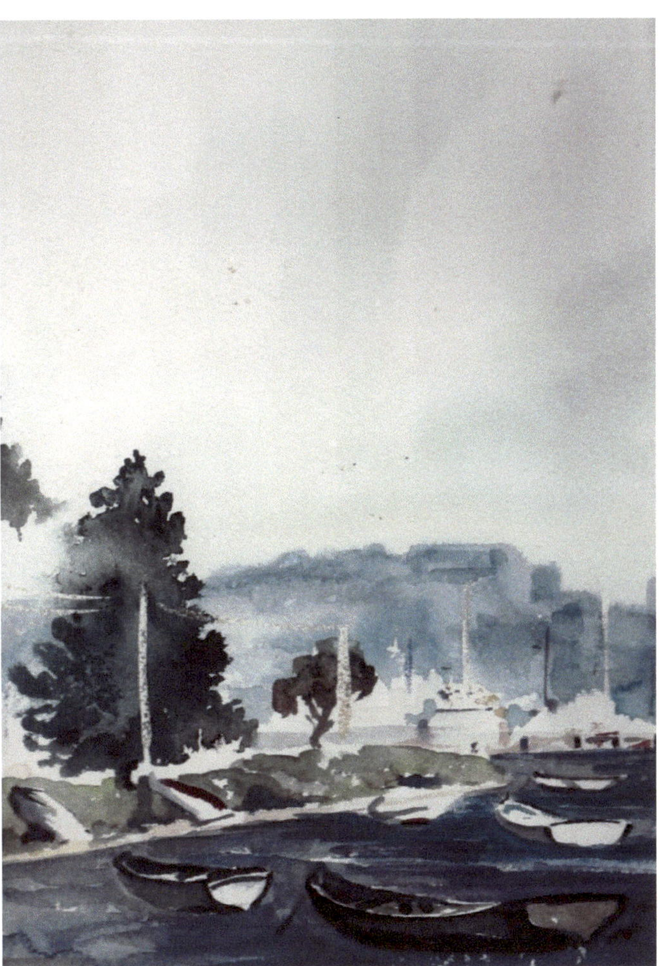

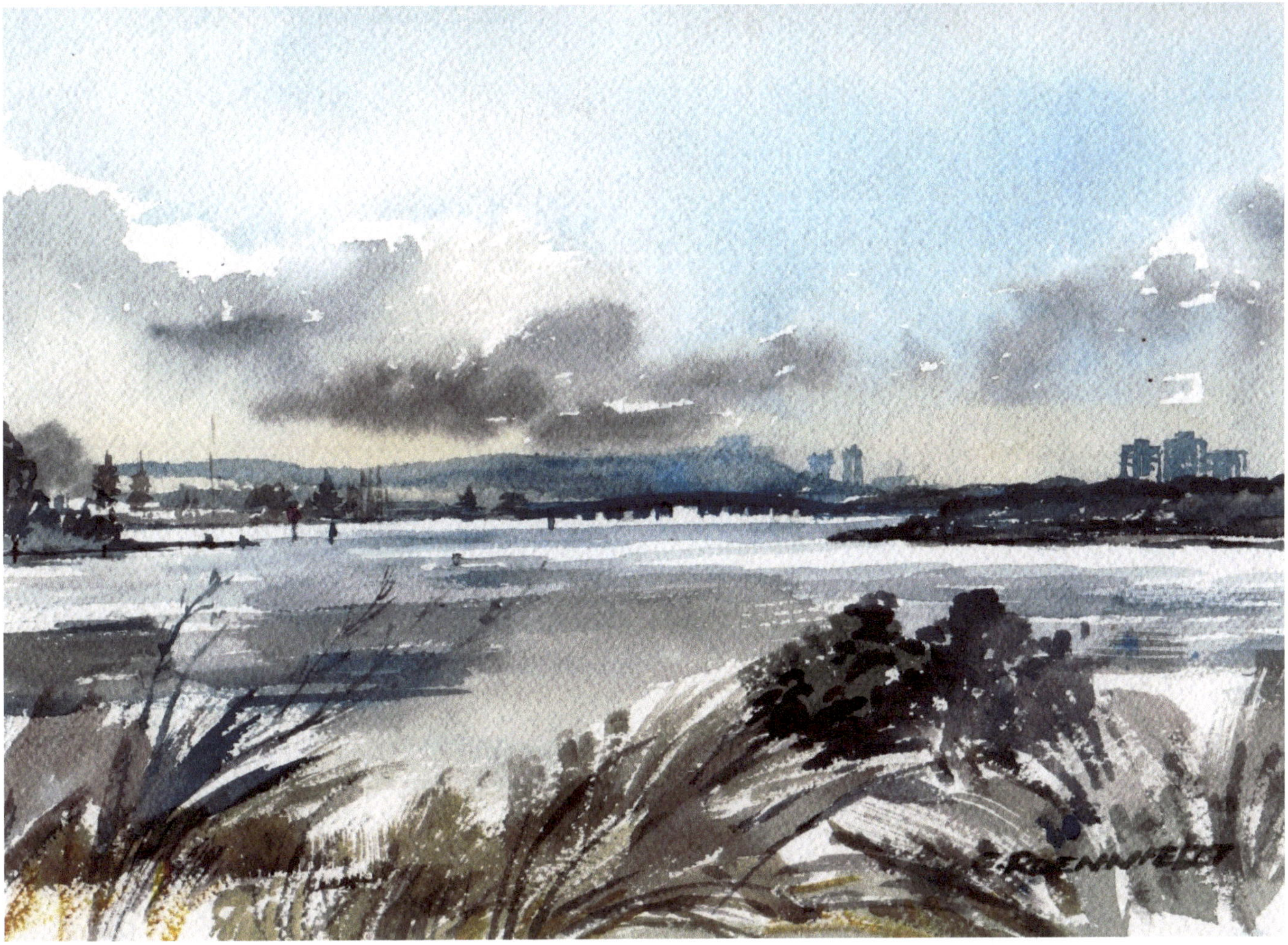

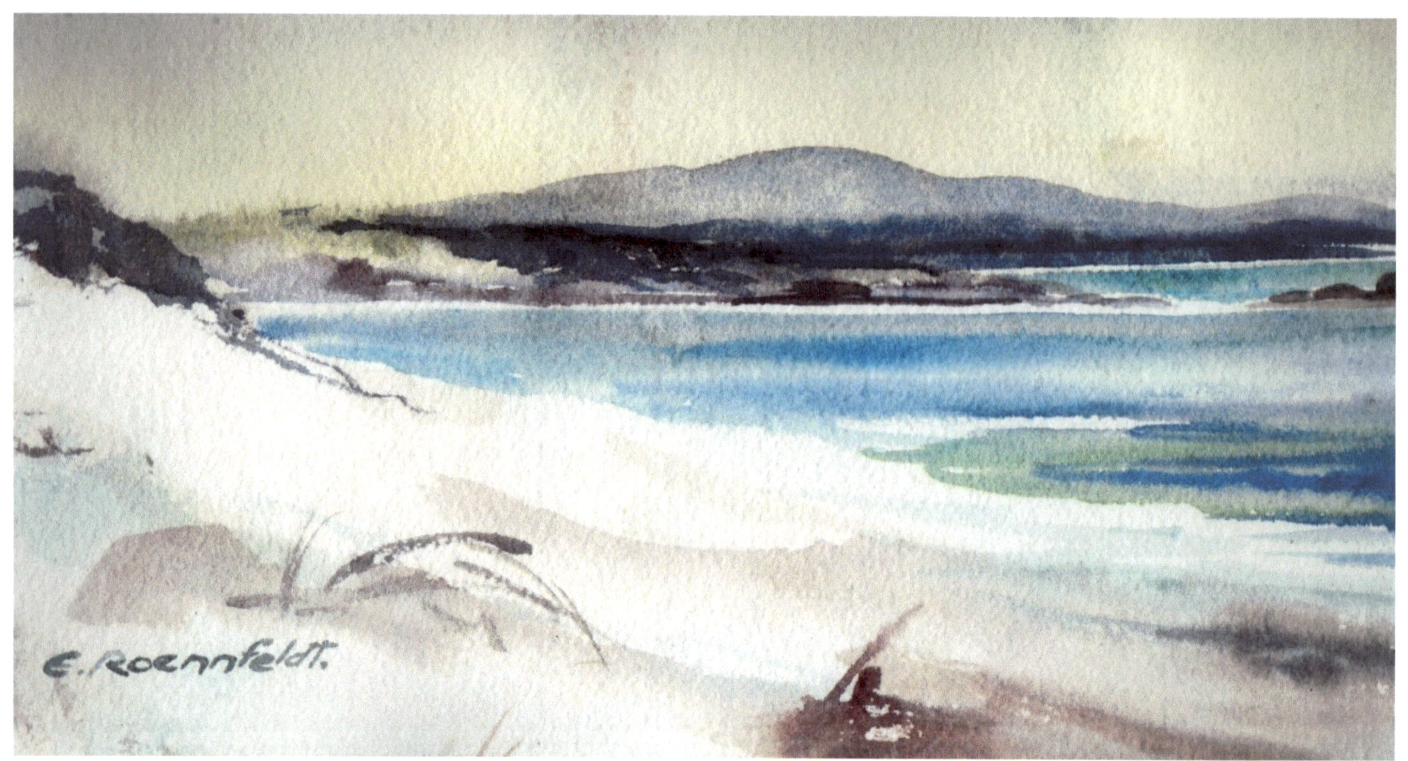
E.Roennfeldt.

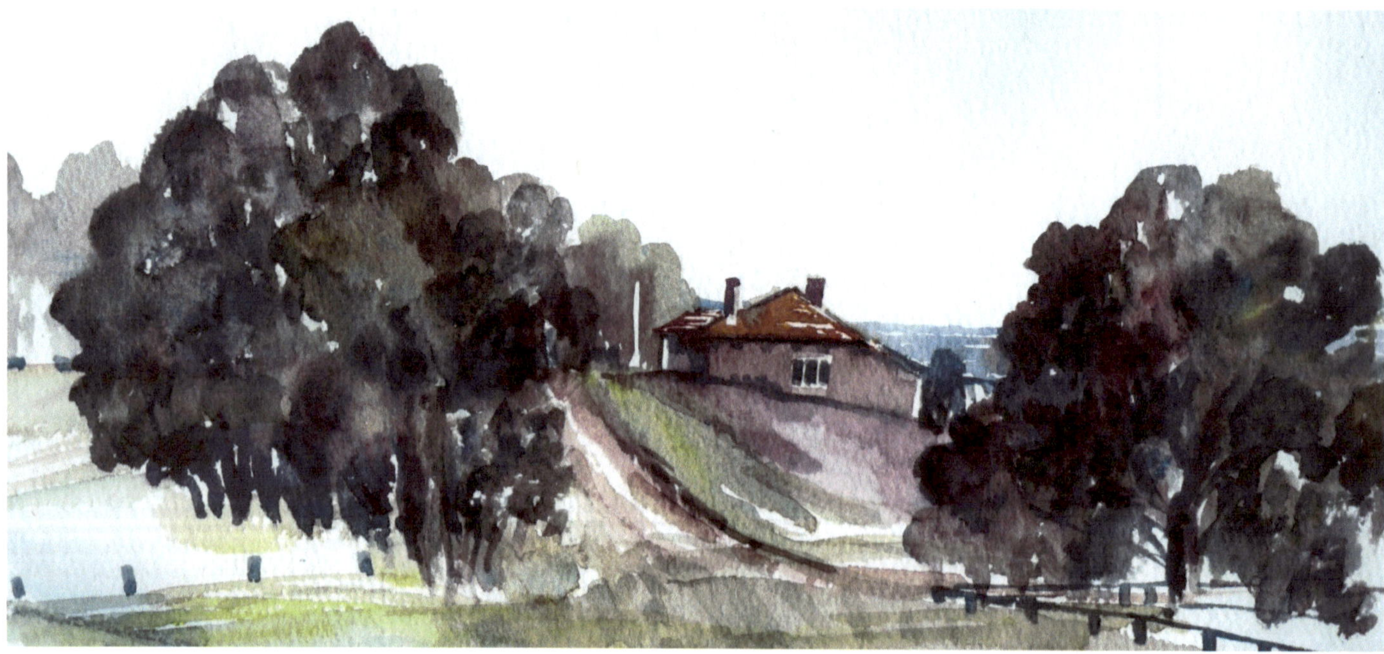

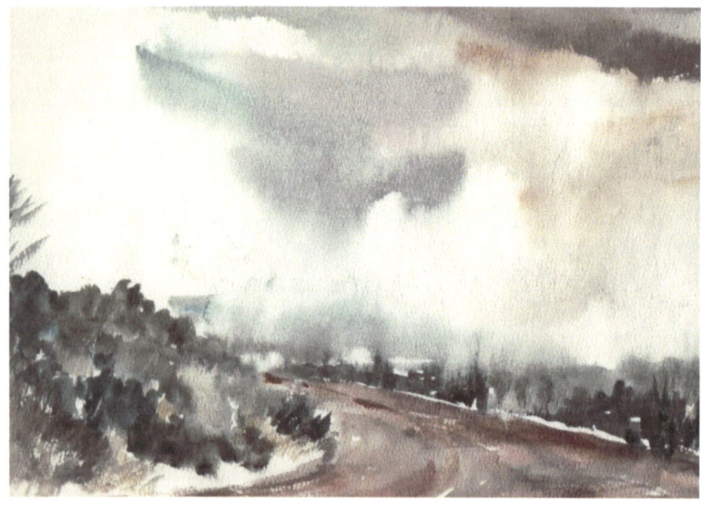

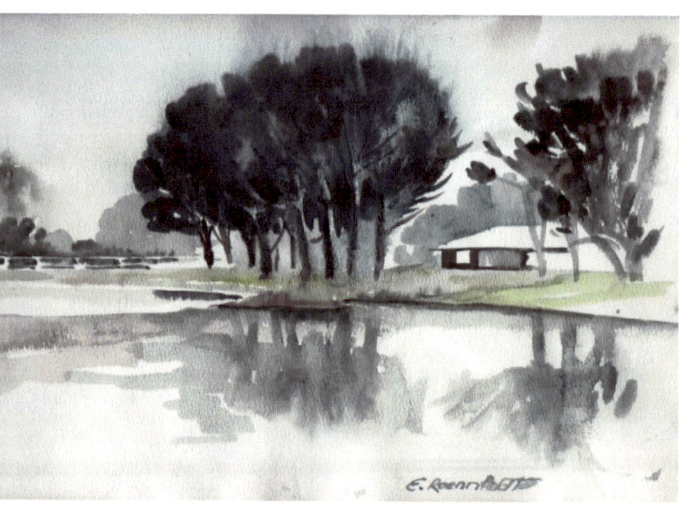
E.Roennfeldt

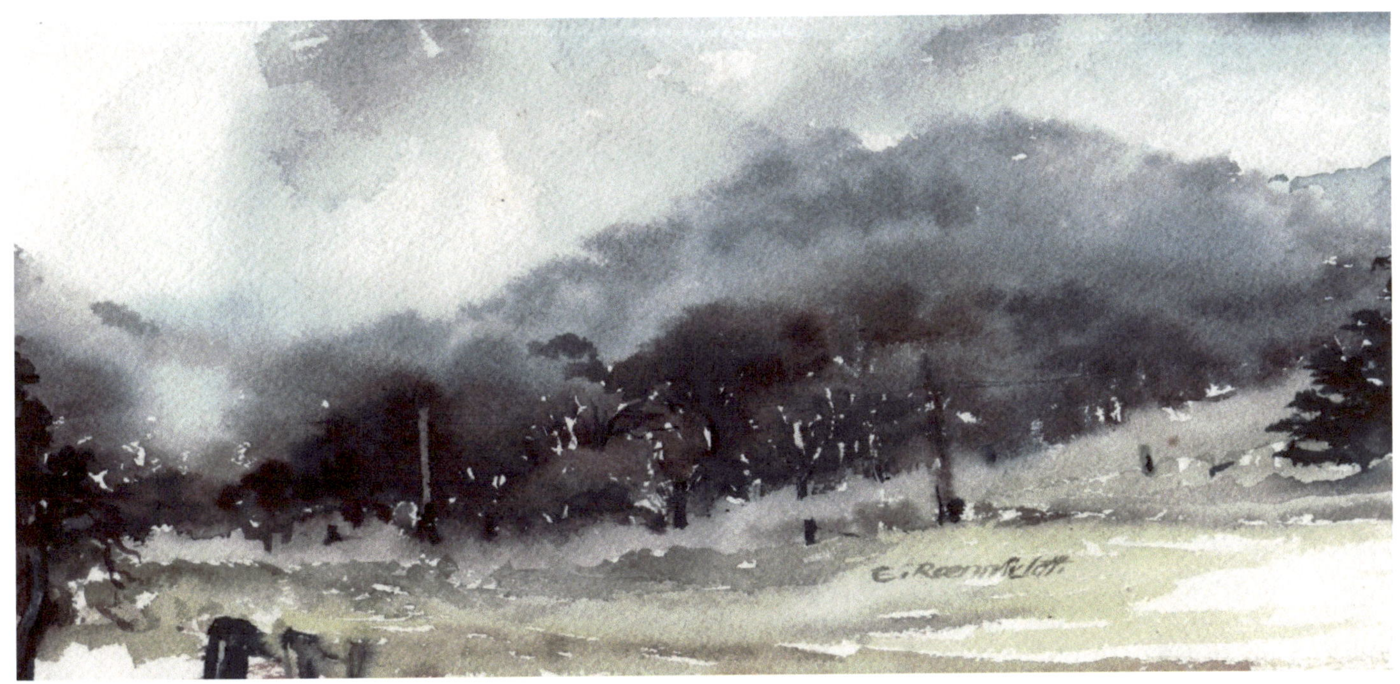

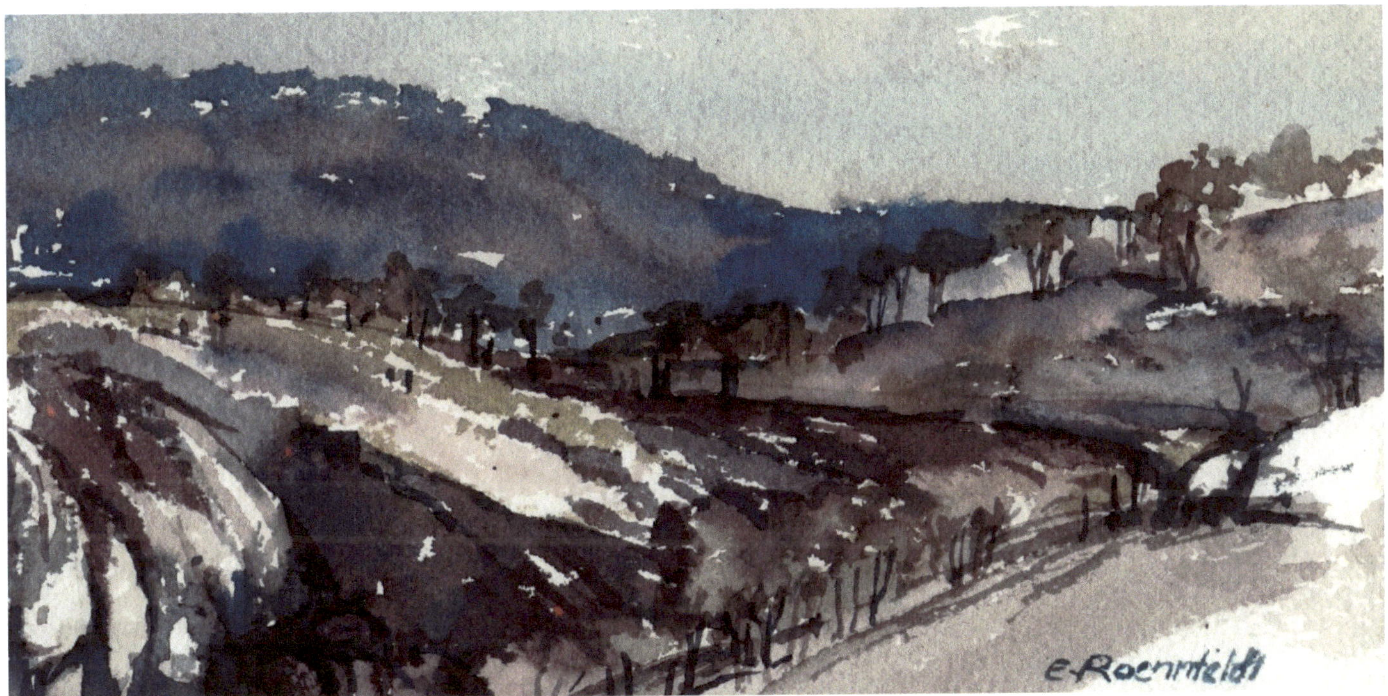

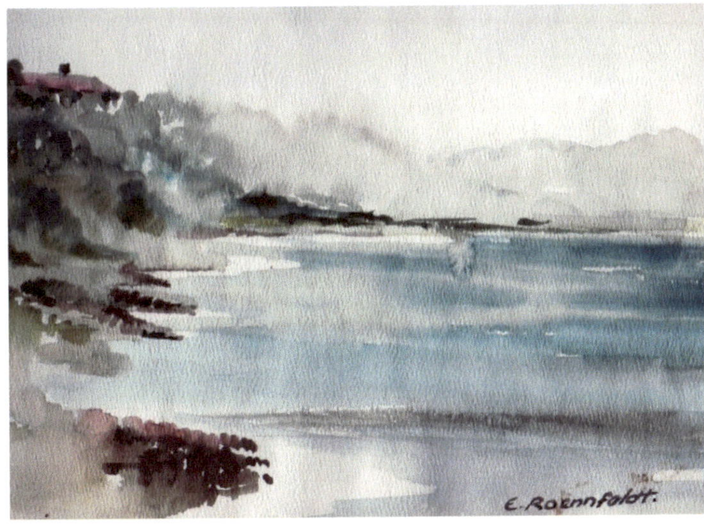

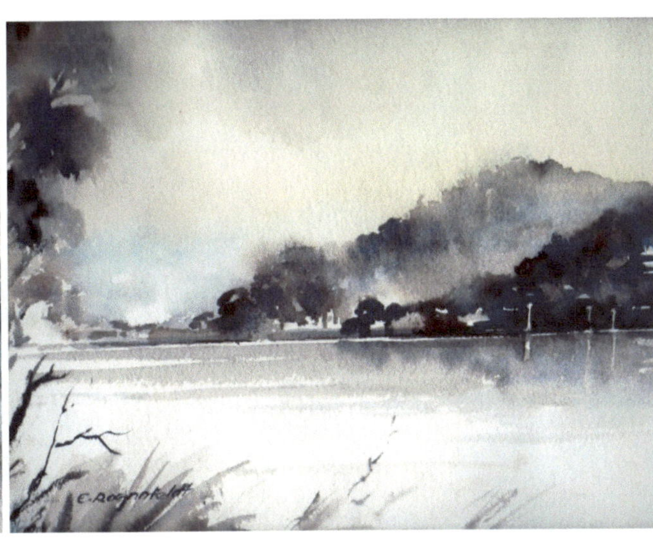

Rottnest and beaches

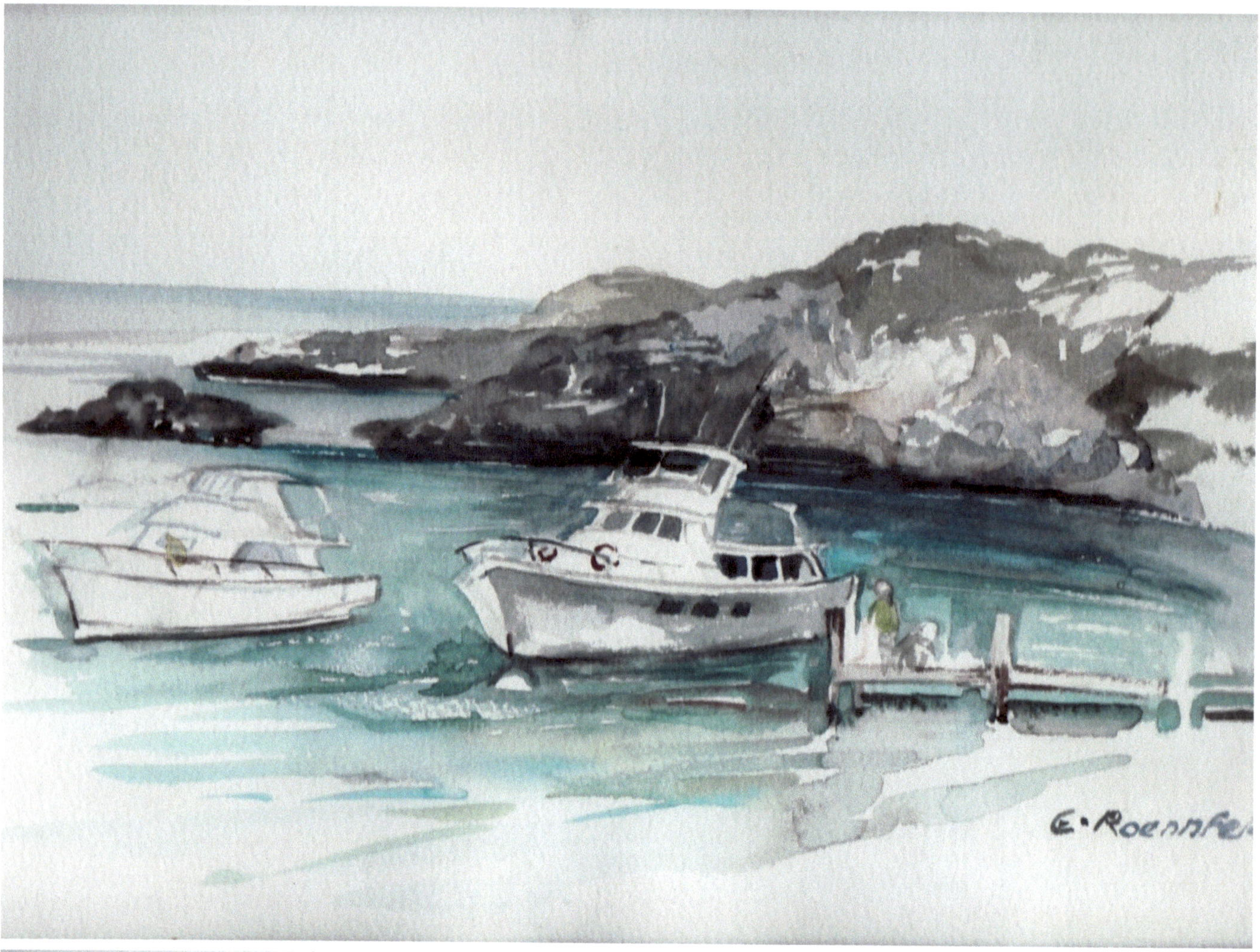

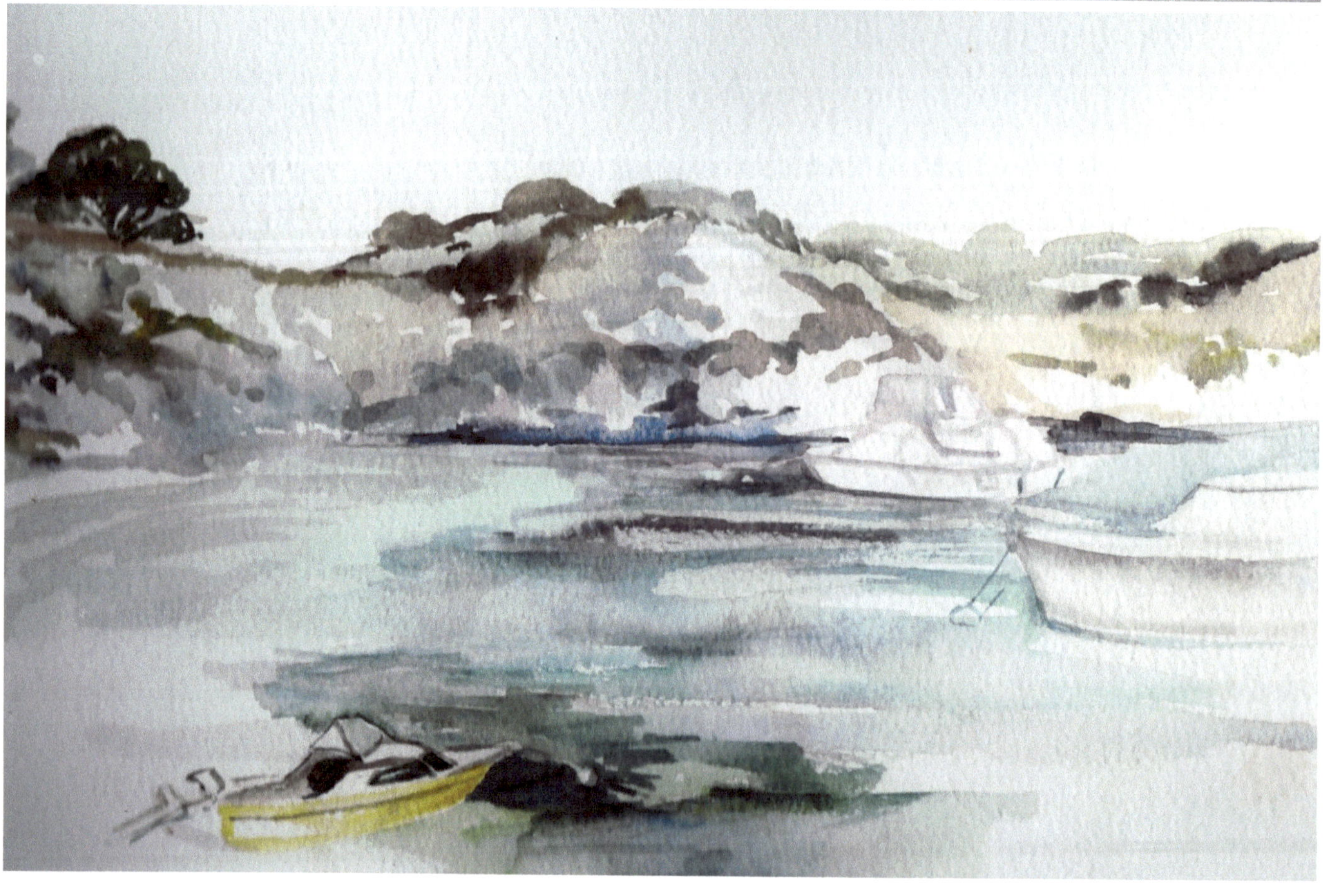

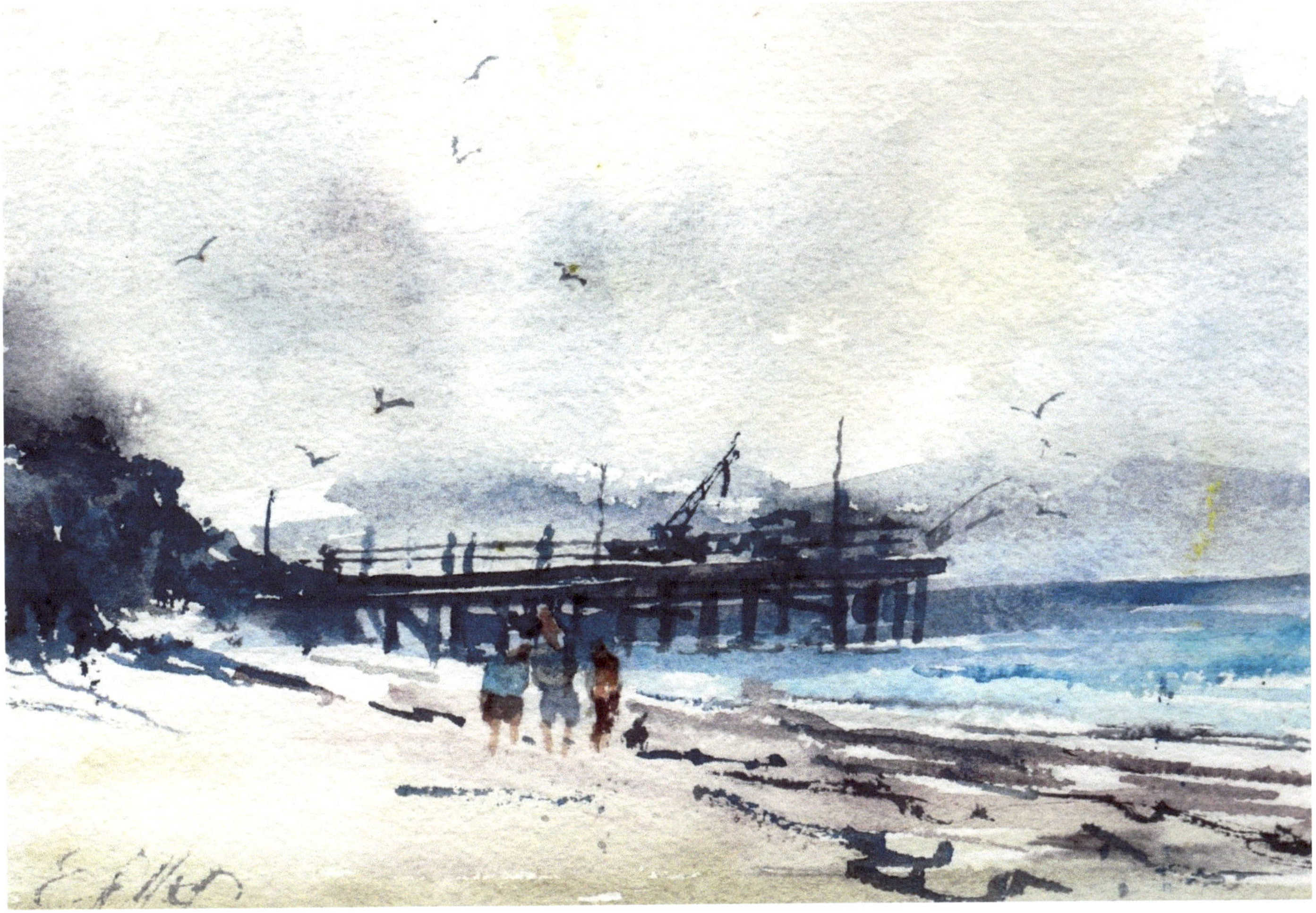

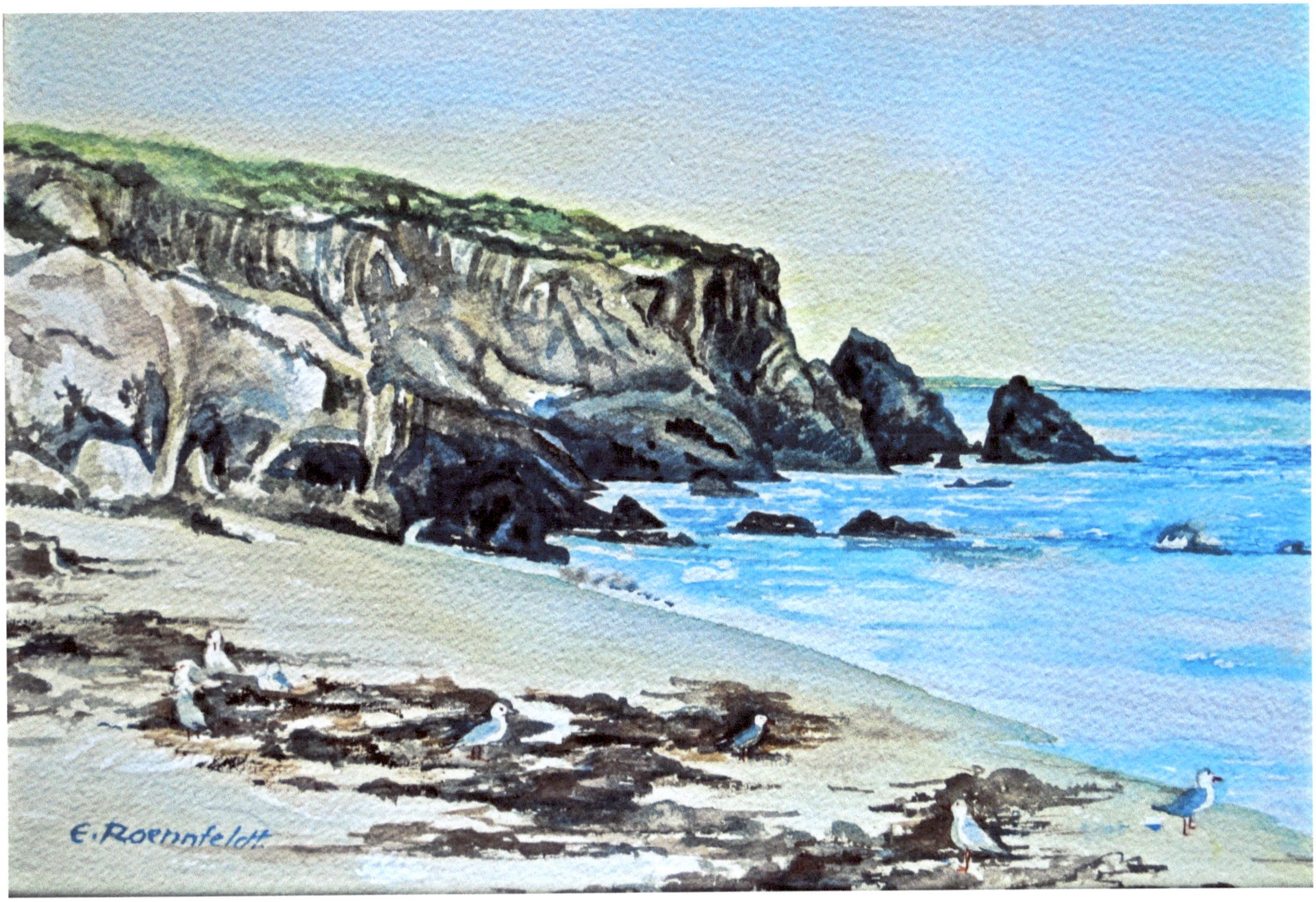

E.Roennfeldt

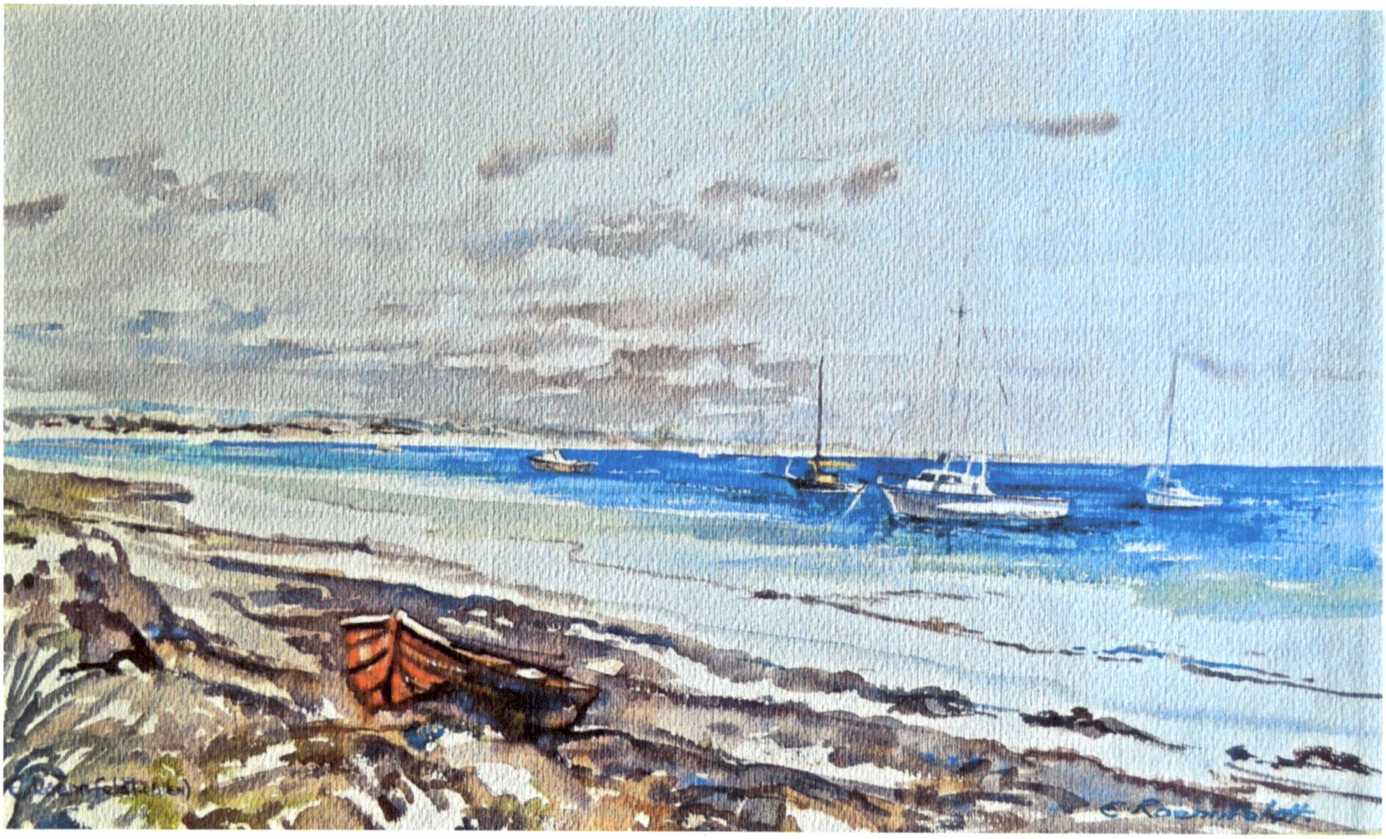

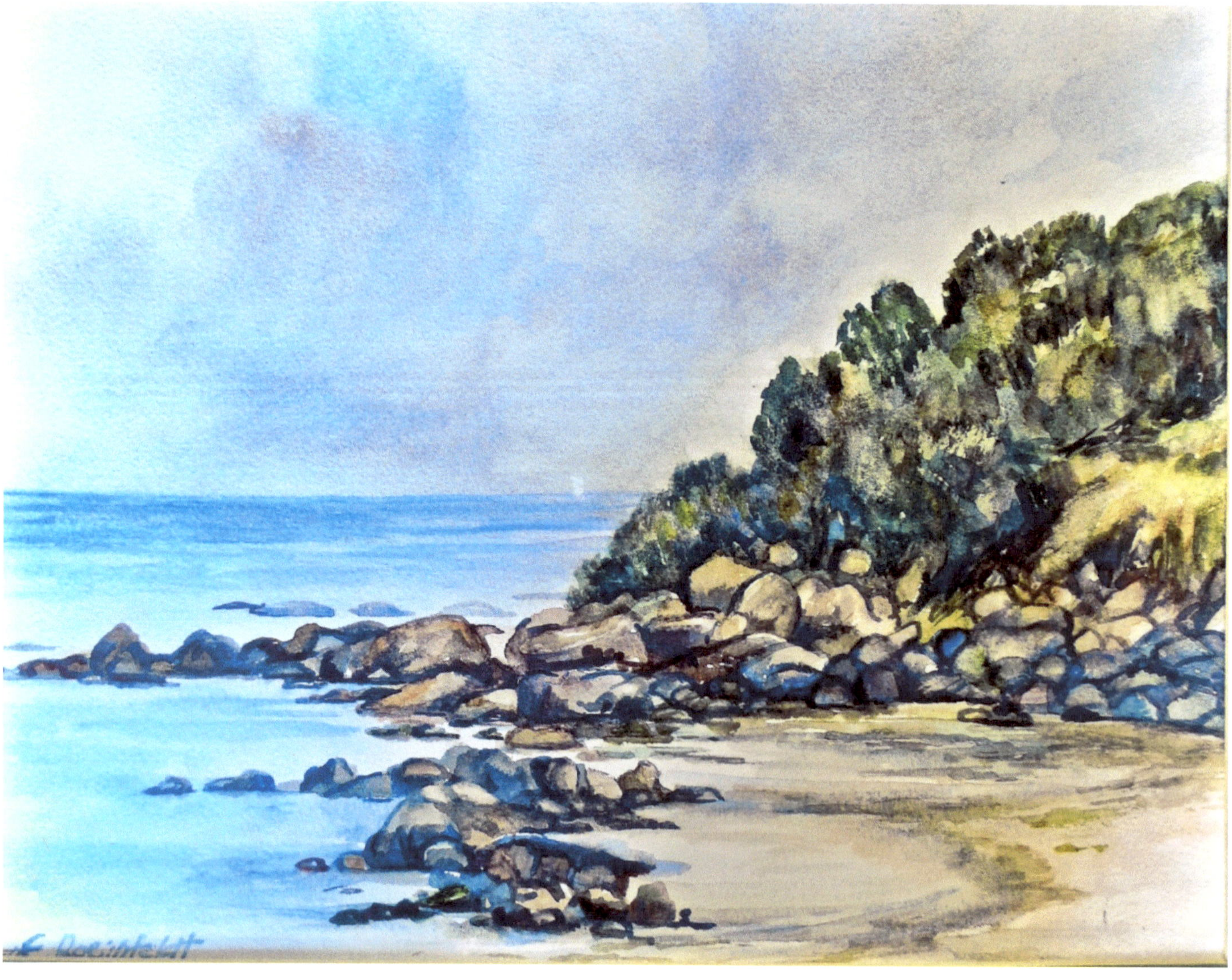

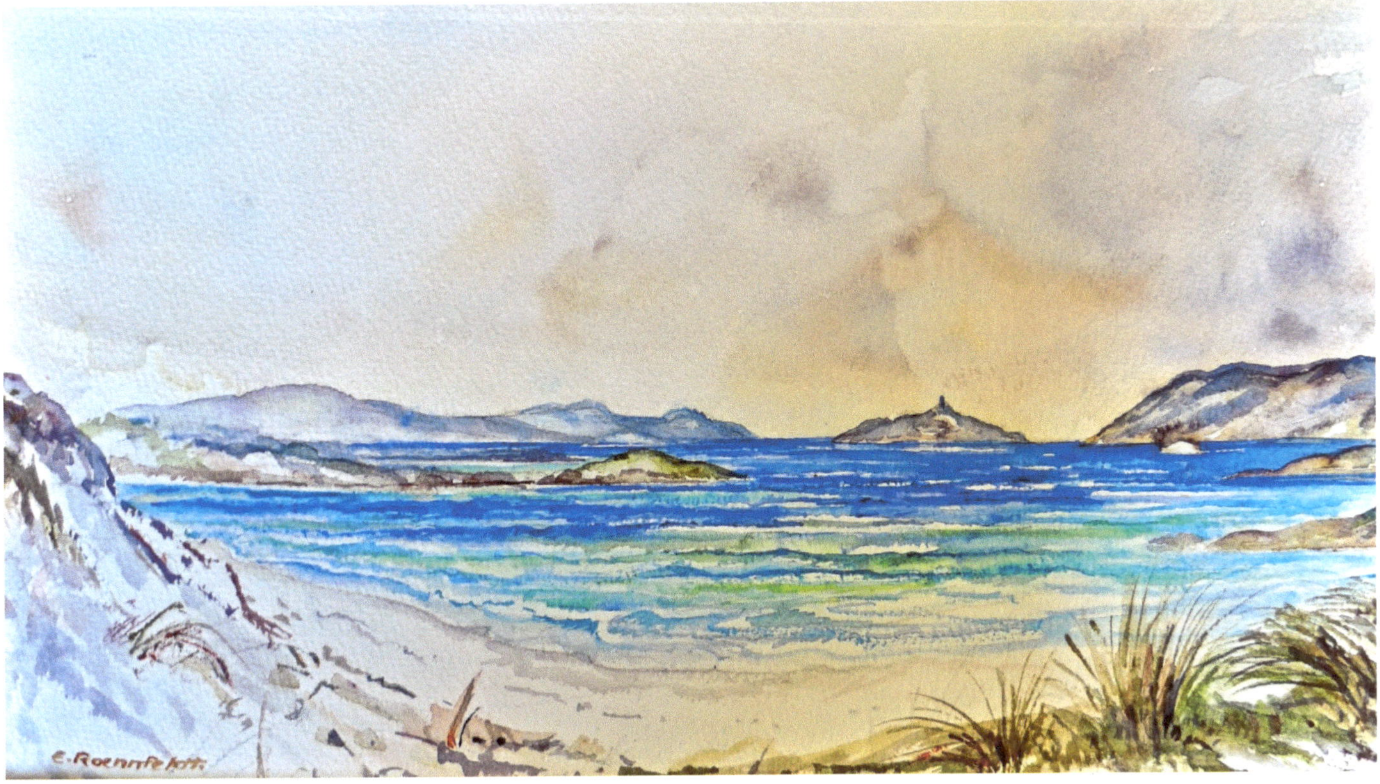

E. Roennfeldt

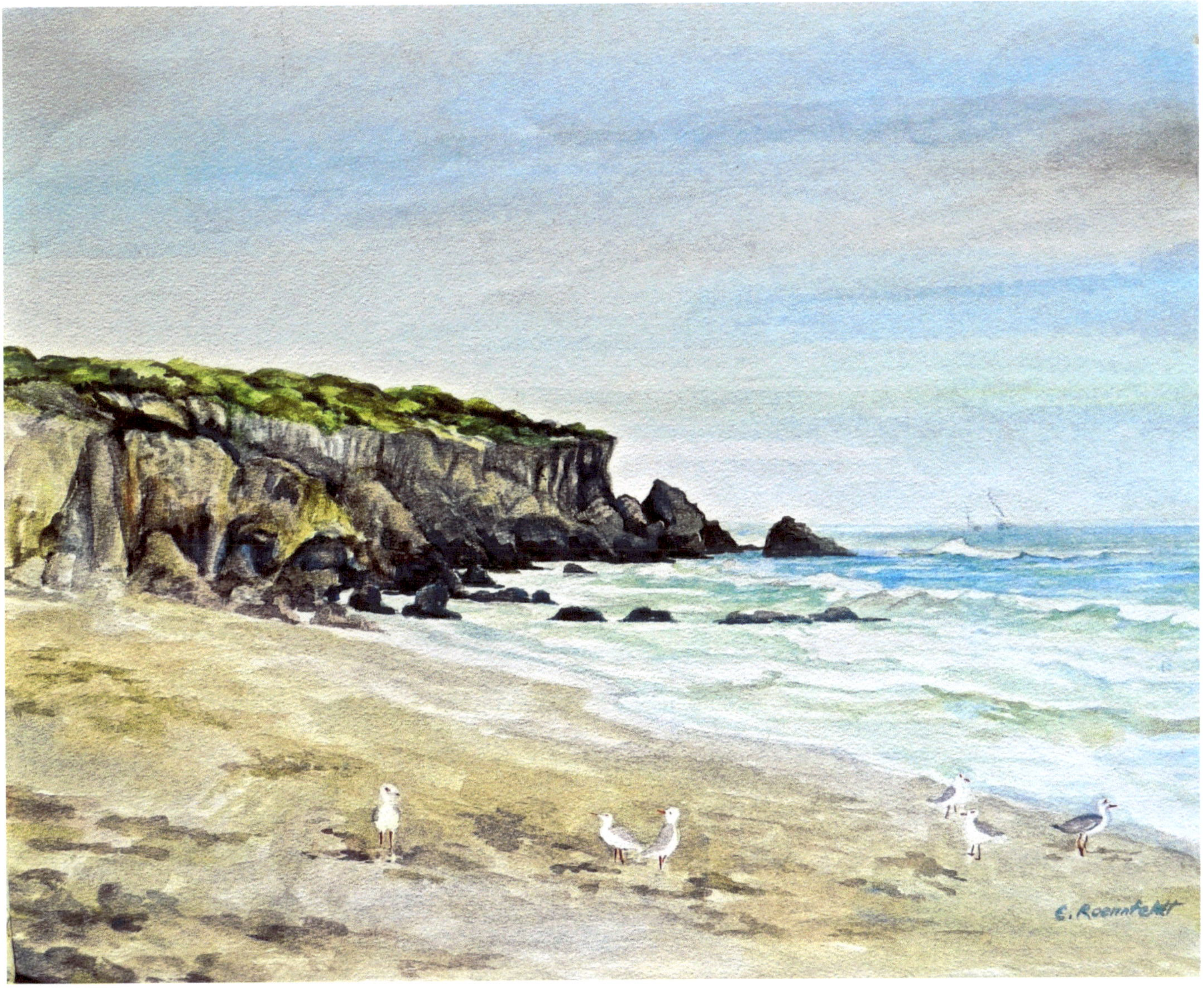

E. Roennfeldt

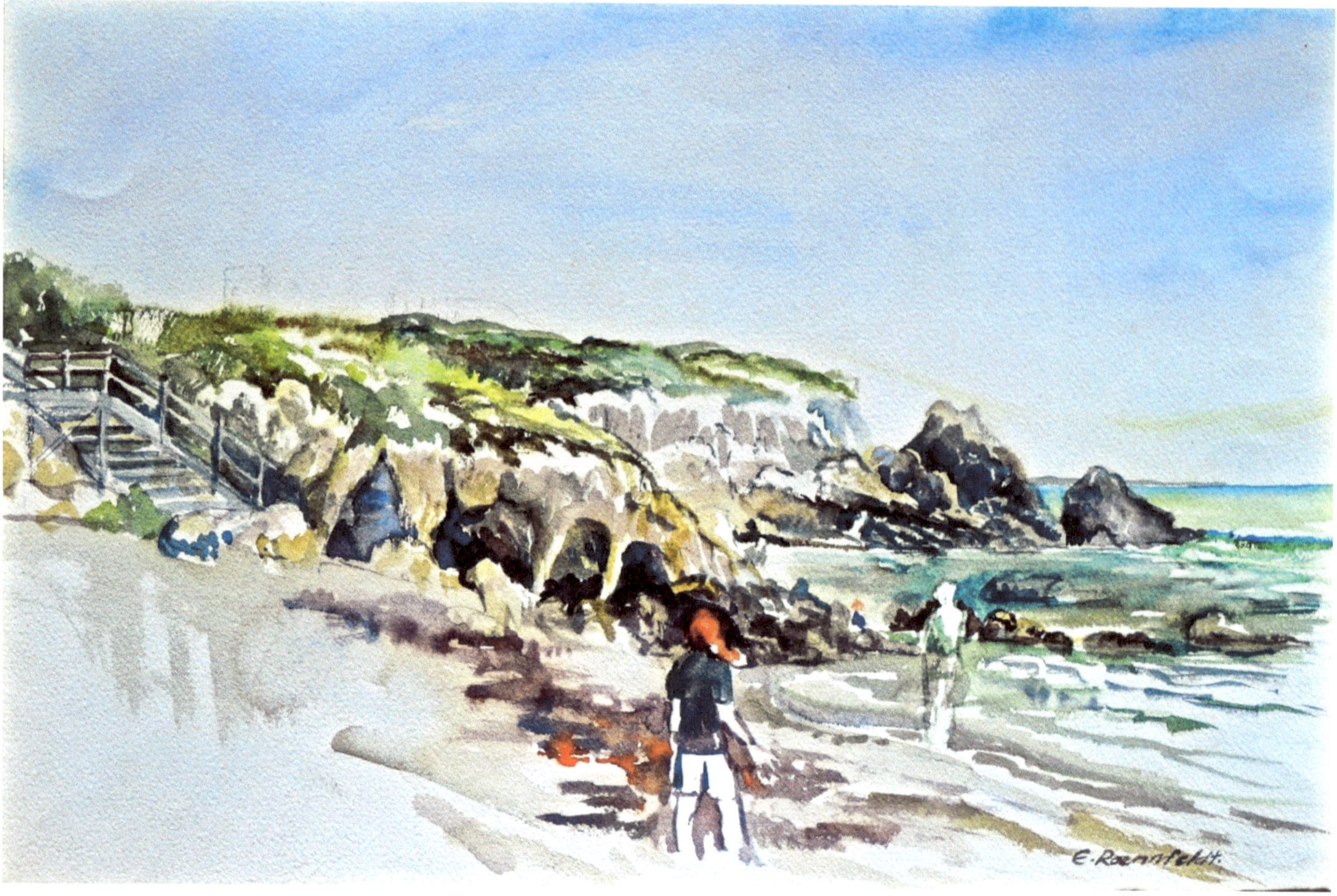
E. Roennfeldt

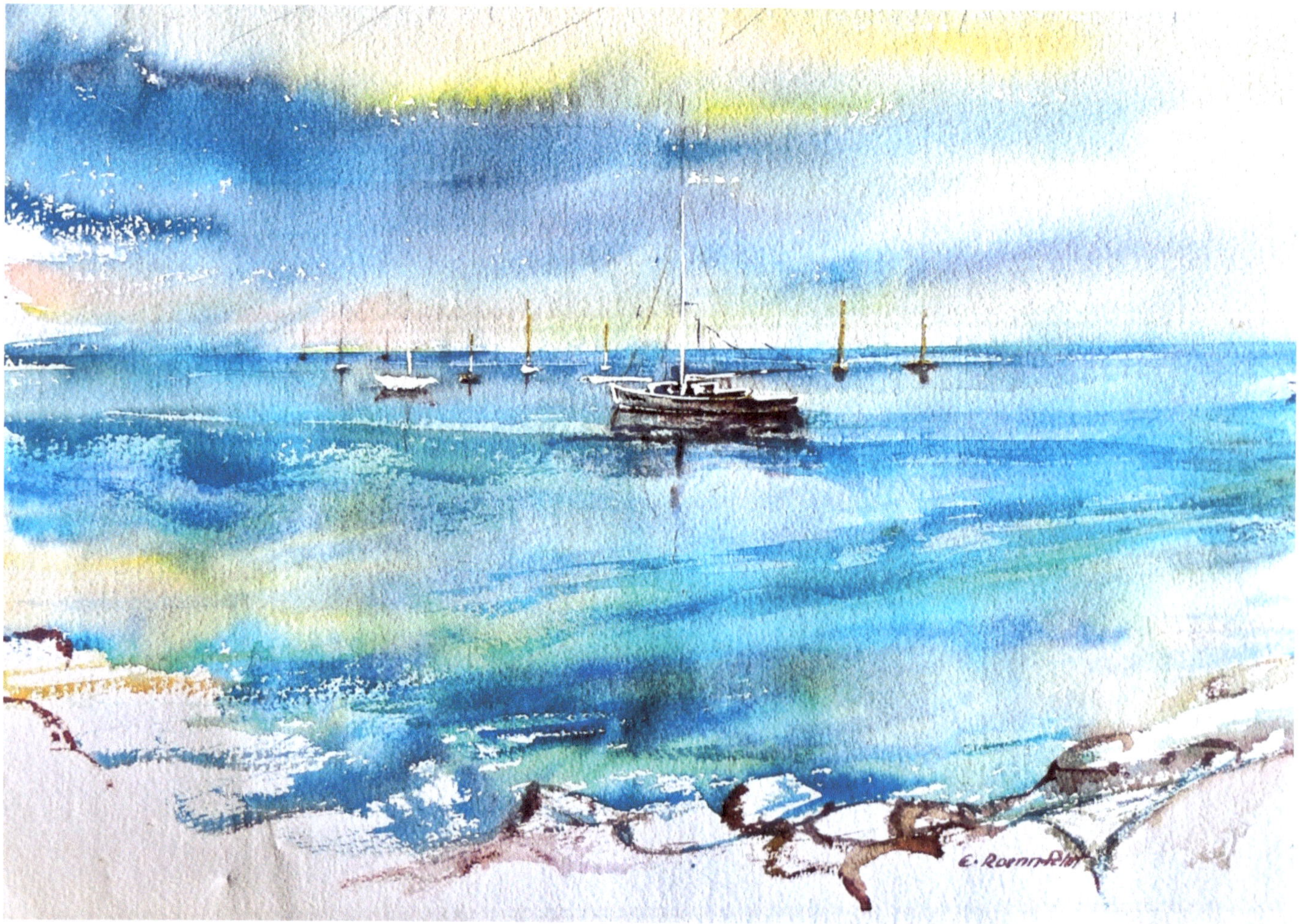
E. Roennfeldt

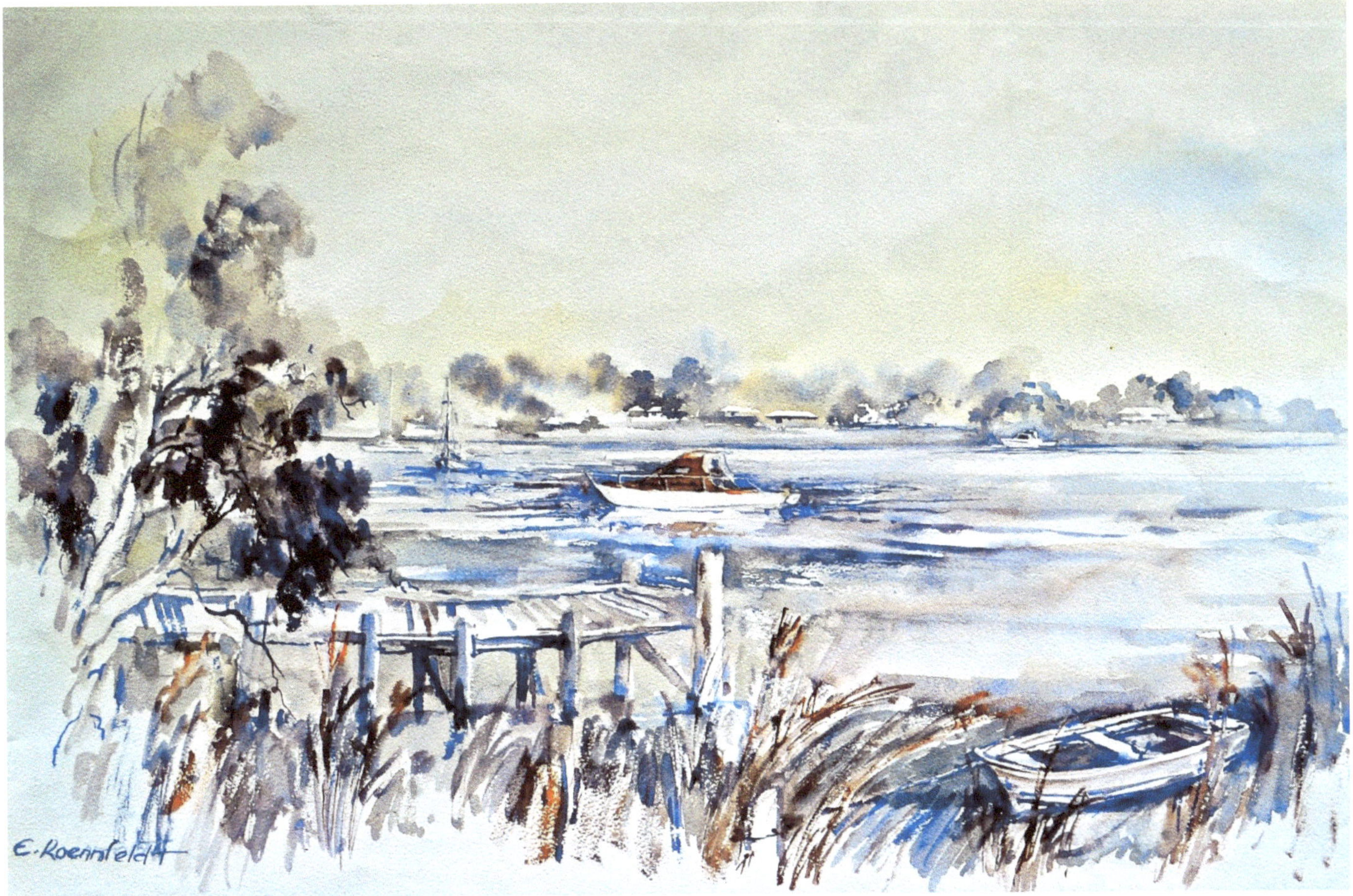

E. Roennfeldt

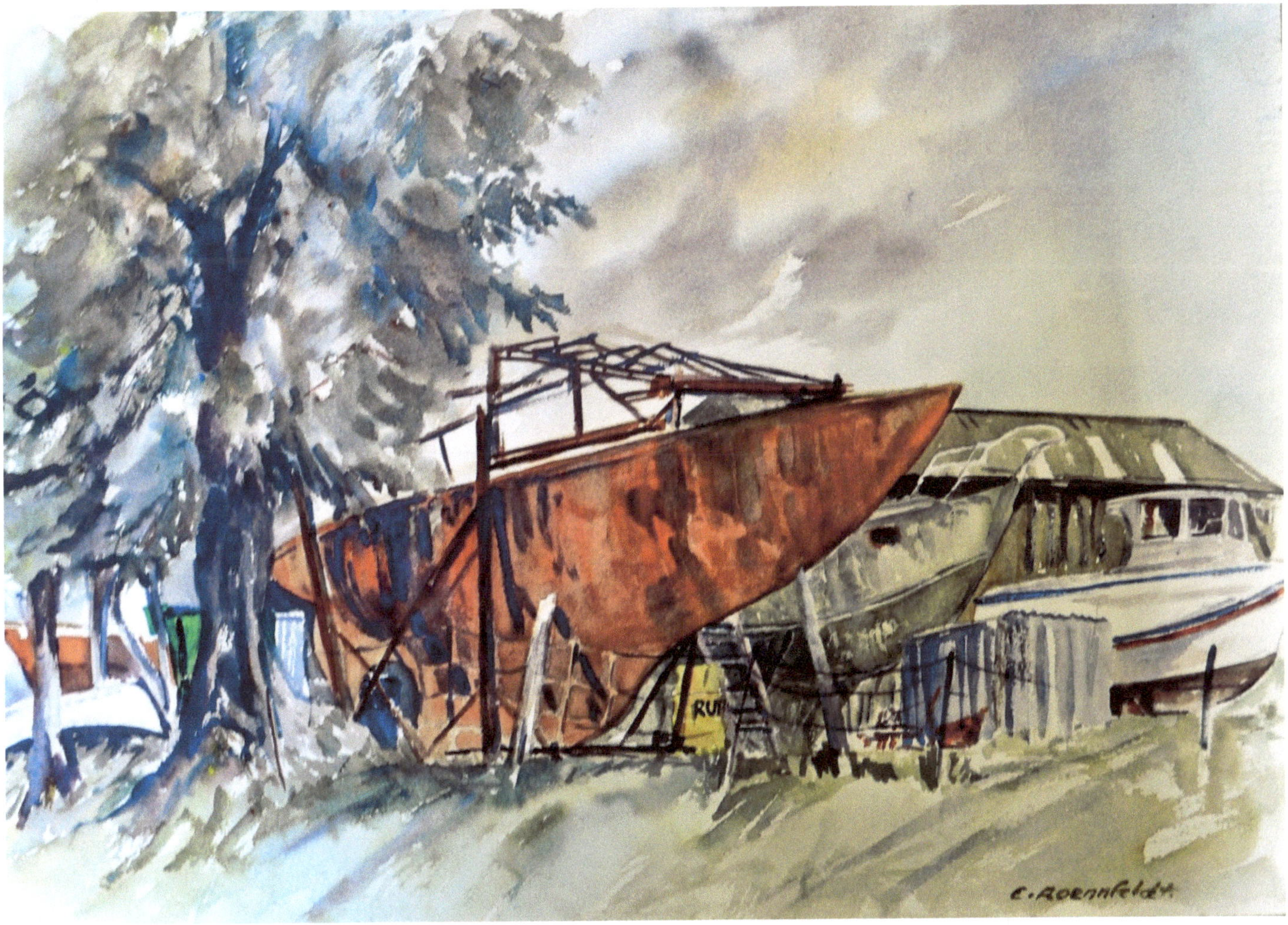

E. Roennfeldt

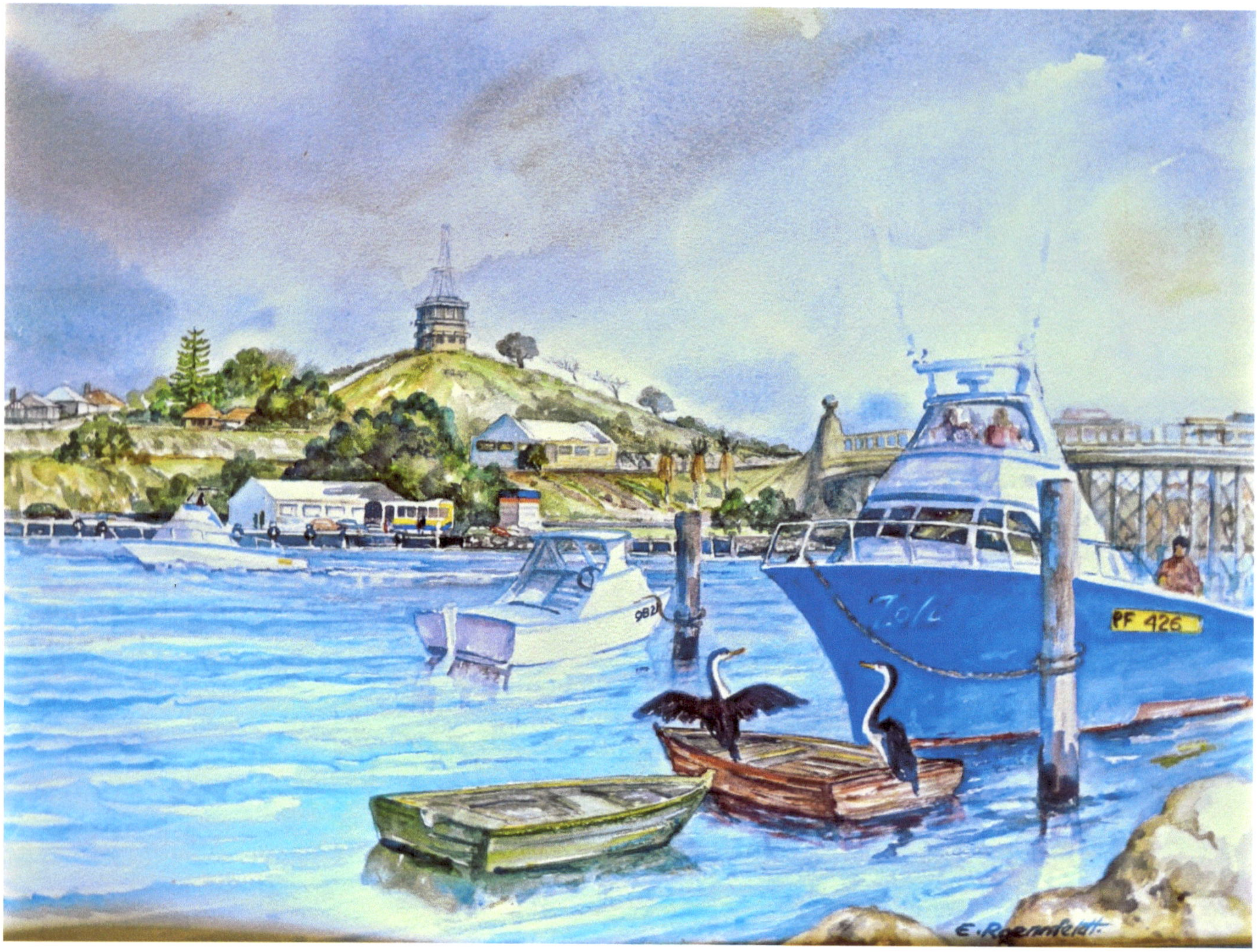

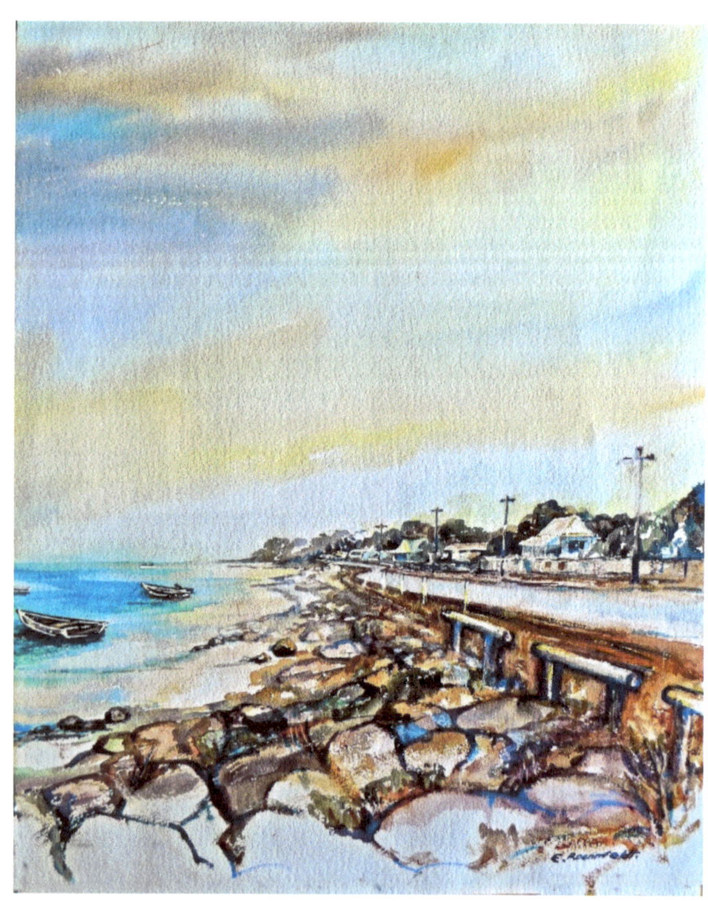

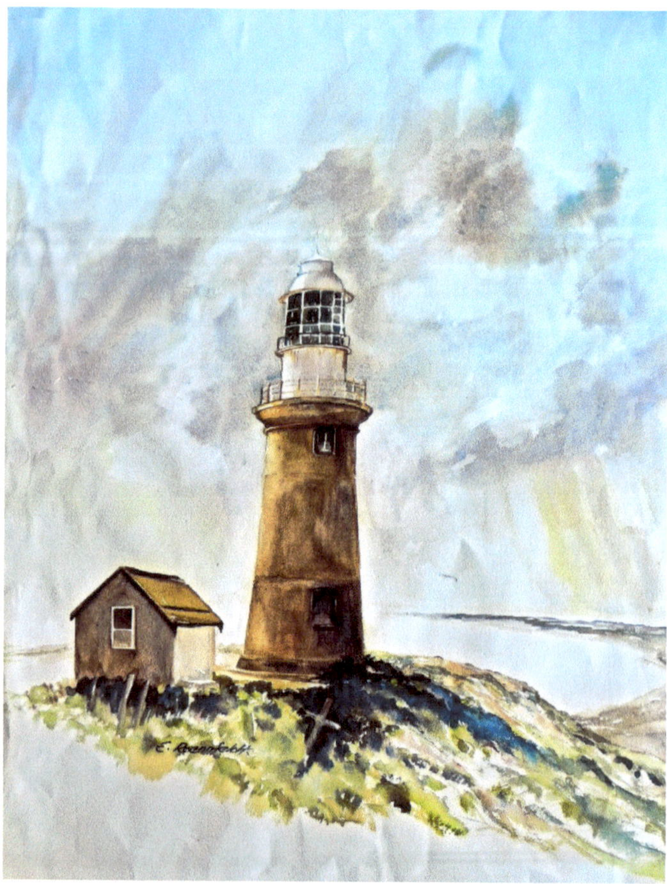

Fowl

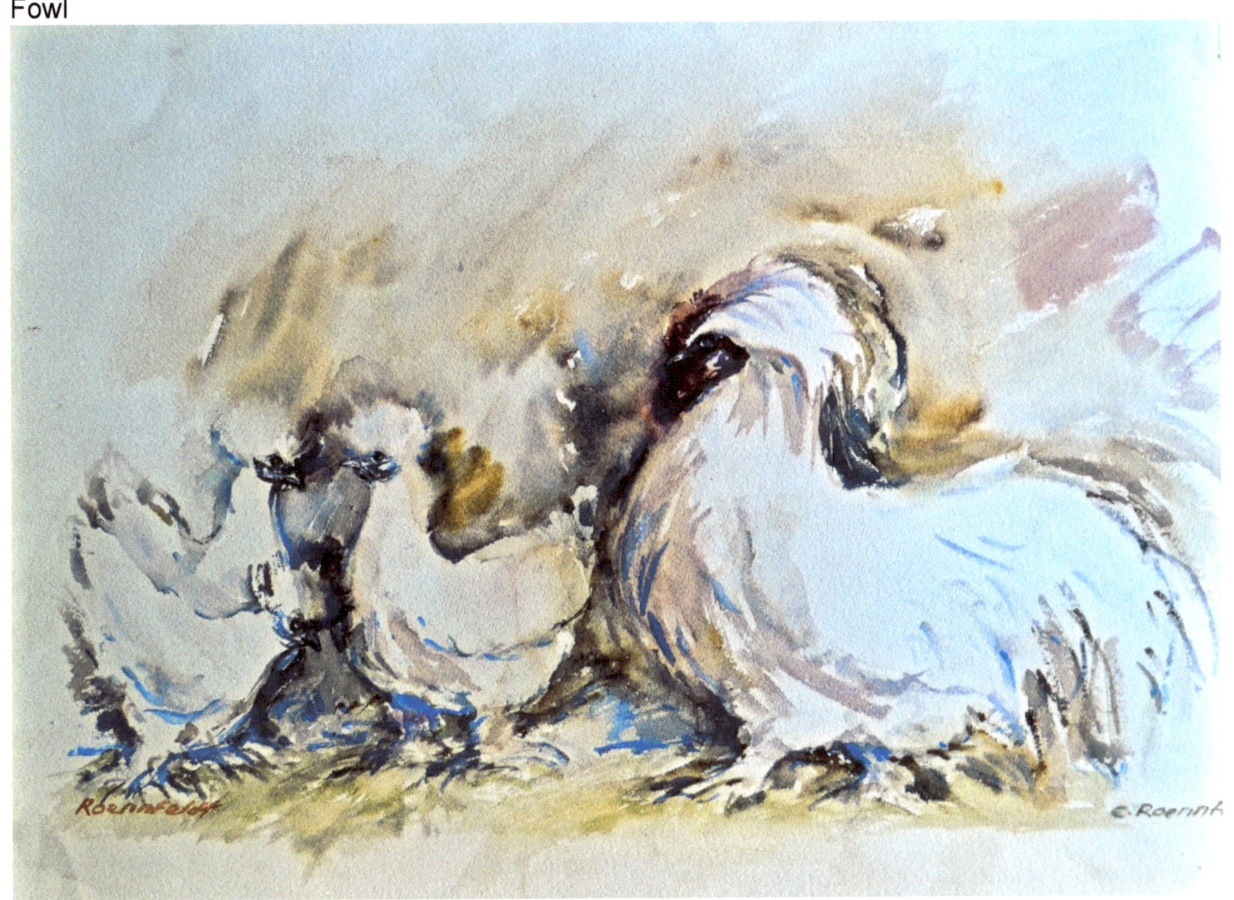

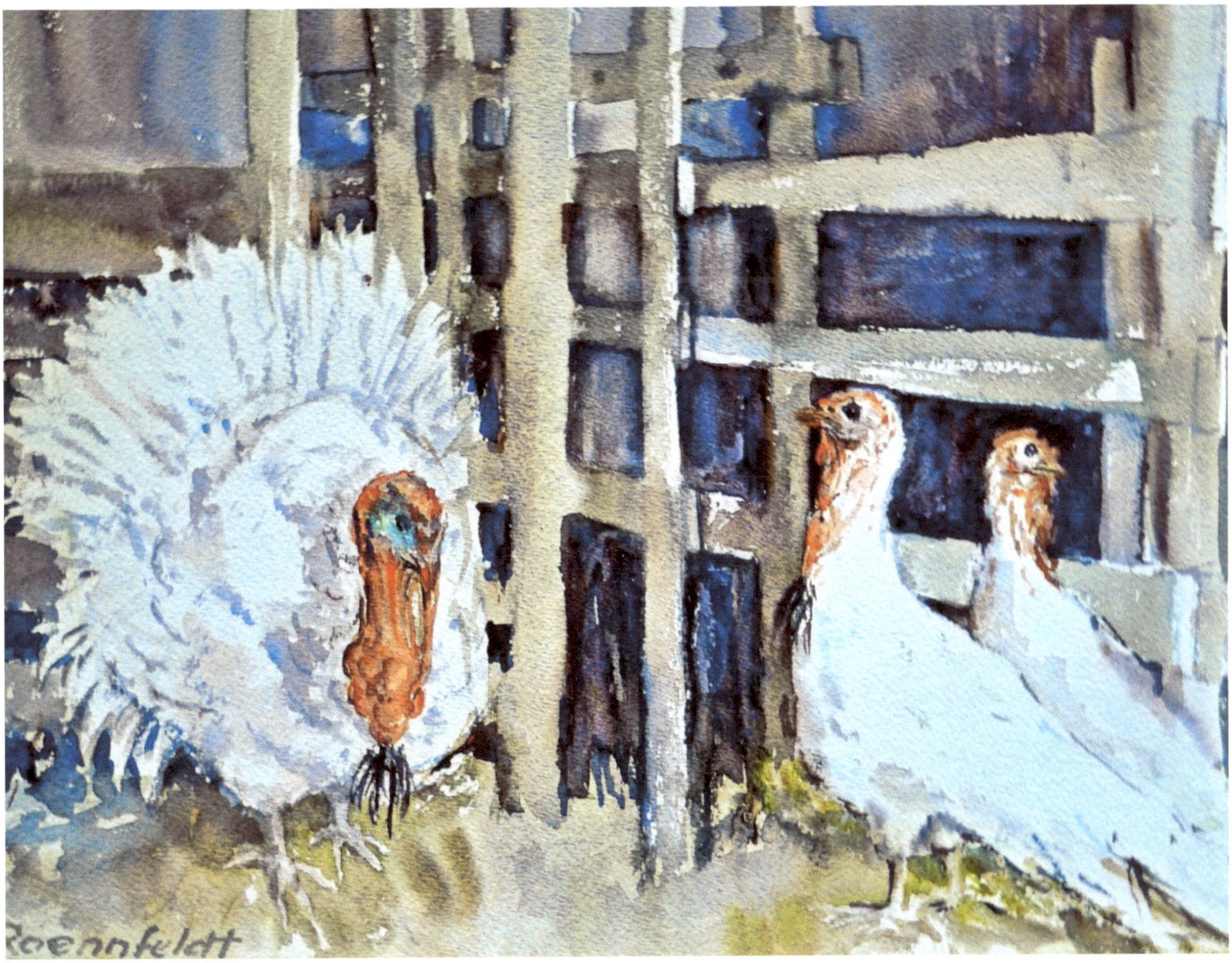

ELAINE (ROENNFELDT) ALLEN

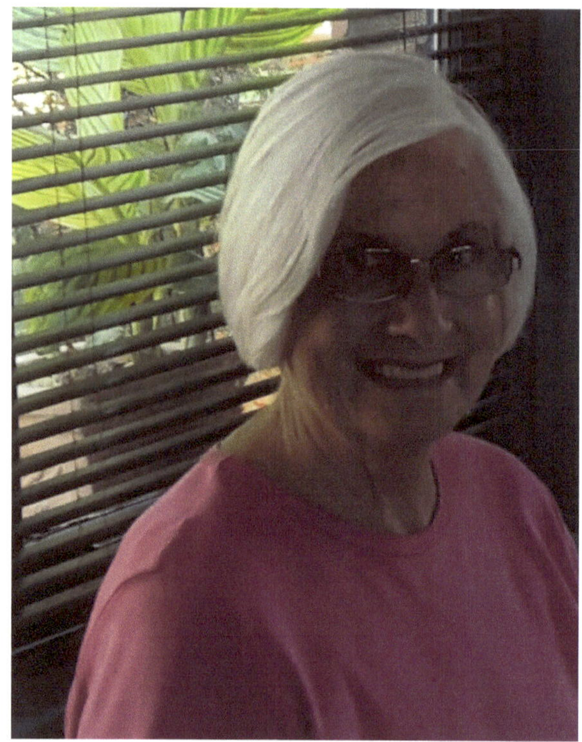

Elaine Roennfeldt Allen

Elaine Roennfeldt was born in the small farming town of Tambellup, Western Australia in 1936.

Her parents were Frank and Doris Roennfeldt and her father's earlier family were from Hamburg in Germany and had settled in the Barossa Valley in 1851.

"Happy Days"

There is a place called "Happy Days"
On the banks of the River King
Midst softly swaying Gum Trees
And the creepers as they cling.

Where the birds all lend their voices
In a very worthy cause
To give you tender moments
Should you decide to pause.

And the waters swiftly flowing
Hear the ripples as they churn
In defiance where they're going
For she knows she can't return.

But Lady Luck has smiled on you
As on the tracks you blaze
For you will find there're places few
As lovely "Happy Days."

GEORGE McARDLE

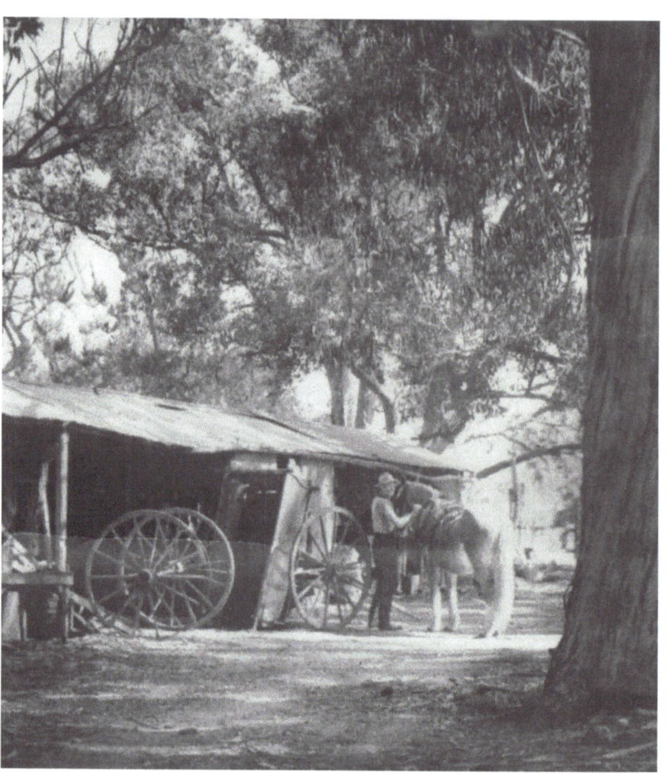

Elaine's father at Happy Days, King River Albany

Shortly after her birth, her parents sold their farm and purchased the Tea Rooms and Guest house of 'Happy Days' located on the King River about 11 kilometres from Albany.

It was a particularly busy and disruptive time for the family to establish a new business; the Second World War was in progress and Neville, Elaine's eldest brother had been posted to the Middle East with Denis, Elaine's other brother about to enlist. The strain on Elaine's mother proved to be too much and she died when Elaine was just four years old.

Elaine's father continued to run the business and coped with the added burden of caring for Elaine. She began primary school at King River but when a bus service began, she attended school in Albany. It was a teacher that recognised Elaine's artistic skills and arranged for her to take art lessons with Leach Barker, who ran classes on Saturdays. He was the teacher's husband and a noted water colourist. It was the beginning of a long association with art.

Elaine completed her schooling as a boarder at St Mary's Anglican Girls' School in West Perth.

Art was a favourite subject at High School in Albany, and also at Mitcham where she attended school while on an extended visit to relatives in South Australia. Elaine completed her schooling at St Mary's Anglican Girls' School in West Perth. A teacher at the school assisted her in obtaining a position as a drafting assistant in a Perth architectural office.

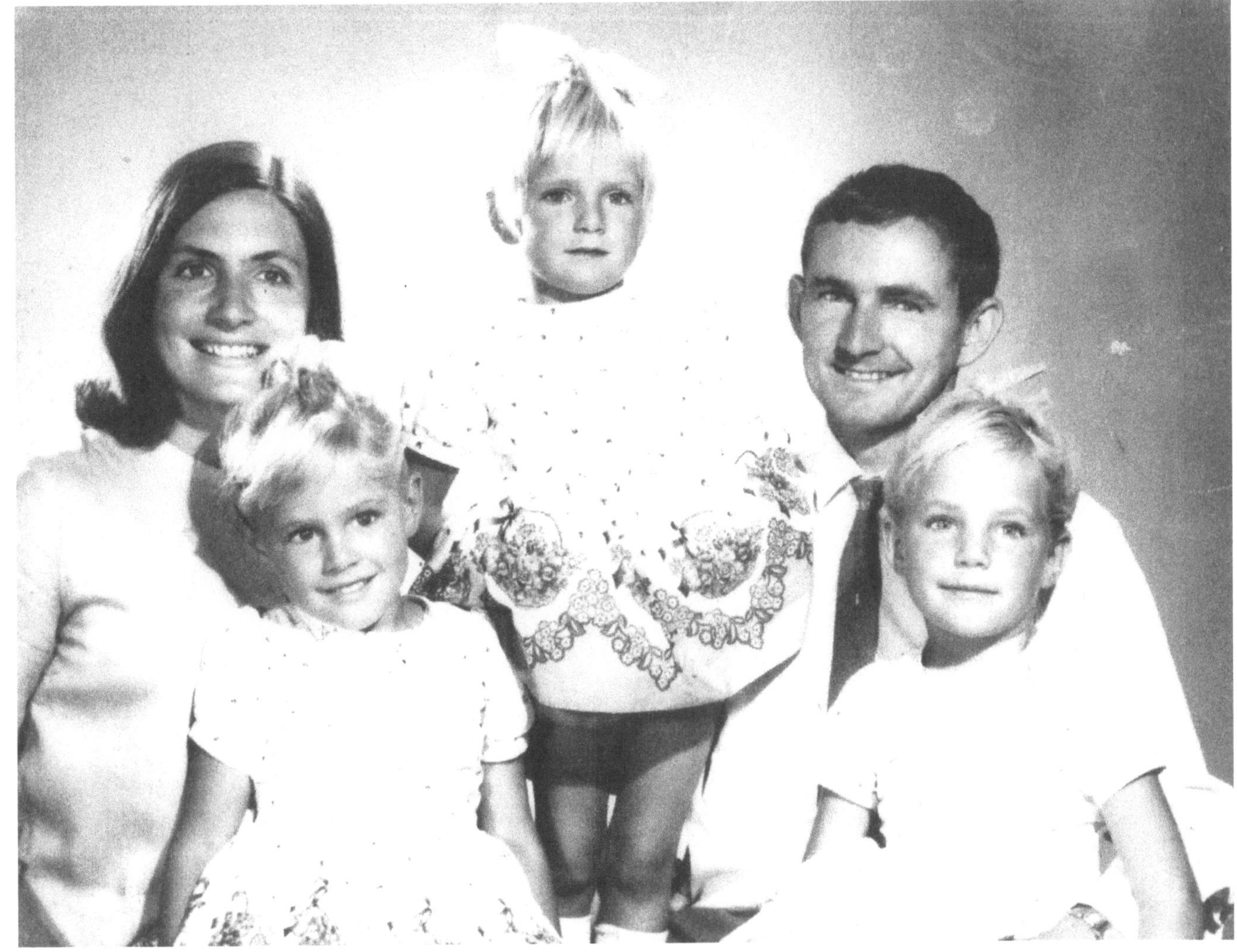

Elaine and David Allen and their three daughters: Beverly, Jennifer and Lisa

Besides her art, Elaine's great love was for horses. She rode in many local gymkhanas and country shows including the Royal Agricultural Show. Over the years she won many ribbons and her favourite horse was Shady (Shadrack).

In 1958 Elaine married David Allen and in 1959 they moved to Kalamunda. Elaine continued with her water colour art and instruction from artists such as Cyril Landor, Alexander Hills, Vlaise Zanalis and David Thornton.

Elaine and David Allen have three daughters. As well as attending to the needs of her family, she has managed to carry on with her painting and an active membership with the Kalamunda Arts and Crafts Group.

Two or three times a week Elaine met up with fellow artists: Anne Silverton, Helen Sounness and Jean Mc Diamid and they visited numerous locations seeking out subjects of interest to paint: 'anything falling down or rusting away, very old homes and places with atmosphere like bush fires, water, mist and smoke'.

Elaine always signed her paintings using her maiden name, Roennfeldt.

Most of Elaine's art is of old houses and trees, bush scenes and landscapes of Kalamunda and surrounds and includes the vineyards in the Swan Valley, horses in local paddocks, the Swan River, views of Perth from Maylands and The Hills and beaches.

Elaine was a prolific painter, painting at every opportunity in water colours and during her 52 year stay in Kalamunda her husband estimates that she painted in excess of 1,000 paintings. Elaine also taught art at Mary's Mount School in Gooseberry Hill.

Her additional activities are associated with her church, various charitable organisations and as a deliverer for the Kalamunda Meals on Wheels for over 50 years.

Over the years Elaine has exhibited her work throughout Western Australia and her paintings are in many Local Government and private collections.

www.ingramcontent.com/pod-product-compliance
Lightning Source LLC
LaVergne TN
LVHW070147110826
845147LV00002B/336
* 9 7 8 0 9 9 4 6 1 9 2 2 8 *